The Art of Rapid Prototyping

USER INTERFACE DESIGN FOR WINDOWS™ AND OS/2®

SCOTT ISENSEE
JAMES RUDD

INTERNATIONAL THOMSON COMPUTER PRESS

I(T)P™ An International Thomson Publishing Company

London • Bonn • Boston • Johannesburg• Madrid • Melbourne • Mexico City • New York • Paris
Singapore • Tokyo • Toronto • Albany, NY • Belmont, CA • Cincinnati, OH • Detroit, MI

COPYRIGHT © 1996 International Thomson Computer Press

I(T)P· A division of International Thomson Publishing Inc.
The ITP logo is a trademark under license.

Printed in the United States of America
For more information, contact:

International Thomson Computer Press
20 Park Place, Suite 1001
Boston, MA 02116
USA

International Thomson Publishing
Königswinterer Strasse 418
53227 Bonn
Germany

International Thomson Publishing Europe
Berkshire House 168-173
High Holborn
London, WC1V 7AA
England

International Thomson Publishing Asia
221 Henderson Road #05-10
Henderson Building
Singapore 0315

Thomas Nelson Australia
102 Dodds Street
South Melbourne, 3205
Victoria, Australia

International Publishing Japan
Hirakawacho Kyowa Building, 3F
2-2-1 Hirakawacho
Chiyoda-ku, 102 Tokyo
Japan

Nelson Canada
1120 Birchmont Road
Scarborough, Ontario
Canada, M1K 5G4

International Thomson Editores
Campos Eliseos 385, Piso 7
Col. Polanco
11560 Mexico D. F. Mexico

International Thomson Publishing France
1, rue st. Georges
75 009 Paris
France

International Thomson Publishing
Southern Africa
Building 19, Constantia Park
239 Old Pretoria Road, P.O. Box 2459
Halfway House, 1685 South Africa

1 2 3 4 5 6 7 8 9 10   01 00 99 98 97 96 95

Library of Congress Cataloging-in-Publication Data (available upon request)
ISBN 1 850-32215 5

rt of
id
ping

DESIGN
ND OS/2®

01

CONTENTS

Acknowledgments   ix

Preface   xi

Chapter 1: What Is Rapid Prototyping?   1
  1.1 The Need for Usable Interfaces   1
  1.2 Description of a Prototype   3
  1.3 Types of Prototypes   5
    1.3.1 Paper-and-Pencil Prototypes   5
    1.3.2 Storyboard Prototypes   6
    1.3.3 Domain-Specific Prototypes   7
    1.3.4 Interface-Builder Prototypes   7
    1.3.5 Model-Based Prototypes   9
    1.3.6 Language Prototypes   10
    1.3.7 Comparisons of Prototyping Types   11
  1.4 Scope of Prototypes   12
    1.4.1 Horizontal and Vertical Prototypes   12
    1.4.2 Global and Local Prototypes   13
  1.5 History of Prototyping   13

Chapter 2: Why Prototype?   15
  2.1 Software Life Cycle   15
  2.2 Advantages of Prototyping   17
    2.2.1 Cost Saving   17
    2.2.2 Better Collection of Customer Requirements 18
    2.2.3 Increased Quality   19
    2.2.4 Evaluation of New Interface Techniques and Functions 19
    2.2.5 Demonstration of Feasibility   20
    2.2.6 Sales Tool   20
    2.2.7 A Clear Specification   20
    2.2.8 Early Testing   21
    2.2.9 Demonstration of Early Progress   21
    2.2.10 User Satisfaction   21
    2.2.11 Better Design   22
    2.2.12 Hardware Design Evaluation   23
  2.3 Prototyping Pitfalls   24
    2.3.1 Learning Curve   24
    2.3.2 Tool Efficiency   24

2.3.3 New Roles for Personnel   25
2.3.4 Prototype Representativeness   25
2.3.5 The Prototype Is Not a Product   25
2.3.6 The Prototype Is Not a Toy   26
2.3.7 Accuracy   27
2.3.8 Ending Prototyping   27

Chapter 3: The Rapid Prototyping Process   **29**
3.1 The Basis for Successful Prototyping   30
3.2 The Process   31
   3.2.1 Identification of Customer Wants and Needs   32
   3.2.2 Concept Validation   36
   3.2.3 Final Prototype Development   39
   3.2.4 Products of the Prototyping Process   41
   3.2.5 Conclusion   42
3.3 The Future of Prototyping   42

Chapter 4: Secrets of Success   **45**
4.1 Low- versus High-Fidelity Prototyping   45
   4.1.1 Types of Prototypes   46
   4.1.2 Low-Fidelity Prototypes   47
   4.1.3 High-Fidelity Prototypes   49
   4.1.4 Using Low-Fidelity Prototypes   51
   4.1.5 Using High-Fidelity Prototypes   52
   4.1.6 Summary and Conclusions   53
4.2 Twenty-two Tips for a Happier, Healthier Prototype   53
   4.2.1 Obtain Upper-Level Development Management Support 55
   4.2.2 Throw Away Your Prototype   55
   4.2.3 Make Prototypes with High Fidelity   55
   4.2.4 Take Every Opportunity to Show the Prototype 55
   4.2.5 Don't Waste Your Time Prototyping Add-ons   56
   4.2.6 Start Early   56
   4.2.7 Make the Prototype the Functional Specification 56
   4.2.8 Keep Control of the Prototype in Your Shop   57
   4.2.9 Disseminate to All Technical Leaders and Developers 57
   4.2.10 Develop Idealistic Instead of Realistic Prototypes 57
   4.2.11 Use the Best Tools   58
   4.2.12 Grab a Piece of the Action   58
   4.2.13 The User Is King   58
   4.2.14 Look Outside the United States   58
   4.2.15 Pay Attention to Aesthetics   59
   4.2.16 Don't Delegate the Prototyping   59
   4.2.17 Become Multidisciplinary   59

4.2.18 Spread the Word   59
4.2.19 Understand Your Corporate Design Guidelines   60
4.2.20 Research the Key Interface Issues   60
4.2.21 Know the Competition   60
4.2.22 Don't Become a Traditional (Schedule-Driven) Developer   60

Chapter 5: Tools for Rapid Prototyping   **61**
5.1 Process for Selecting a Tool   70
    5.1.1 Identifying Tools   70
    5.1.2 Determining Project-Specific Criteria   70
    5.1.3 Prioritizing Project-Specific Criteria   72
    5.1.4 Important Features   72
5.2 Tool Reviews   77
    5.2.1 Smalltalk   77
    5.2.2 KASE:VIP   87
    5.2.3 XVT   92
    5.2.4 Visual Basic   96
    5.2.5 PowerBuilder   100
    5.2.6 Easel   104

Chapter 6: Prototyping Examples   **111**
6.1 Multimedia Kiosk   111
    6.1.1 Branch Locator   112
    6.1.2 Product Information   113
    6.1.3 Automated Teller Machine (ATM) Instructions   113
    6.1.4 Account Information   113
    6.1.5 Customer Service   114
    6.1.6 Implementation of Kiosk   114
6.2 Power Company Customer Service System   121
    6.2.1 Operational Description   121
    6.2.2 Program Logic   126
    6.2.3 Code Listings   128
    6.2.4 Supporting OS/2 Files   156
6.3 Banking Kiosk   156
    6.3.1 Operational Description   157
    6.3.2 Conclusion   164
    6.3.3 Code Listings   165
6.4 Credit Card Workstation   173
    6.4.1 Operational Description   174
    6.4.2 Code Listings   183

Bibliography   **203**

Index   **237**

ACKNOWLEDGMENTS

This book grew out of our experiences prototyping for IBM and its clients. We would like to thank the company for supporting this work, providing us with the opportunity to learn and try new things, and giving us permission to tell the world about it. We would also like to thank the many coworkers who assisted us in our prototyping efforts and helped us over the years to refine the rapid prototyping methodology described in this book.

Thanks to Dr. Mark Ominsky, our manager during our first prototyping projects, who gave us the freedom to experiment. Special thanks to Dr. Ken Stern for his assistance in developing the high- and low-fidelity prototyping comparisons described in this book.

We would also like to thank Risa Cohen, Jim DeWolf, Chris Grisonich, and Kathleen Raftery from International Thomson Computer Press, and Joanne Crerand, of Editorial Services of New England, who shepherded the book through the publishing process and helped motivate us to keep it moving.

Most of all, we would like to thank our families, Dawn Isensee and Ann and Holden Rudd, for their love, patience, and support throughout the writing of this book.

PREFACE

Software prototyping is one of the most promising techniques for improving not only the speed and cost of software development but also the quality and usability of the software produced. As hardware costs have declined, software development expenses have taken an increasingly larger share of the computing dollar. There is a general recognition throughout the industry that improvements to the software development process are needed. Programmers who know the techniques of prototyping and master the tools that allow them to prototype rapidly and efficiently are critical to improving the software development process, and they will be in great demand as the need for software productivity improvements becomes ever more critical.

The prototyping process we describe in this book is applicable to all computer platforms, from the smallest personal computer through the largest mainframe. It doesn't matter which computer language you are familiar with or what operating system you run. In the tools and examples sections, however, we chose to emphasize the Microsoft Windows and IBM OS/2 operating systems and describe some of the major tools for these environments. We based this choice on the popularity of these environments and our own experience with them. Whatever the language you choose, this book will make you better skilled in the art of rapid prototyping.

This book is appropriate for user interface designers and developers looking for more efficient ways to create software, researchers in software engineering, human factors professionals, and students looking for practical advice on software design and rapid prototyping.

We are practitioners, not teachers, so this book emphasizes practical advice over theory. We have personally used the processes and tools we advocate in this book in our work as software developers and consultants. We have found prototyping to be effective, rewarding, and fun. This book provides the information that will help you become an expert in the successful art of rapid prototyping.

Scott Isensee
isensee@aol.com

James Rudd
jimrudd@cltum1.unet.ibm.com

1

WHAT IS RAPID PROTOTYPING?

Example is a bright looking-glass, universal and for all shapes to look into.

Michel de Montaigne

1.1 THE NEED FOR USABLE INTERFACES

Not so many years ago, the typical computer user was an engineer or programmer—someone quite comfortable with technology, at ease with the world of bits and bytes, and who considered IBM System 370 Assembler a friendly environment. To noncomputer users, mastering a computer was like conquering the Alaskan tundra: only the bold ventured forth—only the hardy returned. *User friendly* was not yet a term used to describe computer software. There were so many other disturbing factors to be concerned with (e.g., system crashes, intermittent bugs, poor performance) that usability was, at most, a subordinate concern.

Personal computing has changed the landscape of software usability forever. What started as a trickle in the mid-1970s with the introduction of machines from Altair, Radio Shack, and Atari, to the opening of the floodgates in the early 1980s with the IBM PC and the Apple II, the roster of typical computer users grew to include teachers, students, secretaries, farmers, and even preschool children. Where performance and functionality had previously been the sole considerations, there was now an emphasis on utilization and productivity. The call for usable and graphically attractive software end user interfaces was sounded.

The progenitor of the user-friendly graphical user interface was the Star developed at the Xerox Palo Alto Research Center (PARC) during the mid-1970s and introduced commercially on the Star Information System in 1981. Many of the concepts embodied in today's user-friendly interfaces had their beginnings at Xerox PARC, including the windowed environment, menus, mouse-driven input, and the virtual workplace.

Adroit technologists and marketers envisioned the role a user-friendly interface could play in gaining market advantage and used it effectively to sell their products. The rise of

Apple Computer as a blue-chip computer maker had much to do with Apple's commitment to providing an operating system end user interface that was, and still is, graphically appealing, functionally consistent, and metaphorically intuitive. User-friendly user interfaces continue to sell machines, and even mainframe manufacturers recognize this. A recent survey of 500 IBM customers asked, "What characteristics do you think define quality software?" The most frequent response, by a substantial margin, was "ease of use" or "user friendliness." Interface style guidelines like IBM's Common User Access (CUA) and Apple's Human Interface Guidelines provide the basis for consistent interface design but cannot by themselves ensure that the interface will be usable or will meet user requirements.

User-friendly graphical interfaces, a boon to users, have often been the bane of programmers. It is hard to design and code a graphical interface and harder still to design one that successfully meets the needs of the end users. That is not to say there are not design guidelines. There are plenty of them. But most of them are long on rules for picking colors, word capitalization rules, and other trivial matters and short on practical guidelines for effectively designing user interfaces that end users will find usable. There is a desperate need for techniques that will allow software to be designed more appropriately and written more quickly.

Brooks (1987) observes, "Of all the monsters which fill the nightmares of our folklore, none terrify more than werewolves, because they transform unexpectedly from the familiar into horrors. For these, one seeks bullets of silver which can magically lay them to rest. The software project, at least as seen by the nontechnical manager, has something of this character; it is usually innocent and straightforward, but is capable of becoming a monster of missed schedules, blown budgets, and flawed products. So we hear desperate cries for a silver bullet—something to make computer software costs drop as rapidly as hardware costs do."

Hardware costs have dropped dramatically in the past ten years. The processing power of a 1980-vintage million-dollar IBM System 370 can today be found in mail-order Pentium-based PCs. When computers cost millions of dollars, the expense of software development was a small portion of the costs of running a computer. Programmers' salaries do not drop as hardware costs do, and increases in programming productivity have been small relative to the improvements in performance and price of computer hardware. At the same time, programs are becoming increasingly complex. Each release of a product is expected to have more function to match competitors, and customers expect easy-to-use programs with graphical interfaces, on-line help systems, wizards, and other features. Many commercial PC applications have over a million lines of code. The search is on for techniques that will improve the efficiency of the software development process.

With many companies striving to bring out higher-quality software on shorter schedules, rapid prototyping may be the silver bullet that makes these goals possible. Prototyping can help ensure that a program meets the customer's needs and that developers thoroughly understand requirements before the first line of code is written. It can forestall numerous changes to a program during development.

1.2 DESCRIPTION OF A PROTOTYPE

When people hear the word *prototype,* they often think of those cars of the future that automakers tow around to the shows (Figure 1-1). The automaker promises it will have a toaster in the glove box and get 200 miles to the gallon. If you look closely, though, you will see there's no engine and the body is made of papier-mâché. That's a prototype, isn't it? Yes, that papier-mâché car is a prototype, but prototypes are often more realistic. They are an important part of the development of any product. The automobile company built its show car to collect customer reaction to new styles. It is also building small quantities of engines, frames, and other components to evaluate them for attributes like reliability, cost, and ease of manufacture. Later, it will put all the components together into complete cars. Only then will it consider putting the car into volume production.

All hardware engineering disciplines practice prototyping. Electrical engineers bread-board their circuit designs, mechanical engineers fabricate mechanisms, and chemical engineers experiment with processes and reactions. Software engineers, however, have not been as enthusiastic about prototyping. They often start with just a vague idea of how a program should function. It grows and blossoms as they work. They are more like artists creating a sculpture than engineers meticulously refining a design. Nevertheless, many of these designers are now realizing that prototyping is just as important in software design as it is in hardware. A software prototype is a dynamic, visual model of an application (Figure 1-2). It simulates the user interface and important functions of the program being modeled.

Connell and Shafer (1989) listed the following properties as descriptive of a software prototype:

- Functional quickly

- A miniature model of a proposed system

- Easy to modify

- A working model written in a fourth-generation language

Figure 1-1. *Automobile Prototype*

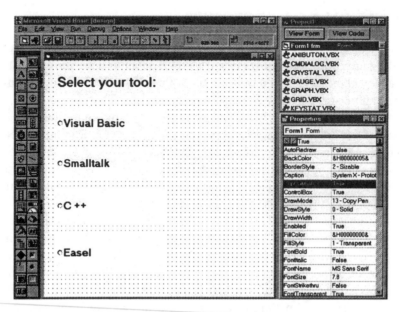

Figure 1-2. *Creating a Software Prototype*

- Often rewritten in a procedural language for implementation
- A model used to determine design correctness
- A quick way to approximate a problem solution
- Often discarded
- Something that models human interfaces to computers
- Something that promotes communication between developers and users
- The nucleus of an evolving system
- Not operating at high-performance levels
- Not intended to be the final system
- Not having advanced system features
- A display-only mockup of reports and screens
- A feasibility study
- Always used with "live" data
- A requirements definition strategy

To this list we can add:

- A blueprint for programmers to follow in writing the final program
- A vehicle for conducting early usability testing
- A marketing tool for early customer demonstrations
- A method of creating a clear and understandable interface specification
- A method of comparing alternative implementations
- An early aid for writing user documentation and help information

Not all of these characteristics will be true of any given prototype, but most prototypes will have a large subset of these properties. The particular properties will depend on the purpose of the prototype constructed and the tools used.

1.3 TYPES OF PROTOTYPES

In choosing from the variety of approaches to prototyping, you must trade off between factors, such as the speed with which the prototype can be constructed, where you are in the development process, the degree of programming skill required on the part of the person doing the prototyping, the degree to which the prototype must faithfully represent the look and interaction of the final product, and whether you want to use the prototype code in the product.

1.3.1 Paper-and-Pencil Prototypes

The simplest form is paper-and-pencil prototyping. You sketch the windows or screens for the application on paper and make diagrams of control flow. This work obviously takes no programming skill and can be done very quickly. It can be sufficient to show the overall design direction and to serve as a straw man, eliciting comments from users.

The main strength of this technique is that it is easy. It is very quick, and almost anyone can do it. You do not even need artistic ability since you can always add annotations or verbal descriptions to tell others what you are trying to show. Paper-and-pencil prototyping is great for team design because many people can draw at once, particularly if you use a blackboard or large sheet of paper. Lack of graphic detail can help to focus a team on the fundamental design questions rather than debating the artistic details of the interface early in the design process. Paper-and-pencil prototypes are good initial prototypes when the design is evolving and changing rapidly. They can serve as a complement to other prototyping techniques.

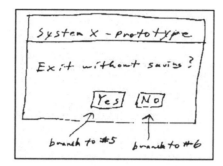

Figure 1-3. *Paper-and-Pencil Prototype*

There are disadvantages to paper-and-pencil prototypes. One is low fidelity. Another is that they cannot accurately show the user interactions, particularly if you are prototyping a graphical interface that makes use of drag-and-drop interaction. It may do a good job of capturing the look of the interface, but not the feel. It is, however, often sufficient to get design ideas across.

1.3.2 Storyboard Prototypes

Storyboard prototypes are essentially screen shows (Figure 1-4). The screens are designed on the computer, but little or no programming is provided to implement function. Many storyboard tools allow an accurate representation of the look of the program you are prototyping by providing visual representations of the interface controls for the target platform. Those with limited artistic ability can produce a professional-looking storyboard on a computer more easily than drawing the same interface with paper and pencil.

Storyboard prototypes have most of the benefits of paper and pencil while providing a degree of interactivity. Some storyboard prototyping tools allow limited behavior to be added—for example, branching from one screen to the next when a menu choice is made. The displays are "canned" rather than dynamic. It is possible to produce a storyboard prototype with sufficient fidelity that it gives a user the impression of using a real application. It can then be a vehicle for collecting reliable feedback from end users.

Storyboard prototypes do not produce code that can be used to build the real application. It produces throwaway prototypes. Storyboard prototypes are typically developed by a different team of people from those who code the application, so there is the danger that some of the lessons learned in creating the prototype will not carry over into implementation of the system and will be lost. Also, it is easy to get carried away with a storyboard prototype and oversell the capabilities of the application.

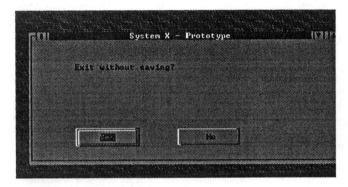

Figure 1-4. *Storyboard Prototype*

1.3.3 Domain-Specific Prototypes

Domain-specific prototypes are created with tools designed for building special kinds of applications or applications with specific styles of interfaces. They focus on a narrow domain and provide facilities for constructing applications very quickly. These are not prototyping tools per se, but the effort required to create a prototype with one is often so small that it compares favorably to other tools designed specifically for prototyping (Figure 1-5).

Fourth-generation languages are special-purpose programming languages that provide powerful help for creating certain types of applications. A number of database-building tools with user interface generation capabilities fall in this category.

Domain-specific prototyping tools have weaknesses. They have a narrow domain of applicability, are slow to execute, and are hard to use compared to tools designed specifically for prototyping.

Visual Basic, Hypercard, and a number of fourth-generation languages fall into this category. Some prototyping tools, such as Hypercard, fit in more than one category depending on the way they are used.

1.3.4 Interface-Builder Prototypes

Interface builders are interface construction tools rather than interface prototyping tools (Figure 1-6). Their main strength is that they give interface developers a drawing-like ability to specify an interface. This design capability is similar to the storyboard tool but with the added advantage of generating executable code. The developer can quickly switch between build and run modes.

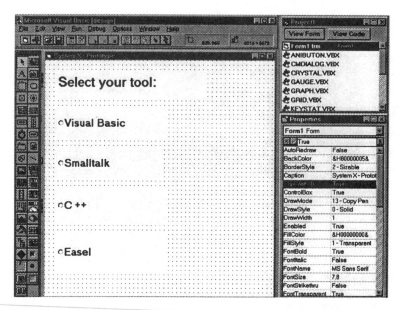

Figure 1-5. *Creating a Domain-Specific Prototype*

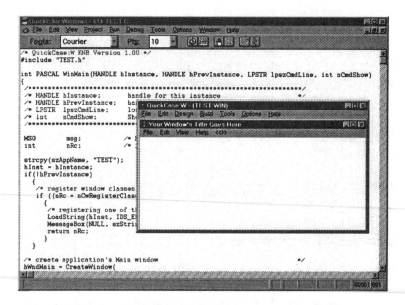

Figure 1-6. *Creating an Interface-Builder Prototype*

Interface builder prototypes can have the look, feel, and function of the real product. They differ from the actual product in that some functions may be smoke and mirrors (that is, they mimic but do not actually perform the functions to be included in the final product), performance may not accurately reflect that of the production application, and they may not provide error checking.

Interface-builder tools provide interface code that can be used in the product. These tools typically have a WYSIWYG (what you see is what you get) screen editor that allows the designer to lay out the interface. From input to this editor, the tool generates some or all of the interface code. Extensive control over properties such as layout, font, and color is typically provided.

This approach is a step removed from actually coding in the production language. The interface-builder tool approach eliminates an inefficiency of the paper-and-pencil or storyboard prototype approaches where the prototype needs to be rewritten in the native language of the product. It also avoids any errors and misjudgments that may occur in the translation process.

On the negative side, it tends to take more time and resources to produce a prototype in this way and requires more programming skill on the part of the prototyper. Significant amounts of coding are sometimes required. Because only static parts of the interface can be constructed without programming, the ability to iterate on the design can be greatly reduced. To be used effectively, these tools must be handled by experienced programmers rather than interface experts, graphic designers, or domain experts, who may be more skilled at designing the interface.

Many programming languages now come with interface builders bundled. Stand-alone interface builders include the NeXT Interface Builder, Prototyper for the Macintosh, WindowsMAKER for Microsoft Windows, and UIMX for X Windows and Motif.

1.3.5 Model-Based Prototypes

Model-based prototyping is the newest of the prototyping paradigms. A central description, called the model, is stored in a database. This model contains information such as the tasks that users are expected to perform using the application, the characteristics of users, and the presentation and behavior of the interface. This model information is processed by an interface generator, which maps the model into the windows, and other interface elements, which will appear on the user's screen. A run-time system executes the interface and accepts user input. Developers specify the features the interface should have rather than specifying how to make the computer exhibit the desired behavior.

This model-based approach allows the construction of tools that make interface design and application development much faster and more efficient. These tools blur the distinction between prototyping and implementation. They allow the designer to specify the interface at varying levels of abstraction.

Model building is easier than programming but harder than drawing pictures. The designer typically has only moderate control over the details of the interface. Model-based technology is not mature yet, but much research is going on in this area, so improvements can be expected. Tools in this category include UIDE and Humanoid.

1.3.6 Language Prototypes

Language prototypes are written in the language of the product (Figure 1-7). This is typically not quick or easy. There are no specific tools to help in the prototyping process other than the standard programming libraries and debuggers. The differences between this form of prototyping and normal product coding are in procedure and mind-set. The prototype is developed with an eye toward speed of creation and iteration. You may, for instance, code a function in the most expedient manner. Only after receiving customer feedback and deciding the interface approach is correct, do you begin to optimize the code, add extensive error checking, add the comments and formatting required by your company procedures, and so forth.

Figure 1-7. Creating a Language Prototype

Another form of language prototype is rapid application development (RAD). In the RAD approach, the prototype evolves into the product. RAD tools typically provide a quick, visual programming front end to aid in prototyping but generate code with the performance and robustness required of a real product.

Any programming language can be used for a language prototype. Languages designed for iterative development, such as Smalltalk, are best suited, however.

1.3.7 Comparisons of Prototyping Types

Table 1-1 shows the ability of different classes of prototyping tools and techniques to help developers collect the kinds of information needed for effective user interface development. Table 1-2 compares the extent to which different classes of prototyping tools and techniques satisfy a variety of requirements for effective interface prototyping. It shows that no single technique or class of tools is uniformly best at satisfying all the requirements of the prototyping process.

	Paper and Pencil	Storyboard	Interface Builder	Model Based	Domain Specific	Language
Task specification	Yes	No	No	Yes	No	No
System functionality	Yes	No	No	Yes	Yes	Yes
Interface functionality	Yes	Implicit	Implicit	Yes	Implicit	Implicit
Screen layout and behavior	Yes	Yes	Yes (static) No (dynamic)	Yes	Yes	Yes
Design rationale	Yes	No	No	Partially	No	No
User feedback record	Yes	No	No	No	No	No
Benchmarks	No	Yes	Yes	Yes	Yes	Yes
Reusable code	No	No	Yes	Yes	Yes	Yes

Source: Szekely (1994).

Table 1-1. *Characteristics of Prototyping Techniques*

	Paper and Pencil	Storyboard	Interface Builder	Model Based	Domain Specific	Language
Ease of use	Excellent	Good	Good	Fair	Good, moderate	Poor
Fast turnaround	Excellent	Excellent	Good	Excellent	Good	Poor
Extensive control	Excellent	Excellent	Good	Moderate	Fair; good within domain	Excellent
Data collection	Good	Fair	Fair	Excellent	Good	Good
Executable prototypes	None	Moderate	Good	Excellent	Excellent	Excellent
Lifecycle support	Good	Moderate	Moderate	Good	Moderate	Poor
Team design	Good	Poor	Poor	Poor	Poor	Fair
Version control	Poor	Poor	Poor	Poor	Poor	Fair

Source: Szekely (1994).

Table 1-2. *Comparison of Prototyping Techniques and Effective Prototyping Requirements*

1.4 SCOPE OF PROTOTYPES

1.4.1 Horizontal and Vertical Prototypes

Nielsen (1987) categorizes prototypes according to the depth and breadth of function they implement. A *horizontal prototype* implements a broad range of features but does not provide much depth. For example, the prototype may provide all the menu paths intended for the application but not include details such as help messages or actually process any of the data the user enters into dialogs. *Vertical prototypes* cover a narrow range of functions but are more detailed. For example, only one menu path may be followed, but along that path, the prototype may be completely representative of the user interface for the final product.

Horizontal prototypes are better for early prototyping because they can be used to evaluate general concepts and to assess proposed functionality. They are suited for use in requirements assessment activities and to guide other members of the development team. Vertical prototypes are more appropriate for later phases of a prototyping effort when the design is stable enough to warrant the effort required to produce a detailed prototype. Vertical prototypes are good vehicles for usability testing.

1.4.2 Global and Local Prototypes

Hix and Hartson (1993) classify prototypes as global or local. *Global prototypes* represent the whole system and allow a user to get a sense of the final product. They often start out not providing much depth (similar to a horizontal prototype) but evolve over time to represent the entire system in more detail (a combination of a horizontal and a vertical prototype).

A *local prototype* is written to represent a specific design detail. It is usually used to evaluate particular, isolated interaction details such as the user action to perform a function, the design of an icon, or the wording of a message. A local prototype is typically a small, stand-alone prototype with a short life span. It is used to make decisions on design issues. Hix and Hartson suggest a five-minute rule: If a design discussion on a particular issue lasts more than five minutes with disagreement among the designers, the design alternatives should be prototyped and a usability test conducted. User testing allows difficult decisions to be resolved by objective data.

1.5 HISTORY OF PROTOTYPING

Software prototyping is not a new idea, but it started to become popular only in the early 1980s. Prior to that, few tools were available to allow efficient prototyping. The demand for shorter software development cycles and increased quality over the past fifteen years has generated significant interest in prototyping.

The scientific approach toward achieving correct systems, called *software engineering*, began around 1968. In 1970, the waterfall life cycle model was proposed by W. W. Royce. Related systems design methods were proposed by Horowitz (1975), Boehm (1976), Hice, Turner, and Cashwell (1978), Andriole (1983), Dee (1984), Leslie (1986), and Pressman (1987). These techniques all described a sequential model of systems design with a single stage for identifying, defining, and validating user requirements. These methods reassuringly portray the design process as orderly and manageable; however, they require that user requirements be defined correctly early in the design process. Experience has shown this is seldom true. These conventional design processes ignore the iterative nature of development that is necessary when requirements are imprecise.

In 1978, Tom DeMarco wrote *Structured Analysis and System Specification*; in 1979, and Edward Yourdon and Larry Constantine published *Structured Design: Fundamentals of a Discipline of Computer Programming and Systems Design*. These books paved the way for structured rapid prototyping by helping to bridge the gap between structured programming and structured analysis. They proposed extensive modeling of a system before beginning to code. Today it is recognized that creating a prototype and soliciting user feedback is an important part of preparing the model.

In 1987, Fred Brooks wrote "No Silver Bullet—Essence and Accidents of Software Engineering" in which he stated that software construction involves essential tasks (e.g., fashioning the complex conceptual structures) and accidental ones (e.g., implementation details such as high-level programming languages and programming environments). He points out much more attention has been focused on the accidental than the essential tasks. Prototyping is a key to providing the required focus on the essential tasks. Rapid prototyping provides a vehicle for the customer to test the conceptual structure for consistency and usability. (The terms *rapid prototyping* and *software prototyping* are synonymous and are used interchangeably in this book.)

Chapter

2

WHY PROTOTYPE?

*If you can determine exactly how much it will cost, exactly how long it will take,
and exactly what the result will be, you are doing the same old thing again.*

Mark Mullin

2.1 SOFTWARE LIFE CYCLE

Most software development for the past twenty years has been based on a life cycle that is
linear and phase oriented. The life cycle consists of distinct stages for requirements analysis,
requirements specification, design, implementation, validation, verification, operation, and
maintenance. Increasing dissatisfaction with this process and with the quality and timeliness
of software produced by it, however, has motivated researchers to pay greater attention to the
earlier stages of software development (Ramamoorthy, Garg, and Prakash 1986).

Better requirements are needed up front in software development. Traditional design
methodologies require that the clients or end users have a clear idea of what they want a
program to do and how they want it implemented, but users rarely have this level of understanding and vision. They just know they have a problem and seek an expert to design a
solution. Boar (1984) reported that 20 to 40 percent of all system problems can be traced to
problems in the design process, while 60 to 80 percent can be traced to inaccurate requirements definitions. Clearly, it is vital for the designer to know the user.

Because computers are predictable machines, people expect software development to be
a predictable process. They expect that because they are using Yourdon's methodology, or
Wirfs-Brock's, or some other specified process, the project is guaranteed to be a success.
This is not the case. Software development involves people, with all the variability and
judgment that implies. Software development is as much art as science.

There is a need to shorten the development process, overlap the phases, and provide for
ongoing changes (change from waterfall to spiral). Too many programmers are following the

15

waterfall process because "it is the way things have always been done." Jerry Pournelle, *BYTE* magazine columnist, has likened COBOL programmers to a bunch of dinosaurs standing around discussing whether to grow another horn, thicker armor, another spike, or a longer tail while failing to notice that mammals are eating their eggs. Despite fifteen years of evidence that prototyping works, many software development shops still consider prototyping to be new and radical.

The cost to correct an error in a program increases dramatically as the life cycle progresses, so it is critical to catch errors in requirements and design before coding starts. The need for an iterative development cycle is now hitting home with most developers. Myers and Rosson (1992) surveyed seventy-four software development projects and found that 87 percent of the developers interviewed reported using iterative design. Some of the best examples of interactive software that have been developed using iterative design are the Xerox Star (Bewely et al. 1983), the Apple Macintosh and Lisa (Morgan, Williams, and Lemmons 1983), and the Olympic Messaging System (Boies et al. 1985).

Boehm, Gray, and Seewaldt (1984) conducted a study at the University of California, Los Angeles, in which some development teams used conventional development methodologies and others included prototypes in their software development. The groups employing prototyping were more successful on a variety of measures:

- The systems were judged to be easier to learn and to use than those produced by the other groups.

- The code size of the final product was only 40 percent as large for the prototyping groups as for the conventional methodology groups.

- The prototyping groups produced their software with 45 percent less effort than the other groups.

- The groups using prototyping appeared to be less affected by deadline pressures.

Alavi (1984) conducted a similar study and also found the prototyping approach to be advantageous:

- Users reported a higher level of satisfaction than those using systems developed without prototyping. They were also more enthusiastic about projects in which they were involved through the use and evaluation of prototypes.

- Developers reported that prototyping improved communication about the proposed system.

- Prototyping facilitated discussions between the programmers and end users about good and bad features in the evolving design.

There are many other reports in the research literature that report anecdotal evidence of prototyping's improving a development process. It is rare to find a report of prototyping having any significant negative effects on a project. Rapid prototyping is an important step in reengineering the software development process. This chapter describes significant advantages that rapid prototyping provides, as well as some pitfalls to avoid.

2.2 ADVANTAGES OF PROTOTYPING

2.2.1 Cost Saving

Protoyping can provide dramatic savings in total life cycle costs (Connell and Shafer 1989).

Traditional software design methods, which evolved in the 1960s and 1970s, are primarily focused on the conversion of paper-based systems to electronic systems (Mullin 1990). The requirements are typically well defined because the process has been done previously in a manual form. It is easy for computer-based systems to show productivity improvements. The typical new application today is not replacing a manual system. It is typically an improvement on a previous software solution or something that has never been done before. The requirements are thus not well defined. Prototypes allow us to refine the program design quickly without starting to code designs that may turn out to be blind alleys.

Fred Brooks (1973) advises planning to throw away the first version of any newly developed system because it is nearly impossible to do it right the first time. Protoyping provides an economical way of doing this. An inexpensively produced prototype that is easy to modify can be done the wrong way the first time. In prototyping, changes are encouraged; they are not in the common waterfall life cycle process of freezing incorrect specifications.

Clients do not understand traditional design walk-throughs. Their job is not to be experts on design. (If we had a nickel for every time a customer complained about something that had already been approved in a design walk-through, we would be on a beach in Tahiti.) Customers are, however, quite capable of determining what they like and do not like when they have a chance to try it themselves. If customers can interact with the software while it is being developed, problems can be caught quickly, and it isn't necessary to throw a lot of expensive work out the window.

Most of the time and most of the cost of software is spent in maintenance rather than initial development. Estimates of the proportion of software cost spent on maintenance are as high as 80 percent. Changes made during the maintenance phase cost at least ten times as much as those made during the design phase. Software created using prototyping will better meet user requirements and thus need fewer enhancements during the maintenance cycle. That prototypes are developed in a modular and easily modified fashion aids the development team in making the product modular and easily modifiable as well so that maintenance is simpler.

Gains due to prototyping occur in the other development cycle phases as well. Requirements gathering proceeds more smoothly because the prototype acts as a straw man to elicit feedback from users. The specification phase is quicker because the prototype serves as the specification. There is less thrashing during coding because the prototype provides clear direction to the programmers. And, there will be fewer surprises in the testing phase because end users have been evaluating the product via the prototype since the requirements phase. Connell and Shafer (1989) estimated the savings in each phase of the development process when following a prototyping approach and found a total of 41 percent reduction in development expense. The actual amount will vary from one project to another, but the reduction should always be significant.

Prototyping increases programmer productivity, and this is becoming increasingly important. Software development is a complex and difficult job, and those who do it well are paid high salaries. Between 1964 and 1979, the price-performance ratio for hardware increased one thousandfold, while programming productivity increased only fivefold.

Prototyping, in sum, is a risk avoidance approach rather than a risky approach.

2.2.2 Better Collection of Customer Requirements

One of the most important goals in designing a user interface is to make sure it meets the needs of the customer. Incorrect specifications account for 60 to 80 percent of the errors in software, according to Boar (1984). A prototype provides a means for the designer to communicate with the customer. It puts the designer's ideas in a tangible form that the customer can evaluate. It verifies that the designer has correctly understood the tasks to be performed.

Users seldom have a clear idea of how they want a program implemented at the beginning of development. Alavi (1984) observed that users are very good at criticizing an existing system (i.e., the prototype) but are not good at anticipating or articulating needs. Wasserman and Shewmake (1985) found that users often change their view about what they want a system to do after trying a prototype of it. Rapid prototyping reduces the need for extensive and concrete requirements at the beginning of a project. It allows the definition of the problem to be developed and refined over time. The prototype provides an excellent mechanism of extracting specifications from the user.

An example of the value of a prototype in extracting customers' requirements was demonstrated in an OS/2-based program we developed in the late 1980s. The predecessor product was a DOS-based program with character menus. We met with customers using the DOS version of the product and asked them what type of interface they would like in the OS/2 version. Their response was "more of the same," that is, incremental improvements to the menus. We asked them if they would be interested in a graphical user interface (GUI), and they replied they would not. They could not visualize how a graphical interface could improve the product.

Suspecting that a GUI would provide a better solution, we went back to the development lab and prototyped two interfaces: a character-based menu, which was exactly what the customers had asked for, and a GUI. Seeing the two side by side and getting the opportunity to try them out, the users were almost unanimous in asking for the GUI. Without the prototype, we could not have determined if this change would be accepted by our customers. We would have evolved the product more slowly and risked being overtaken by more innovative competitors. Through successive iterations of the prototype, we were able to try many design variations, implementing the ones our customers found useful and discarding those they did not.

In many situations, users must make a paradigm shift. They must consider software designs that change the way they work rather than just supporting existing processes. Prototypes are an effective vehicle for demonstrating the value of alternative approaches and facilitating this paradigm shift.

Creating software is both an art and a science. Successful design requires a good imagination. You must be able to see the solution to a customer's problem in your mind's eye before you begin implementing the solution. Make end users members of the development team, if possible, and use another group of end users who have no vested interest in the design as reviewers and test participants throughout the design process.

2.2.3 Increased Quality

Prototypes can dramatically raise the level of customer satisfaction with software. Customer reviews and checks are built into the process from beginning to end, so the delivered software will contain fewer functional defects. Testing can begin very early in the process by using the prototype to do usability testing with end users.

Defects are identified early in the development process when they are easiest to correct.

2.2.4 Evaluation of New Interface Techniques and Functions

Interface designers typically generate many alternative approaches early in the design process, and a prototype can be used to present design alternatives to customers for critique. These alternatives may take the form of several prototypes, each demonstrating different approaches to the interface or minor variations on the presentation of a function in a given prototype.

Users request more from software than any development organizaion can deliver. The size of this application backlog is common knowledge and frequently discourages users from requesting all the features they really want and would ask for if they could actually expect them to be delivered. Prototypes provide a quick way to assess which changes are really needed. Unnecessary or less critical requests can be removed from the backlog, with the most important changes developed first.

2.2.5 Demonstration of Feasibility

A prototype helps to demonstrate the feasibility of a product. If the desired function can be implemented in a prototype, the chances are good it can be implemented in the actual product. Market research conducted with the prototype can demonstrate that the product is salable.

Prototypes need not be done with a special prototyping tool. If there is a question as to whether a particular function can be implemented in the product, a prototype of that function can be written in the development language that will be used for the product.

2.2.6 Sales Tool

A prototype may serve as an effective sales tool. Customers who have helped to evaluate the prototype are more likely to see the product as meeting their needs than one developed by developers sitting in their ivory tower. A prototype can convince potential customers they want the product even when previous sales pitches and product descriptions had left them unconvinced. The main problem now is often explaining why they have to wait to buy the product. A high-fidelity prototype may look like a finished product even though there may be much function below the interface level that needs to be written.

2.2.7 A Clear Specification

Prototypes may serve as a dynamic specification for the product. The traditional process was to write a specification, often hundreds of pages in length. These specifications were typically time-consuming to write, difficult to understand, and out of date by the time they were finished. A prototype provides an easy-to-understand specification that programmers can use to code the product. It can show the nuances of behavior that are difficult to capture in writing. Having a good specification to follow allows programmers to proceed confidently in coding the product and avoid many blind alleys. Many programmers work less productively in the abstract; they need a clear and specific example to follow.

2.2.8 Early Testing

Prototypes provide a vehicle for early usability testing, with problems identified early in the development cycle while changes are still easy to make. If multiple design alternatives are being considered, they can be prototyped and evaluated so that only the best design choices are included in the product. The prototype can even be instrumented to collect data. Typical usability testing measurements include time to perform a task, errors, and user satisfaction ratings. Users are also asked for suggestions on how they would improve the interface.

2.2.9 Demonstration of Early Progress

It seems that nearly every software development project comes in late and over budget, and many large projects never even reach completion. Given this track record, management typically watches software development very closely and defines milestones to allow measurement of where the project is at on a schedule. Project managers can be greatly reassured if visible progress can be shown early in the project. A prototype is a good way to demonstrate progress. It can be a morale booster for the development team to be able to show tangible progress early in a project.

A large proportion of the code for most programs—as high as 80 percent—is user interface code. Having a clear definition of what the product externals will be helps to ensure that this large and important portion of the code can be written correctly the first time.

On one large development project we were involved with, a programming team was called in for a project audit in the second year of a three-year development project. All of the low-level code (the plumbing) had been written, but the team had not yet started the user interface. They could show the executives stacks of code listings and progress charts, but there was little that the executives, being nontechnical types, could really see of the product. A small outside company had taken the opposite approach. It had prototyped the user interface but had not yet written any product code or clearly defined the plumbing. This outside company offered to sell the product to the execute team. Because of the prototype, it appeared to the executives of Big Corp. that this outside company was making better progress, and the internal development effort was scrapped. The moral of this story is that it is essential, as you make progress on a project, to be able to demonstrate this progress. A prototype can serve this purpose.

2.2.10 User Satisfaction

Users have input into software design from the beginning with a prototype. They influence the design so it will provide just the function they want, and the way they want it. They may even be able to specify a design that is fun to use. They develop a sense of ownership that makes them feel better about the system than if the same program were just thrown over the wall from a traditional development process. If it is an in-house program, the users who participated in design can teach their coworkers about the product and spread their enthusiasm.

2.2.11 Better Design

Products that are prototyped have better user interfaces than those that are not. It is impossible to have a complete and accurate understanding of requirements at the beginning of a project. Good design is an iterative process: You collect requirements, design an interface, prototype it, collect feedback, and then start the design cycle again. Each iteration improves the design. The more quickly you can make this cycle, the more iterations you can achieve within a development schedule.

This is similar to the edit-compile-test loop that programmers work in during code production. They write the code, fiddle with it until it compiles, try to run it, and then return to the edit cycle. This process happens over and over again until the shipping date or a point of diminishing returns is reached. It is seldom the case that code is considered perfect. Code is not immutable; it has an evolutionary inertia.

It is important to keep track of the iterations in the prototyping cycle. They may be useful to keep from repeating previous work, to educate those who come on the project midway, and as a demonstration of a successful process for future projects. Saving a copy of the code at each iteration is the best technique. Screen dumps, screen shows, and videotapes are other alternatives.

This prototype and feedback process is much more efficient than traditional design reviews. In a design review, programmers typically quibble about whether some algorithm should have been implemented recursively or whether a loop is as efficient as it could be. End users reviewing a prototype do not care about loops and recursion. Their concern is whether the software does what they want. End users measure software efficiency in system response time, not in raw algorithmic efficiency.

We once worked on a banking product in which tellers entered information, then waited while a query was made to a remote host. To cover this awkward pause, the tellers had to make small talk with the customers. They grew tired of discussing the weather a hundred times a day so we prototyped a modified form of the application, moving the query to a period when the teller was still doing data entry. This slightly lengthened the actual processing time but made the interaction between the teller and customer smoother and decreased the amount of time required to serve a customer. The prototype allowed us to experiment and find a better design that was not obvious during the design cycle for previous versions of the product.

2.2.12 Hardware Design Evaluation

Software prototyping can be used to prototype hardware too. A software prototype of hardware can typically be constructed much more quickly and cheaply than a hardware prototype—saving cost, decreasing cycle time, and allowing the designer to evaluate more alternatives than would otherwise be possible.

We were once involved in the design of operator panels for the IBM Proprinter line of dot matrix PC printers. Constructing hardware prototypes was a lengthy process. It involved:

- Proposing an interface design

- Translating the interface design into mechanical, electrical, and microcode designs

- Finding suppliers for the components

- Constructing a hardware prototype of the operator panel

- Conducting usability testing

Because of the high cost, we did not have the luxury of prototyping more than one design at a time. If problems were found in usability testing, there was no time to go through the design cycle again, so we were limited to making minor changes.

We were able to improve the process of operator panel design by introducing software prototypes of operator panels. The operator panels were realistically shown on the monitor of a PC. A touch panel allowed the user to press the buttons and receive the normal feedback he or she would get using the printer (a click from pressing the button, LED or LCD readouts, error sounds, etc.). The only feedback missing was the tactile feedback of pressing a real key. A printer attached to the PC accepted the settings the user made on the prototype operator panel and printed accordingly so that the users could verify whether they were making the settings correctly. This software prototype of the operator panel was months faster and far cheaper to construct than actual hardware prototypes had been. We were able to prototype several design alternatives at once and test them head to head. When problems were found, we could redesign and test again.

Many companies are now making use of software prototypes and simulations in their design process. *PC Magazine* (September 26, 1995) describes how the Boeing 777 was "flown" into Miami International Airport via a software simulation before the first plane was ever built. Hewlett-Packard reduced a nine- to twelve-month design cycle by two months using a software prototype of computer motherboard designs. Motorola uses prototypes to create interactive working models of cellular telephones.

2.3 PROTOTYPING PITFALLS

There are pitfalls that must be avoided to ensure the success of a prototyping effort. These are not disadvantages but, rather, areas where caution is necessary.

2.3.1 Learning Curve

Prototyping has been successful in so many instances that expectations are typically very high when a group first starts to prototype. They expect high productivity right away and do not anticipate the learning curve.

Before starting a prototyping effort, it is important to take time to select the right prototyping tool for the project, train personnel on using the tool, and decide how prototyping will fit into the development process.

2.3.2 Tool Efficiency

Prototyping tools are generally less efficient than conventional programming languages. The prototype typically will execute more slowly, require more memory, and have a larger code size than would a program written in a programming language. In practice, we have found that the larger code size and memory requirements seldom cause problems. When they do, we use a larger, faster computer for the prototype than we expect our target user audience to have.

Execution speed is more frequently a problem. If performance is poor, it may be hard for users to evaluate the system properly. We once worked on a prototype that was to highlight the object the user clicked on to give feedback that he or she had selected the right object. It acted on the mouse-down event and added a constant to the RGB value of each pixel. In the product, the design goal for this operation was to take approximately 1/10 second. In the prototype, it took up to 2 seconds for large objects to highlight. This slowed users, and they disliked this technique, which we thought they would like if it performed as designed. We switched to a faster computer and tried a number of optimization techniques on the prototype code. This still did not provide an adequate speed increase so we finally had to go outside the prototyping tool and code a dynamic link library (DLL) that could be called from the prototype. In other similar instances, we have substituted smoke-and-mirrors techniques that execute faster than performing an actual operation. For example, we have simulated a database query by reading a local text file rather than actually connecting to a remote database.

Tool efficiency may sometimes be a problem, but there are almost always ways to compensate.

2.3.3 New Roles for Personnel

In traditional development processes, programs are designed with little user input. Developers like this system because they are not bothered by end users' telling them what to do. End users, however, seldom get a product that meets their needs well. If this process is used for prototyping, little will be gained. There will be no iteration on the prototype because there is no feedback loop.

For prototyping to work well, the roles must change. Users must define the requirements for the software and provide feedback throughout the development process. Developers must seek out user input and be willing to make changes based on it. Both groups must buy into this process.

It is also important to get buy-in from management. Prototyping changes the development life cycle, which makes planning and scheduling different from what managers may be accustomed to. Managers may view the allocation of resources to building a prototype, especially a throwaway one, as wasteful.

Agreement among all parties should be reached before the development process begins.

2.3.4 Prototype Representativeness

It is easy to produce a prototype that looks and acts nothing like what the product will:

- The prototyper may put features in the product that the development team does not have time to implement.

- The prototyping tool may contain features that are very difficult to duplicate in the programming language chosen for the product.

- The prototyper may put features into the prototype that are not accepted by the developers or the user advocates.

A prototype that differs greatly from the product it represents can mislead or overpromise.

It is important for the prototyper to keep in close contact with both the developers and the end users and seek their feedback throughout the prototyping cycle. Putting some questionable features into the prototype is acceptable as a means of soliciting feedback, but those features should be removed on the next iteration of the prototype if they are not accepted. The goal of a prototype is to define the interface of the product. It should not drift far from this.

2.3.5 The Prototype Is Not a Product

On customer visits, we have seen people get very excited about a prototype and want to buy it immediately. They may not understand that the product is a year away from shipping because it appears to be working before their eyes. We have heard stories of managers seeing a prototype they like and profusely congratulating the development team on delivery so far ahead of schedule. When this happens, products may be rushed to market long before they are ready. The moral of this story is that it is important to explain the purposes and limitations of a prototype and not let expectations get out of hand.

Viewing the prototype as a product can also lead to too much expenditure of effort on it. Prototypes must be quick and easily modified to be of value. If the programmers spend too much time optimizing the algorithms used, implementing every last detail or restructuring the code, for example, the prototype will take as much effort to develop as the real product. These are all appropriate activities for a product but must be done in moderation in a prototype.

You must determine the right level of complexity and effort to devote to a prototype for your product. The Federal Aviation Administration (FAA) built a full-function prototype of the next-generation air traffic control system that took nearly two years and cost millions of dollars to develop. This may be appropriate for a multibillion dollar project with serious safety implications if the final system does not work correctly. More typically, however, prototypes are developed in a matter of days or weeks by a single programmer or, at most, a small team.

2.3.6 The Prototype Is Not a Toy

It is easy to view the prototype as a sandbox to play in while avoiding writing the code for the real product or to view it as an exercise that is preventing the programmers from getting down to real work. Alavi (1984) noticed a reduction in programmer discipline, possibly because the process of developing the prototype was viewed as an exercise rather than the real thing.

Viewing the prototype as a toy can lead to tossing it into a traditional development cycle without making the necessary changes to the development process. This can result in the loss of many of the advantages a prototype can provide and, in the worst case, may result in a prototype that no one makes use of.

At the beginning of a project, it is important to educate the programming team on the goals and importance of prototyping. Providing some examples of how it has helped other projects can be useful. A programmer who has had experience with prototyping could be included on the team to give firsthand reports and act as the prototyping advocate to build enthusiasm among the team.

2.3.7 Accuracy

It can be difficult to get the prototype to represent the interface design in all respects. Most prototyping tools are less flexible than programming languages. These accuracy trade-offs must be reviewed on a case-by-case basis. Sometimes it is acceptable to ignore or explain away an inaccuracy; other times you must work hard to find a way to make the prototype more accurate.

Prototypes often target one aspect of a system in which accuracy is most important. The user interface, system functionality, or system performance are three common areas to prioritize and then trade off accuracy in one area for another.

Accuracy is most important when performing user testing. Some deviations are so minor that they have no effect. You may be able to counteract others just by explaining to the user that the prototype does not represent the design and describing how it should work. In other cases, an inaccuracy will bias the test. Someone skilled in user testing should work with the prototyper to identify these potential problem areas and develop solutions.

2.3.8 Ending Prototyping

It can be difficult to stop prototyping (Mantei 1986). If each iteration is still bringing improvements to the design, it is tempting to continue. The client may think of more new features each time a new version of the prototype is presented. All good things must come to an end, however. Like an endless loop in code, a perpetual prototyping cycle chews up resources without making real progress. It is important to have some criterion to judge when prototyping should end—for example, performance measurements, customer satisfaction criteria, and a scheduled end date. These criteria are best set at the beginning of the project; once you are into prototyping, it is always tempting to try to squeeze in just a few more changes. Prototyping is fun, and fun is addictive. Prototyping is sometimes so much fun that programmers lose enthusiasm for developing the real product (Alavi 1984).

One good way to determine that the time has come to end prototyping is when the changes being made are purely cosmetic. It is not that cosmetic changes are unimportant, but they can easily degenerate into long discussions over whether the background should be blue or green.

Once the prototype is finished, the rest of the coding can be completed with confidence. Traditional development techniques generally work well from this point on. The prototype provides a specification that allows everyone to know what the user interface will look like and allows them to estimate the time and effort required to complete the project. From this point on, the prototype should be changed only if an important requirement changes and the prototype needs to be modified accordingly.

Chapter

3

THE RAPID PROTOTYPING PROCESS

Ritual will always mean throwing away something: destroying our corn or wine upon the altar of our gods.

G. K. Chesterton

For a multitude of reasons that the average computer user would never understand, software makers just don't seem to understand that usability is the burning issue for the average user. As user interface designers, we are always having lively discussions with our product planners and programmers about how important usability is. They are still too many developers who believe usability is spelled I-C-O-N-S (and plenty of them, especially the really colorful one with lots of little doodads). But when we meet with the average user, the burning issue is usability, and these users do not spell usability, I-C-O-N-S.

User interface guidelines play an important role in design of a user interface and development of a prototype. But guidelines alone will never make for a 100 percent usable user interface. Nor is understanding how to write a prototype sufficient. The key to successful prototyping is adherence to a well-defined process in which the advantages of prototyping can be realized.

Every usability lab has examples of software that it has tested over years that is incredibly unusable. To avoid this outcome, follow the prototyping process outlined in this chapter. There are three requirements for being a superstar in the fine art of prototyping: (1) knowing prototyping tools, (2) knowing the design guidelines, and, perhaps most overlooked, underappreciated, minimized, and forgotten, (3) understanding the prototyping process itself.

As consultants and mentors, our biggest challenge in teaching the fine art of rapid prototyping is getting people to understand and appreciate the importance of a sound, verifiable, and methodical process for ensuring prototyping success. On a recent project, we worked closely with a programmer, whom we will call Bob. Bob is a very skilled programmer who knows all the ins and outs of OS/2 Presentation Manager (PM). His technical know-how is unequaled. And in terms of understanding and familiarization with the corporate user interface guidelines, Bob's knowledge is impressive by any measure. This knowledge over the years has earned him a couple of promotions, but he has never made it to senior-level programmer, because, despite his in-depth technical knowledge, he never took the time to learn and perfect the prototyping process. Although Bob could crank out prototypes that were technically correct and guideline correct, he often failed at producing prototypes that were deemed usable. No matter how much we prodded, he never took the time to learn the prototyping process.

Prototyping is much, much more than reading the guidelines and cranking out the code. Successful prototypes are developed as part of a methodical prototyping process.

3.1 THE BASIS FOR SUCCESSFUL PROTOTYPING

The bases for a successful prototyping process are speed, iterative design, domain expertise, and early completion.

First, prototyping is done quickly. Code should be developed in a modular fashion with reuse in mind. New prototypes can be created from existing blocks of code. A well-maintained library of reusable code can make the difference between finishing on time and getting follow-up business, or not delivering on time and being put out of business by a competing department or another organization.

Initially, this "library" can be a drive on a file server or even a diskette. At the start, the focus should be more on writing quality code so that the team can use it later. As you get further along on the road to successful prototyping, you can use your existing corporate change management facility to manage your code. But it is best to start small, so you will not be tied up in the overhead and bureaucracy of managing the effort. As long as you and others understand your code and know where to find it, you will be on the right path to establishing a library.

Some of the modules that are included in our library are:

- **Open object dialog windows,** such as those used for opening files. They should be written in such a fashion that the object being opened (such as a file or a record) is passed as an argument into the module.

- **Folders.** Containers are windows that hold other objects. These objects can be files, records, or any other object that can be placed in a folder. Some of the associated behaviors that should be coded into these modules include opening and closing the folder, sorting objects in the folder, and, where applicable, enabling dragging and dropping objects to and from the folder.

- **Industry-specific scenarios.** Some industry applications have task sequences that can be found in every application. For example, every branch banking application has a "welcome customer" scenario. In this scenario, the user welcomes the customer by collecting some information about the customer, such as whether the customer has an existing account and the customer's tax identification number.

Since we do a lot of finance industry prototypes, we have a library of scenario code that includes customer welcomes, IRA openings, deposits, and withdrawals. We even have code to support banking printers and magnetic stripe readers. By being able to draw on this library, we are able to move fast, efficiently, and with great confidence. It is important for any prototyping effort to begin developing this library immediately. The library can make the difference between winning prototyping contracts and sitting on the sidelines.

The second key to successful prototyping is iterative development. Seldom does the designer get it right the first time. One reason is that the requirements are almost always fuzzy, and even when the technical leader or project manager indicates that the requirements are "firm," they seldom are. Have you noticed that "firm" functional requirements almost always translate into squishy user interface requirements, especially when the requirements are being handed down by the project leader? It is rare to work with a project leader who has any idea of what makes a usable interface besides a "gut" feeling. The project leader's "gut" sense of what makes a user interface usable is often the user interface designer's worst enemy.

A key to successful prototyping is to accept that perfect prototyping requires iteration over many imperfect predecessor prototypes. The first prototype is often based on requirements gathered through structured requirements-gathering techniques. Subsequent prototype refinement is based on customer critique of the prototype.

The third element of successful prototyping is that prototypes are built with the aid of domain experts: those who are familiar with the user tasks because they are current users or performed these job duties in the past. The domain expert works with the user interface designer to develop the prototype. With a qualified domain expert, a prototype will be more likely to hit the mark earlier in the iteration process.

Finally, and perhaps most important, successful rapid prototyping efforts are launched and completed early in the design process—before a single line of low-level code is written. By the time programmers crank out the code to turn the design into a product, every design feature of the user interface has been demonstrated, critiqued, and refined through customer involvement.

3.2 THE PROCESS

Figure 3-1 shows the details of the prototyping process. The major components are (1) identification of customer wants and needs, (2) concept validation, and (3) final prototype development.

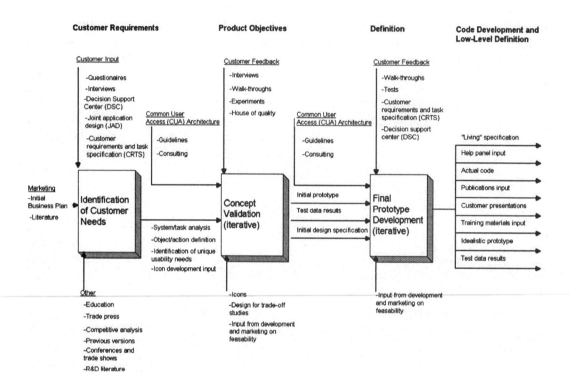

Figure 3-1. *Prototyping Process*

3.2.1 Identification of Customer Wants and Needs

Customer wants and needs must be met in order for the customer to acquire, install, configure, customize, and use the product effectively in the workplace. These customer wants and needs must be translated into operational requirements and refined into a user interface design that is usable and intuitive. Operational needs complement functional needs; both must be met to ensure the delivery of a satisfactory application.

The interface designer and the development team gain an understanding of the customer's operational needs and environment by determining the depth and range of design sophistication required for each of the major user interfaces, understanding the work complexity required of end users, and understanding the wants and needs of the customer. The designer should select and document the method that will be used, such as interviews, survey questionnaires, customer requirements and task specification (CRTS) methodology, or joint application design (JAD) methodology. Sources for the needed understanding are: marketing (lists of wants and needs from the customer), technical and architectural engineers (application direction or vision), and domain experts (task information from experienced users). This activity should result in documented system usability needs, interface design requirements, and an understanding of system characteristics, constraints, and features. The design team should map these end user characteristics against user conceptual models. This activity should result in documented user tasks and scenarios used for the initial prototype.

There are a number of important reasons for understanding the customer's operational needs. First, it allows the design team to determine the depth and range of design sophistication required for each of the major user interfaces. This is an obvious reason, but one missed by many design teams. In essence, it means not to underdesign—and not to overdesign. One company we have worked with does a good job of designing and developing middle-of-the-road software. They seldom blow your doors off with their software, but it is also seldom the case that they overdesign to the point that it misses the mark and becomes unusable. Conversely, another large software company we work with often overdesigns. Designers and developers spend an inordinate amount of time designing for every possible error condition and exception that could occur. As a result, not enough time is spent on polishing the most frequently used functions. They make sure the software responds appropriately when the user presses twelve function keys and the Print Screen key all at once. This bias is left over from the days when the user was a tad more ignorant and, for whatever reason, had an inclination to want to press twelve function keys and the Print Screen key all at once. Good design is not overdesign. Good design is based on an understanding of operational needs, which provides a basis for estimating and planning for levels of design sophistication.

Second, understanding the degree of work complexity is often another overlooked key to understanding customer wants and needs. Software designers frequently approach user interface as an exercise in replacing mainframe "green screens" with the direct equivalent in software. Understanding the degree of work complexity required of end users leads to the identification of work simplification features for the new application.

Third, understanding the wants and needs of the customer allows the design team to focus more attention on those user interface components that are seen as most important by the customer.

Finally, identifying the customer's wants and needs provides the fundamental basis for defining the new application's performance and productivity requirements. Ultimately, all of these factors play a significant role in establishing product appeal and competitiveness.

One of the first steps in this phase is defining end user characteristics, such as education level, skill level, experience with certain software applications and tools, and past work experience. This knowledge provides a focus for the design team's effort to design applications that meet customer expectations. The design team can map these end user characteristics against user conceptual models.

Another major step in identifying customer needs is to analyze and understand the operational environment of those who will be using the product. Applications designed for, say, a self-service kiosk will have certain interface characteristics and attributes completely different from applications designed for repetitive, high-volume environments. Other attributes of the operational environment that need to be identified to match the application to customer needs are customer productivity expectations, error performance goals, impact of errors on job and system performance, and personnel turnover rates. For example, high turnover rates are a key design issue that should cultivate the development of an application that is easy to learn and to use. Knowledge of customer expectations for a high transaction throughput rate will help foster the development of a product with fast system response time. An awareness that user-keyed errors may result in catastrophic system malfunctions should lead to the development of code that is as bullet-proof as possible to user-keying errors.

Among the ways to help identify customer needs and wants are: marketing and customer input. Marketing will have a list of customer wants and needs at a functional level. (Of course, one of these functional requirements typically is that the system be easy to use.) It is the designer's job to take the list of functions put together by marketing and make them usable. With the marketing requirements sheet, the designer can begin conceptualizing the type of user conceptual models and templates appropriate for the application user.

Naturally, the customer will be the primary source of input at this stage. Typically, a number of customers will be involved in helping to identify usability and functional requirements. The key technical and architectural engineers will have the vision of where they believe the application should be headed. They will have ideas of what sort of new and different user interface technologies should be considered for the application. These people are very good at brainstorming how the new technologies may fit into their application. The other type of customer to have involved at this point are the domain experts: the experienced users in the business. They know both the business and the current application (if it exists) inside and out. The domain experts help guide early design decisions and facilitate the identification of potential design directions. They are also very good at aiding in the task and system analyses that will serve as the basis for the task scenarios developed in the concept validation stage.

There are a number of mechanisms for collecting customer input during this phase. Interviews and survey questionnaires are two common methods. In general, the information collected during interviews is of higher qualitative value than that of surveys because the interviewer has more control over ensuring that the right types of information are collected. On the other hand, surveys are better at eliminating interviewer bias, allow the interviewee to remain anonymous, and are more effective when the customer population is large. In addition, all respondents' answers carry the same weight in the analysis.

When there are more than a handful of people to collect information from, data collection can be streamlined with the CRTS methodology, a means for capturing, organizing, and prioritizing customers' application requirements based on direct customer input (Di Angelo and Petrun 1995). Customer input is collected in a decision support center, a room of LAN-connected PCs running groupware software called TeamFocus (a trademark of the IBM

Corporation). The CRTS methodology has a number of advantages over traditional interview and survey methodologies:

- **Efficient use of time.** Participants seated at workstations use the keyboard to enter their thoughts and ideas on a topic. By entering comments at the keyboard, all participants can "talk" at the same time, saving hours in meeting time.

- **Equal participation.** The process avoids domination by senior-ranking individuals or strong personalities. It allows all members to participate equally.

- **Anonymous exchange of ideas.** The TeamFocus software allows participants to generate ideas anonymously. The anonymity helps to encourage the free-flowing exchange of ideas, particularly by those who may remain quiet otherwise.

CRTS provides a mechanism for allowing the design team to learn quickly what customers do and what tasks they consider important to their jobs. It allows the design team to define end-to-end task scenarios to serve as input to the concept validation phase.

Another methodology, which has been used successfully for more than fifteen years, is JAD. Whereas CRTS is aimed at collecting requirements from people who will actually be using the product, JAD is aimed at collecting requirements from those who will be handling the data processing characteristics of the system. The user interface designer must be concerned with both aspects in design, since much of the functionality of the user interface will be dictated by the characteristics of the system.

JAD is a technique used to define and design operational systems that help meet real information needs. As a team, the users and information systems personnel participate in intensive plan and design sessions under the guidance and facilitation of an experienced JAD leader and analyst(s). Using a step-by-step logical approach and tailored material, the leader and analyst guide the group through the definition of the system.

JAD has three basic objectives with regard to application design: (1) it is aimed at improving the quality and completeness of the design, (2) it accelerates this phase of the prototyping process by systematically identifying application requirements, and (3) it collects data requirements through the use of entity-relationship diagrams, definition of data elements and their characteristics, and the construction of data flow diagrams. Taken to a deep enough level, preliminary screen layouts and interface flows can be identified.

At the same time, the design team should be collecting information on competing products and previous versions of the application (if they exist). The trade press and trade shows provide good forums for identifying new technologies or adapting technologies and ideas from other lines of business that may fit into the target application.

Once customer information is obtained from all these sources, the following activities are performed:

1. List key problems in the work environment.

2. Group problems into appropriate categories.

3. Rate problems on difficulty and importance.

4. Brainstorm on solutions to problems.

5. Provide detail on key elements of the solution.

6. Review and validate the solutions.

7. Rate each solution on how strongly its implementation would affect customer satisfaction.

At the end of the requirements-gathering phase, the designer will have the following outputs:

- Feature and function specifications

- Competitive information

- Price and schedule constraints

- Customer's primary business concerns

- Task domain preferences

- Solution alternatives

- Task analyses

- Product usability plan

3.2.2 Concept Validation

The main objective of this phase is to select and develop working, high-level user interface prototypes for design and validation. These prototypes will allow you to evaluate and endorse key concepts, approaches, and techniques.

To provide a better understanding of the feasibility of various design candidates, one or more straw man prototypes are constructed during this period. The prototyping effort has a number of fundamental objectives. First, the prototypes will allow the design team to implement previously identified usability concepts in the form of actual working models that help verify the feasibility of particular design approaches. A number of alternatives can be mocked up quickly and reviewed with the customer to validate a design approach. One approach is to use the decision support center, with input from twelve to fifteen users gathered to quickly evaluate the various designs.

Concept validation is an iterative process whereby a prospective prototype is mocked up and made available to end users for review. Based on feedback from these and other groups, modifications and improvements will be made to the prototype.

There are a number of inputs to this phase of the prototyping process:

- **Customer feedback.** The customer walk-throughs of the prototypes are probably the most important input during this phase. Although these walk-throughs are sometimes very painful for the user interface designer, they are also among the most useful forms of input since these critiques can identify very quickly design approaches that are not feasible. The walk-throughs allow both customers and developers to see an actual working model of the proposed product and identify benefits and the feasibility of various design alternatives. The walk-through also enables the development team to identify user interface and operational weaknesses and to propose solutions for these problems. The greater the customer involvement, the better for the product. Walk-throughs on a daily basis are not uncommon. With rapid prototyping, changes are made overnight or sometimes on the fly, depending on tool expertise, the customer relationship, and the particular goals of the customer.

- **User interface guidelines.** Each operating environment (Windows, OS/2, Macintosh, Motif, VM, etc.) provides a set of user interface guidelines for developers to follow. Conforming to these guidelines will help ensure the application looks and works like other applications that users are likely to utilize. Much expert design and user testing has gone into these guidelines, and the decisions they lead you to are likely to be much better than those you are able to come to on your own without having the luxury of much time and usability test resources.

- **System/task analysis.** The system/task analysis—that is, analyzing a job and breaking it down into a set of tasks—will give the information necessary to understand the user tasks and map these tasks to the application's function. It will also give information necessary to build task scenarios that can be shown to customers for feedback and refinement.

- **Icons.** At this point, preliminary drafts of screen icons will be available, and the design team can place them in the prototype to be tested for legibility and comprehension.

- **Trade-off studies.** Trade-off studies compare alternative approaches to determine the relative advantages and disadvantages of each. Those identified during the identification of customer needs phase are executed during this period. These studies will provide comparative investigation of competing user interface strategies.

Depending on the circumstances, trade-off studies may or may not be required. They should be conducted during this stage if there is uncertainty or dissatisfaction with the user interface design direction. In the case of a new product offering, studies may be needed to examine various aspects of the user-interface. For established products, trade-off studies may not be necessary at all, since the design is already stable and successful. Advanced technologies are a prime target for investigative trade-off studies since there are always risks involved in moving to a new technology.

Straw man prototypes of each of the various design alternatives can be constructed and tested during this phase. Ideally, statistically controlled tests should be conducted, but sometimes this is not possible. We have found that tests with smaller sample sizes, although not statistically conclusive, can be effective for eliminating the most unworkable of designs. Be sure to run more thorough tests later in the development cycle to verify the results you found with the straw man and evaluate the design more thoroughly.

- **Input from development and marketing on feasibility.** It is important to continue development and market planning input on feasibility of the design. That is why an established user interface design team is a critical component of the prototyping process. Regular sessions with development and marketing will keep the user interface designer honest.

The eventual goal of this phase of the prototyping methodology is to establish support for key user interface design concepts, approaches, and techniques. It is during this phase of development that the design team solidifies its support for a particular user interface design position. The straw man prototypes, each with its two or three key task scenarios, will have been reviewed, critiqued, refined, or eliminated. At the end of this phase, the major design direction of the application will be set and ready for full implementation during the final prototype development phase. Formal outputs of this phase of the prototyping process are as follows:

- **Initial prototype.** This prototype will have captured the design direction of the application. The two to three key tasks that were prototyped will be completely flushed out down to the icons, help panels, and error messages. The initial prototype will smooth the way for faster progress on later, more complete prototypes, as well as the application coding.

- **Test data results.** Results from trade-off studies, icon tests, and customer walk-throughs will be documented as an input from this stage. These data will help justify design decisions later.

- **Initial design for the functional specification.** Screen captures from the prototype can be used in the functional specification document. This will make it easier to evaluate the application's initial design and make it easier for others to critique the specification.

3.2.3 Final Prototype Development

During this phase, the prototype is completed. All of the function is prototyped as completely as possible. There is debate as to how much detail needs to be added to the prototype and to what extent functions need to be prototyped. It has been our experience that given the time, money, and resources, it is best to complete the prototype with as much detail as possible, for a number of reasons. First, it helps make sure that there are no design surprises. It uncovers user interface problems that are not always recognized until made visible through prototyping. By focusing on a complete prototype, no design decision is left unvisited. Second, it offers insurance that an inexperienced coder will not jeopardize the consistency of the user interface by making unilateral decisions. Third, it gives comfort to those who are to assess the feasibility of the design by letting them know that all decision points have been investigated.

The following serve as inputs to the final prototype:

- **Customer feedback.** Continued customer feedback will help refine the prototype. Walk-throughs should continue. Depending on how large customer involvement is, these walk-throughs can occur with the aid of the decision support center, TeamFocus, and CRTS. When the prototype is ready and there is enough time, run usability studies with the prototype.

- **Initial prototype.** The initial prototype that made it through the functional specification/concept validation phase serves as initial input for the final prototype.

- **Test data results.** These are gathered from icon studies, trade-off, and concept validation.

- **Development and marketing feedback.** Continue to gather information on the feasibility of the design.

The primary goal for this last phase of the prototyping process is to deliver a prototype that will aid developers in low-level coding. Specifically, these outputs are:

- **Living specification.** The final prototype serves as a living specification for developers. The prototype can be distributed to the developer's workstation and the developer can be running the prototype concurrently with his or her code. By making available the prototype, the developer can have an up-and-running model to aid development. The developer can focus on the function and not worry about how the user interface should look and feel. When we have not been able to provide the prototype to the developer in this form, we have given developers the prototype in the form of a videotape so that they can play the videotape when they have design questions. If the production and distribution of a videotape is not feasible, the user interface can be documented in a user interface specification along with screen dumps and directions for use. This document sometimes can serve as the basis for the user's manual.

- **Help panel input.** We have used the prototype to develop the help panels for products. With OS/2, the help panels are written to the prototype with the Information Presentation Facility (IPF, a trademark of the IBM Corporation) resource identification numbers matched up with the prototype resource IDs. In this way, the help panels can be done early in the process, sometimes before a single line of code is written. When the code is written, the compiled IPF file can be linked to the operating code.

- **Actual code.** Depending on how well the prototyping tool matches the eventual application, the tool can be used to generate actual code. For example, KASE:VIP (a trademark of KaseWorks, Incorporated) is a prototyping tool that generates C and Presentation Manager code. A number of the tools generate their own proprietary language. Easel-EE (a trademark of Mark Corporation) and Smalltalk (a trademark of Parc Place-Digitalk, Incorporated) are two of these languages.

  Our opinion is that there is not a tool good enough to provide both prototyping function and good native code generation for any platform. For the purposes of rapid iterative prototyping and good user interface design, we believe that with the choice between a tool that has good code generation capability but poor prototyping function and a tool with poor code generation capability but good prototyping function, it is better to select the tool with good prototyping function.

- **Publication and training input.** A user interface design specification written in terms of how to use the prototype serves as a good start for the user's manual.

- **Customer presentations.** Many of our prototypes have been used by our marketing support staff at customer presentations, executive conferences, and trade shows. The prototypes give customers at large an early view of the product.

- **Idealistic prototypes.** It is at the functional specification time frame that it will become clear that certain functions that the prototype contains will not make it into the product, typically because of a combination of cost, schedule, and need. Nevertheless, these new functions should not be dropped from the prototype. We keep them in a prototype we call the "idealistic prototype," in order to give people an idea of how some function may look in the future. This idealistic prototype is useful for the next release or perhaps entirely new products and to stimulate thought and creativity.

- **Test data results.** Test data results from continued customer walk-throughs and tests will serve as an audit trail for explaining design decisions.

3.2.4 Products of the Prototyping Process

To build a successful interface, developers need to acquire several kinds of information about the system to be built. Szekely (1994) provided the following categorizations of information required for prototyping and the products of the process:

- **Task specification.** A list of the tasks that users are expected to accomplish using the system. It may also include task-relevant data such as documents and data that users will need or will produce. The task specification is needed in order for developers to understand what services to provide in a system and how to deliver them to the end users in order to help them perform their tasks more effectively. Prototypes help developers better understand the tasks that users need to perform by letting developers see users in action with the system and make determinations about the effectiveness of a system. In addition, successful systems often change the nature of the tasks that users perform, enabling them to do tasks they could not accomplish before. Prototypes let developers see how a system might change the tasks the users perform and allow them to design a better system.

- **System functionality specification.** Describes the functional requirements of a system. It specifies the software modules the interface calls on to retrieve and display data and to modify data in response to user requests. Different interface designs often impose different requirements on system functionality. Tools that can build interface prototypes without requiring that the system functionality be built are especially useful here. They allow interface designers to explore design alternatives without having to wait for programmers to revise the system functionality in order to test the prototypes.

- **Interface functionality specification.** Details the system information and states that need to be presented on the screen and the commands available to the users. This specification captures the content of the interface, abstracting away from style details such as font or color. It is important for developers to understand the interface at this abstract level. For example, before worrying about style issues of a display, developers should understand whether the display presents the right data and the right time to help users perform their tasks.

- **Screen layouts and behavior.** Specify how the system interface looks and behaves. This information is of high importance because it defines what users can see and do. Prototyping is very useful to acquire this information because "look and feel" issues can be a source of endless discussions between members of a design team and there is a wide space of possibilities that need to be explored.

- **Design rationale.** A specification of the reasons that the various design choices were made. This information can be used to achieve consistency in the interface, to guide extensions to the interface of a previous version of the system, or to review and justify decisions with management. In addition, since prototypes may implement only a subset of the system functionality, the design rationale is useful in extrapolating from the prototype to the full system.

- **User feedback.** Collected from a variety of sources such as end users and design reviews. Feedback can take several forms; among them, comments that users express while interacting with a prototype, answers to questionnaires, and usability test data. Collecting and managing feedback is an important, and difficult, task. Prototyping tools or other support tools should provide facilities to collect and manage such feedback so it can be summarized and retrieved when needed.

- **Performance criteria.** Specifications of the required system response times in different situations, learning time goals, number of user errors allowable on different tasks, user satisfaction goals, and so forth. Prototypes let developers see the users in action and understand the requirements for effective system usage.

- **Reusable code.** A by-product of prototyping that is used in the implementation of the real system. This helps to reduce the cost of system development and makes it more certain that the interface design shown in the prototype will be accurately implemented in the final system.

3.2.5 Conclusion

Iterative, rapid user interface prototyping is the key to successful user interface design. It provides a number of key advantages for ensuring a more effective development effort. However, the mere act of creating a prototype will not deliver a specification for superior application design. Only when prototypes are iteratively designed and redesigned as a result of a systematic, ongoing design process, emphasizing customer feedback and involvement, will rapid prototyping lead to the development of superior solutions that delight customers.

3.3 THE FUTURE OF PROTOTYPING

Prototyping is increasing rapidly in popularity. This interest is driving the development of new prototyping tools. Existing tools are receiving frequent updates, and many new tools are coming on the market each year. It is becoming increasingly easier to learn to prototype, quicker to construct the prototype, and prototypes can be constructed with greater fidelity than before.

One consequence of this evolution is that the distinction between throwaway and evolutionary prototypes is blurring. In the future, it will become easier for programmers and interface designers to experiment with new design ideas and then integrate them directly into the product. Advances in object-oriented programming aid this as well; new code can be encapsulated such that it is less likely to cause problems in existing code.

Users today often participate in setting requirements and reviewing prototypes. They are sometimes even on the design team, but only recently have some become active in writing the prototype or the actual product. Easy-to-use prototyping tools will allow many end users to prototype their own applications. Programs developed in this manner will much better meet the needs of the end users who know better than anyone else what their needs are.

Better techniques for translating requirements into prototypes and prototypes into code will evolve. Today there are CASE tools that try to support the entire development process from beginning to end. None of them does a good job in all stages, so most teams use a variety of products. Each one may do well at the task it was designed for, but they seldom work together. The need is well recognized; it is only a matter of time before good beginning-to-end development tool sets are available.

Prototyping tools will evolve with user interfaces. Today the GUI is the standard. Tomorrow it may be speech recognition, virtual reality, or something else. Whatever the interface of the future looks like, someone will provide prototyping tools for it. These tools allow software to be developed more efficiently and to meet customer needs better. Programmers and designers who are knowledgeable about these tools and can create prototypes efficiently will have a tremendous advantage.

Chapter

4

SECRETS OF SUCCESS

There are no secrets better kept than the secrets everybody guesses.

George Bernard Shaw

4.1 LOW- VERSUS HIGH-FIDELITY PROTOTYPING

Although prototyping has been recognized as an efficient and effective means of developing user interfaces for some time (Pfauth, Hammer, and Fissel 1985) and has become an integral part of the development process in many organizations (Rudd and Isensee 1994b; Windsor and Storrs 1992), the optimum methods of prototyping have not yet been agreed upon. We know that prototyping provides the means to model software applications to support the evaluation of design alternatives early in the product development cycle. We understand that the use of iterative design promotes the refinement and optimization of interfaces through discussion, exploration, testing, and iterative revision. The experiences of many designers in developing and evaluating user interface prototypes provide testimonials regarding the many applications and benefits of prototypes (Greitzer, Wunderlich, and Weinberg 1993; Kinoe and Horikawa 1991).

An ongoing controversy exists in the prototyping community about how closely in form and function a user interface prototype should represent the final product. This polemic is referred to as the "low- versus high-fidelity prototyping debate." In this chapter, we discuss arguments for and against low- and high-fidelity prototypes, guidelines for their use in rapid user interface development, and the implications for user interface designers. The debate lies in the fidelity of prototype required to illustrate a concept, model design alternatives, or test an application. Do prototypes need to be complete, realistic, or reusable to be effective?

4.1.1 Types of Prototypes

Low-fidelity prototypes are generally limited-function, limited-interaction prototyping efforts. They are constructed to depict concepts, design alternatives, and screen layouts rather than to model the user interaction with a system. Storyboard presentations and proof-of-concept prototypes fall into this category. In general, low-fidelity prototypes are constructed quickly and provide limited or no functionality. They demonstrate the general look and perhaps the feel of the interface; they are not intended to show in detail how the application operates. These prototypes are created to communicate, educate, and inform but not to train, test, or serve as a basis from which to code.

Tullis (1990) contends that the fidelity of a prototype is judged by how it appears to the person viewing it and not its similarity to the actual application. In other words, the degree to which the prototype accurately represents the appearance and interaction of the product is the determining factor in prototype fidelity, not the degree to which the code and other attributes invisible to the user are accurate.

The mind-set for low-fidelity prototypes is that prototyping is rapid, with the prototype code not reused once product coding is initiated. Heaton (1992) believes that rapid prototyping should solve 80 percent of the major interface problems, with the speed of producing a prototype early (during the requirements specification phase) outweighing the need to produce a final model.

Low-fidelity prototypes can consist of a series of static windows or menus that can be rapidly generated and displayed, either singly or in a storyboard presentation. Mark van Harmelen (1989) classifies these noninteractive prototypes as scenario tools. Despite limited functionality, these scenarios can play an important role in visualizing the use of an interface. These low-fidelity prototypes are created to show visuals, including colors, icons, and the placement of controls. They will show design direction but not provide details such as navigation and interaction. Low-fidelity prototypes have very little functionality built in; users can see what the product is supposed to do, but the prototype may not respond to user input. Users do not exercise a low-fidelity prototype to get a firsthand idea of how it operates; rather, low-fidelity prototypes are demonstrated by someone skilled at operating the prototype. The presentation of a low-fidelity prototype is typically carefully scripted to allow the presenter to tell a story about how the product will eventually operate. Low-fidelity prototypes are often used early in the design cycle to show general conceptual approaches without much investment in development. A low-fidelity prototype may be as simple as a paper-and-pencil mockup that shows general flow through the screens.

Low-fidelity prototypes generally require a facilitator, who knows the application thoroughly, to demonstrate or to test the application. Interactivity by the user is restricted. The user is dependent on the facilitator to respond to the user's commands to turn cards or advance screens to simulate the flow of the application.

In contrast, *high-fidelity* prototypes are fully interactive. Users can enter data in entry fields, respond to messages, select icons to open windows, and in general interact with the user interface as though it were a real product. They are high fidelity because they represent the core functionality of the product's user interface. High-fidelity prototypes are typically built with fourth-generation programming tools such as Smalltalk or VisualBasic and can be programmed to simulate much of the function in the final product.

High-fidelity prototypes trade off speed for accuracy. They are not as quick and easy to create as low-fidelity prototypes, but they faithfully represent the interface to be implemented in the product. They can be made so realistic that the user cannot distinguish them from the actual product.

When time is a factor, it is still possible to develop what is called a *vertical prototype*: an interactive, high-fidelity prototype of only a subset of the product's available functions. Another approach is to create *horizontal prototypes*: prototypes that contain high-level functionality but no lower-level system detail. These prototypes may be limited in scope, yet they can be quickly created and provide user interface interactivity that may be essential for specific product design decisions.

4.1.2 Low-Fidelity Prototypes

4.1.2.1 Advantages

Low-fidelity prototypes have great value in the early requirements-gathering and analysis phase of product development. Customers and end users often do not know how to articulate their requirements. Verbalizing design requirements is often not an objective, as design concepts may be biased by a customer's mental model of the system. In other words, customers may have difficulty separating what they want a system to do from how they want the tasks to be performed. A low-fidelity prototype can be the communication medium by which requirements can be articulated. It can serve as the common language to which users and developers can relate. Low-fidelity prototypes are well suited for use in user interface design teams (UIDT) (Kinoe and Horikawa 1991; Telek and Schell 1992), allowing developers to maintain an early focus on users.

Low-fidelity prototypes can be constructed early in the development cycle without a large investment in time and development dollars. Because they are constructed with paper-and-pencil or simple storyboard tools, they require little or no programming skill on the part of the designer. Moreover, they can be presented on paper, viewgraphs, or whiteboards so they are easily portable.

A low-fidelity prototype can be used as a first step in proposing fundamental design approaches for the user interface. The prototype can be demonstrated to potential users to obtain feedback on how well the design meets their needs or which of several designs is most on target. This feedback can be used to iterate the low-fidelity prototype or used as requirements input for follow-on higher-fidelity prototyping.

Rettig (1994) describes paper prototyping as the fastest of the rapid prototyping techniques. By sketching and designing ideas and concepts onto paper, interface designers are able to focus on design rather than the mechanics of a tool. Rettig used paper prototyping to design and sketch a prototype of an automated menu for a fast food restaurant. In six hours, developers designed an interface, built a paper model, tested it, and improved the initial design. The tools for building a paper prototype are simple: paper, index cards, markers, adhesives, and other common office supplies.

Bellantone and Lanzetta (1992) used a low-fidelity prototyping approach to create and project nonprogrammable terminal user interface panels onto an overhead screen for review and revision. Members of a user interface design team addressed layout and terminology concerns with the panels. A walk-through of the prototype was conducted, with the objective to gain consensus that the prototype was complete and flowed properly. Based on design change recommendations, the panels were iteratively modified and reevaluated until consensus among team members was reached.

4.1.2.2 Disadvantages

Low-fidelity prototypes represent broad-brush approximations to the eventual design. Just because something can be represented in the prototype and artfully demonstrated to a set of users does not mean that the approach will be feasible in the product. Because low-fidelity prototypes are typically crude and can provide little error checking, many important design decisions are often overlooked.

Low-fidelity prototypes are not a good forum for user evaluation. Because they are often demonstrated to the user rather than exercised by him or her, it is more difficult to identify design inconsistencies and shortcomings. Nielson (1990) compared the effectiveness of a high-fidelity interactive prototype with that of a low-fidelity static paper-and-pencil prototype for identifying shortcomings. Two groups of evaluators were asked to evaluate each of the two prototypes. There were fifty usability problems with each of the prototypes, fifteen of them labeled major. Nielson found that evaluators discovered significantly more problems with the high-fidelity prototype than with the low-fidelity prototype.

It is difficult for programmers to code to a low-fidelity prototype. Because the prototype is not fleshed out, the programmer is forced to make personal decisions about such details as user interaction and navigation, the content of error messages, the layout and architecture of help panels, and the design of little-used functions. Programmers with little user interface design experience tend to make bad design decisions about what should and should not be done, even if they use an established design guide as a reference. An interesting study by Tetzlaff and Schwartz (1991) bears this out. They found that programmers inexperienced at user interface development often relied more on the pictures in design guidelines than they did the supporting text in making design decisions. The inexperienced programmers also showed higher levels of frustration than experienced programmers when the design guide did not provide obvious and explicit rules for complex application-specific problems.

4.1.3 High-Fidelity Prototypes

4.1.3.1 Advantages

Unlike low-fidelity prototypes, high-fidelity prototypes have complete functionality and are interactive. While low-fidelity prototypes address the layout and terminology of applications (surface presentation), high-fidelity prototypes address the issues of navigation and flow and of matching the design and user models of a system (van Harmelen 1989).

High-fidelity prototypes are interactive and are used for exploration and test. The user can operate the prototype as if it were the final product, selecting icons on the screen and expecting windows to open or functions to be launched. Messages are delivered at appropriate times. Data can be displayed in a real-time fashion and updated periodically, and the user can take action in response to data updates. Errors and deviations from the expected path will be flagged and identified to the user as if using the real product. The prototype will respond in a manner that represents the behavior of the eventual product. In general, the user can get a sense of how the product will operate and can make informed recommendations about how to improve its user interface.

Usability testing can be conducted early in the design process with the prototype as a test vehicle. Realistic comparisons with competing products can be made via the prototype to ensure that the program is marketable and usable before committing the resources necessary to develop the product fully. A representative prototype can be available months before the product code, allowing usability testing, test case construction, help panel design, and documentation to be initiated much earlier in the development cycle.

High-fidelity prototypes are a good educational and productivity tool for programmers and information developers. The programmer can use the prototype as a living specification of the functional and operating requirements. Whenever the programmer needs design guidance, the prototype is fired up, and the function in question is executed to determine its design. This can save substantial time over the typical development process where programmers sometimes make design decisions on the fly that may require expensive rework to fix later. Information developers can generate more useful help panels and documentation earlier in the development process by running the prototype and identifying where users may have problems. In addition, the information developer will better understand the product because of increased exposure to the product's user interface.

High-fidelity prototypes can be effective marketing and sales tools. Customer input can be solicited at customer sites and trade shows and this feedback used to refine the prototype.

Finally, high-fidelity prototypes can be used effectively to encourage customer buy-in. Because the prototype is more fully functional than a low-fidelity prototype, it provides a better basis for thorough evaluation by end users, whose feedback can be used to fine-tune the prototype. Because changes can be made rapidly, end user feedback can quickly be incorporated into the prototype. This rapid turnaround fosters greater end user acceptance because users can immediately see their design recommendations put into place. End users become constructive, contributing members rather than evaluators of the design team when they see immediate turnaround on their input. A high-fidelity prototyping effort, implemented properly, can provide this buy-in.

4.1.3.2 Disadvantages

There are some serious shortcomings to high-fidelity prototyping. Generally, these prototypes are more expensive and time-consuming to construct than their low-fidelity counterparts. Because high-fidelity prototypes represent function that will appear in the final product, prototype development becomes a development effort in itself, sometimes requiring many weeks of programming support. Although high-level languages and screen builders exist to make this process easier, high-fidelity prototyping still requires a substantial programming effort. This places constraints on who does interface design. It is difficult to find people who are both good interface designers and skilled programmers.

When customers see a high-fidelity prototype it often appears that the product is ready. If the prototype is much better than the product that they are using currently, they may demand it immediately, perhaps not understanding that substantial effort may be required to write the base code and perform the testing required to turn a prototype into a commercial product. In addition, not all the function demonstrated in a prototype may be incorporated into the product. For reasons such as cost, schedule, and perceived customer interest, function may be dropped from the time the customer sees the prototype to the time the product is released.

Often funds are not committed to develop a high-fidelity prototype. Given a choice, developers often would opt not to construct any prototype but to test the interface once it is fully coded, during the test phase. Although this happens much less frequently now, many development groups perceive extensive prototyping as an unnecessary added expense and a duplication of effort of a programmer's job. They fear that a high-fidelity prototype may have an impact on product development costs and schedules, the measures on which most development efforts are rated.

Unlike low-fidelity prototypes, the high-fidelity variety is not good for investigating more than two or three design approaches to the interface because they are too expensive to construct and often the detail provided is extraneous to the more important issues at hand. When we are investigating various design approaches, we do not care about the wording of message boxes or the content of help panels. Rather we are trying to determine if a particular approach is appropriate for the intended set of users. High-fidelity prototyping is not a good tool for identifying conceptual approaches unless the alternatives have been narrowed to two or three, depending on budget and schedule.

A disadvantage of presenting alternative design options in a prototype is that design decisions may be made too quickly. Generally products are tested extensively before being released to the field. Testing ensures that the product meets performance, service, and usability guidelines. Given the speed with which rapid prototypes can be generated, there may be a tendency to make rash decisions regarding design options without ensuring that the proper validations are conducted. There is a time and place in the development process for both low- and high-fidelity prototypes.

4.1.4 Using Low-Fidelity Prototypes

Use low-fidelity prototypes in the following situations:

- **When the team is trying to identify market and user requirements.** The low-fidelity prototype can be used to generate ideas quickly and cost-effectively about how the product might work. Low-fidelity prototypes are useful in providing a broad-brush user interface design (Virzi 1990); alternative designs can be quickly generated and evaluated during the requirements-gathering stage.

- **To provide a common language among development and support groups.** A low-fidelity prototype can provide customers and developers with an understanding of the application that cannot be obtained by reading the functional specifications and can serve as an educational aid in understanding how an application works (Bellantone and Lanzetta 1992).

- **To investigate early concepts about what function the product might have and how it might be presented to the user.** It can allow the team to get an early understanding of approaches to screen design and navigation. The prototype can allow the team to iterate through a number of alternatives without a great investment in time and money. The prototype can provide a degree of comfort regarding the suitability of design approaches early in the development cycle.

- **To evaluate design alternatives and depict concepts.** Do not get bogged down in the details. Evaluate broad-brush approaches to particular user interface design approaches. Constrain the list of tasks to the set of the most common tasks that the user performs. Build the prototype around these tasks and don't worry about the other, less important, tasks the user performs. Structure the use of the prototype (demonstrations, focus groups, interviews) around these common tasks. Thus, the prototype is vertically rather than horizontally integrated.

- **To elicit customer input during requirements gathering.** Users know the tasks that software should help them perform, but they may not know how to express these requirements in ways that are useful for interface design. A low-fidelity prototype gives them some idea of what is possible, providing a starting point for discussion and a target for criticism.

There are places in the design process where low-fidelity prototyping clearly does not belong:

- **After the product requirements have been decided upon and coding has started.** At this point, the prototype is too vague and too incomplete to give the programmers the guidance they need in developing the product.

- **As a vehicle for testing user interface issues pertinent to the product under development.** A low-fidelity prototype may be suitable for conducting qualitative evaluations but will not have the detail necessary to allow the design team to make quantitative decisions with high levels of confidence about user interface nuances.

4.1.5 Using High-Fidelity Prototypes

Use high-fidelity prototypes in the following situations:

- **To create a living specification for programmers and information developers.** High-fidelity prototyping should be done in conjunction with the development of a written specification. Screen captures of the prototype as well as descriptions of its use can be included in the written specification. Give programmers a working version of the prototype to refer to when the written specification does not provide the clarity or the detail they need. Give the information developers a copy of the prototype to help them develop the user's manuals and help panels.

- **At trade shows to show the public how the product will operate prior to the code being fully developed.** This publicity gives the development and marketing team a leg up on getting the word out about future releases.

- **For testing user interface issues.** Because high-fidelity prototypes model the application and have error and help information built in, the actions of the test user will more closely resemble the actions of the eventual users of the product. Because high-fidelity prototypes can be available months before coding is completed, the opportunity exists to affect and test changes before the design has been frozen. It is possible to instrument a prototype to automate some of the data collection for user testing. Add code hooks to collect mouse and keystroke time and error data. These data can be used in statistical analyses.

There are phases in the development process where high-fidelity prototyping clearly does not fit:

- **During requirements gathering.** Developing three or more high-fidelity prototypes at this point is a waste of resources. It is too early in the game to be making huge investments in programming services when the market requirements are not clearly understood.

- **When your skills, schedule, and/or budget don't allow it.** Development of a high-fidelity prototype requires programming skills on the part of the interface designer and may be time-consuming and expensive, and a high-fidelity prototype may not be an option. In this case, consider developing vertical prototypes to design and test a subset of available function.

4.1.6 Summary and Conclusions

Table 4-1 summarizes the various advantages and disadvantages for conducting low- and high-fidelity prototyping efforts. Table 4-2 summarizes some of the key points to consider when deciding whether a low- or high-fidelity prototyping effort would be more appropriate for particular design and development needs.

In many ways, the debate over the relative value of low- versus high-fidelity prototyping is a moot one. Both have a place in the design process.

4.2 TWENTY-TWO TIPS FOR A HAPPIER, HEALTHIER PROTOTYPE

Never before has the user-interface designer had the opportunity to take a leading role in software development. Enabled by a vigorous focus on software usability and the availability of a number of robust prototyping tools, corporate user-interface designers are making significant contributions to software development through prototyping. However, a successful prototyping effort requires more than a prototyping tool and a background in user interface design. It has been our experience that the success of a prototyping effort is dependent on many factors—some obvious, some not so obvious, and others learned only through experience. Following are some of the lessons we've learned on the way to happier and healthier prototyping efforts (Rudd and Isensee 1994b).

Type	Advantages	Disadvantages
Low-fidelity prototype	• Lower development cost • Evaluate multiple design concepts • Useful communication device • Address screen layout issues • Useful for identifying market requirements • Proof of concept	• Limited error checking • Poor detailed specification to code to • Facilitator driven • Limited utility after requirements established • Limitations in usability testing • Navigational and flow limitations
High-fidelity prototype	• Complete functionality • Fully interactive • User driven • Clearly defines navigational scheme • Useful for exploration and testing • Look and feel of final product • Serves as a living specification • Marketing and sales tool	• More expensive to develop • Time-consuming to create • Inefficient for proof-of-concept designs • Not effective for requirements gathering

Table 4-1. *Relative Effectiveness of Low- vs. High-Fidelity Prototypes*

Consideration	Low Fidelity	High Fidelity
Cost constraints	●	
Define market requirements	●	
Schedule constraints	●	
Screen layout	●	●
Navigation and flow		●
Proof of concept	●	
Communications medium	●	●
Training overview	●	
Training tool		●
Usability test		●
Basis for coding		●
User driven		●
Facilitator driven	●	
Data collection		●
Look and feel of product		●

Table 4-2. *Prototyping Considerations*

4.2.1 Obtain Upper-Level Development Management Support

Don't waste your time trying to convince programmers or low-level programming managers that prototyping is a good thing. For that matter, don't even waste your time convincing management that it is beneficial. The people you have to convince are those who hold the purse strings for product development. The best way to do this is to invite them into your lab, tell them about the benefits, relate success stories, and top the pitch off with a demonstration of your prototypes. We have found this to be the most effective way for communicating the power of prototyping and, as a very positive by-product, generating interesting, challenging work.

4.2.2 Throw Away Your Prototype

That's right; tear it into little pieces and start again. Don't expect it to be right the first time. You don't know your audience well enough, you do not fully know the limits of the prototyping tool, you will not know the application inside and out, and you don't know whether the developers can implement what you have prototyped. Prototyping is an iterative process, and you are going to learn as you go along. Leave enough time in your schedule to make radical changes based on the feedback you receive.

4.2.3 Make Prototypes with High Fidelity

Under the right circumstances (see preceding section), we have found that high-fidelity prototypes are more successful at convincing management and development that a particular user interface approach will work. The higher the fidelity of the prototype, the greater is the perception that the design approach is feasible, and the more likely it will be accepted. Don't be lazy. What is intuitive to you may not be to the developer. If you have the time, add minutiae to your prototype. Add error messages and help panels. Make sure that every path leads someplace. Not only does it improve the perception of feasibility, but it lets others know that you have studied the problem in depth and have considered each of the user interface issues.

4.2.4 Take Every Opportunity to Show the Prototype

By showing the prototype to as many people as possible, you build a case for the benefits of prototyping and the feasibility of your approach. It gets people excited. No matter how busy you get and no matter how many deadlines are imminent, when asked to demonstrate the prototype to somebody, do it. Not only do you understand the prototype better than anyone else, but you will be better able to answer any user interface question that may come up. If the prototype is good, it will only be a matter of time before marketing will take over demonstrating the prototype. Take advantage of the exposure. Fame is fleeting.

4.2.5 Don't Waste Your Time Prototyping Add-ons

At some point, we all are assigned to point releases of products. By the time this occurs, the excitement of product development has worn off and all major design changes have been decided upon. You are left with the crumbs and the B team. The name of the game is *influence*. If given the opportunity, move on and take an influential and leading role in the development of new products.

4.2.6 Start Early

You cannot start early enough. We have found that an initial draft of the prototype should be available before the product objectives are published. Don't wait for the product requirements to come out. *You* should be defining the requirements. If you have some background in the application area, take your best shot at defining a set of requirements, prototype it, and then go to the users to find out how close you are to providing what is really needed. The initial prototype serves as a straw man to get the users thinking and talking about their requirements. They may tear it apart, but at least you know where they stand and what they want. We have found straw man prototype critiques to be a great mechanism for generating user involvement and commitment in our development efforts.

4.2.7 Make the Prototype the Functional Specification

When the prototype accurately represents what users are looking for, it provides a specification for the developers to code to. The old style of functional specification typically contains hundreds of pages of obtuse technical detail and is impossible to understand and review fully. A prototype provides a "living spec," which the reviewer can see, touch, and play with. Prototyping can greatly increase the efficiency of the development process by eliminating reviews of obtuse specifications that only a small percentage of reviewers read and understand. If you are not able to get rid of the written specification, at a minimum, the prototype supplements the written word. Dr. Mark Ominsky expresses this approach as: "A picture may be worth a thousand words, but a prototype is worth a thousand pictures."

4.2.8 Keep Control of the Prototype in Your Shop

Along the way, others outside your department may volunteer to do some of the prototyping for you. Adroit technical people know a good thing when they see it. You might be behind in your work or you might be interested in improving your working relationship with those who volunteered. Sounds like a good idea, doesn't it? If you are even slightly concerned about your place in the design process, our recommendation is an emphatic **don't do it**. By letting others from outside your department in on even a small portion of the prototyping work, you give up control of the user interface—maybe not on this application, but potentially on the next. Your contribution is no longer unique; constraints like cost, schedule, and coding complexity begin to influence the design subtly; you begin to slip into the old role of consultant rather than owner. In addition, you are doing the product a disservice since, most likely, the others working on the program, such as developers or marketers, will have limited user interface training. It is imperative that you keep control of the prototype in your shop.

4.2.9 Disseminate to All Technical Leaders and Developers

Everyone involved in the development of the product—planners, developers, marketers, writers, testers, and others—has a different perspective and can provide valuable input. The product should reflect all of these viewpoints. You need miss the mark in only one area for a product to fail. Asking for advice can yield a sense of commitment to the product that fosters teamwork.

4.2.10 Develop Idealistic Instead of Realistic Prototypes

Be idealistic in the prototyping that occurs early in the product development cycle. Add as many features to the prototype as you can. Although you know some may not be feasible for the first release, it is important to get these ideas in front of marketers, developers, and users for a number of reasons. First, customers should determine what is important to be included in the first release. Development priorities on our products have often been modified by user requests. Frequently the users didn't realize they needed a new function until they saw it in the prototype. Second, the new features get the developers to stretch the envelope. If we can prototype it, they have a hard time arguing it is impossible to code. Third, it's good public relations for your shop; it convinces users that your development group is serious about producing best-of-breed software. Fourth, it builds up the reputation of user-interface designers. We become the venerated advanced user interface technology people instead of the traffic cops we are sometimes perceived as.

4.2.11 Use the Best Tools

The ideal tool is quick to learn, fast to prototype with, high in function, executes like lightning, and produces code that can be used in the real product. Unfortunately, this ideal tool doesn't exist yet. You must pick a prototyping tool that has the functions most appropriate for your effort. The tool you select will have a significant impact on the success of your work.

4.2.12 Grab a Piece of the Action

Take on responsibility for part of the project, if necessary. On one of our projects, we volunteered to write the installation program and customization samples because the development group did not have the staffing to meet our specifications. By taking on this responsibility, we ensured our company produced a better product; learned more about programming, our product, and the development process; got an appreciation of the problems developers face; and gained respect from the developers by showing we could work in their arena. It's difficult to be everything to everybody, and we are not advocating that position. However, sometimes volunteering for work that you normally do not do pays off in unexpected ways.

4.2.13 The Customer Is King

Cash may be king to Donald Trump, but for a prototyping effort to succeed, user involvement is essential. You can perform task analyses until you are blue in the face, but you will never know as much about the job as the user who performs it day in and day out. We found repeatedly during development of prototypes that users made suggestions we never would have thought of. Users can also be a powerful driving force in setting requirements. When they see a function they like in the prototype, they can demand that it be included in the product.

4.2.14 Look Outside the United States

In many U.S. companies, we are accustomed to developing products for the U.S. market and we expect them to be used outside the U.S. with little change other than language translation. However, the marketplace is becoming increasingly global. The world market is a market you can't ignore. Differences between countries such as laws, education levels, and customers influence the design of software. Talk to customers, users, and members of your line of business in other countries.

4.2.15 Pay Attention to Aesthetics

In customer demonstrations, we found it important to use professional-looking artwork, good screen design, and pleasing color selections. Appearance gave the users an initial, favorable impression of the prototype, helped convince them to look at it seriously, and allowed us to move past the aesthetics to concentrate on the ease-of-use and function questions that are the bread-and-butter issues of our profession. If you have access to a graphics design department, use it, even if it isn't staffed by computer-literate people. This resource will save you many hours and much heartache arguing over aesthetic issues.

4.2.16 Don't Delegate the Prototyping

It is tempting to define the requirements for the prototype and then get an intern or a programmer to implement it. We recommend against doing this if possible. This breaks the feedback loop that comes from getting an idea, implementing it, showing it to users, and cycling through again. We quickly learned which ideas could and could not be implemented by our prototyping tool. We also got ideas by writing the prototype that we would not have otherwise. In addition, prototyping it ourselves forced us to become familiar with the nuances and intricacies of our user-interface design guidelines. Our experience with assigning prototyping work convinced us of the truth of the old programming adage that the most elegant designs are the product of a single mind.

4.2.17 Become Multidisciplinary

When we were doing user-interface design work on programming tools for the banking industry, we worked very hard trying to keep up with recent developments in all three domains (software usability, programming, and banking). We believe it contributed positively to our prototyping efforts. When prototyping, try to build as much domain expertise as you can.

4.2.18 Spread the Word

The user-interface design profession is moving from hardware to software, from testing to prototyping, from support to ownership. It is important to pass your new knowledge along to others through journal articles, conference presentations, technical interchange groups, and in-house publications.

4.2.19 Understand Your Corporate Design Guidelines

It isn't sufficient just to read your design guides. They are incomplete and imprecise, and represent a single-time-slice picture of a moving target. At IBM, our corporate design guide is called Common User Access (CUA). To stay current with CUA, departments read the electronic bulletin boards, send a representative to CUA meetings, and talk to the people responsible for CUA. Know what the rules are today and what they will be by the time your product hits the market. Be informed enough to challenge the rules when you don't think they're right.

4.2.20 Research the Key Interface Issues

Prototypes allow us to do our testing up front, before the program is written. Rather than just looking for problems, we can design and evaluate multiple alternatives. We see early prototyping efforts as a vehicle for performing advanced technology user-interface studies. For many, this will be a very rewarding side effect of early prototyping efforts. In fact, these early prototyping efforts can often identify patentable software ideas.

4.2.21 Know the Competition

You can't compete in the high jump until you know the height of the bar. No matter how brilliant and creative you are, there are important lessons you can learn from the competition. Get to know the competition by purchasing and experimenting with their software, talking to users who use their software, and visiting trade show exhibits.

4.2.22 Don't Become a Traditional (Schedule-Driven) Developer

You know developers—those nasty little trolls who hide in dark corners throwing out curses like "cost" and "schedule." As user-interface prototypes become a key part of the development process, we come under some of the same pressures. Be careful not to use cost and schedule as excuses for not producing the highest-quality prototype possible.

5

TOOLS FOR RAPID PROTOTYPING

Man is a tool-using animal.... Without tools he is nothing, with tools he is all.

Thomas Carlyle

5.1 PROCESS FOR SELECTING A TOOL

Selecting a prototyping tool is not an easy process. There are a wide variety of tools available, and some are more appropriate for particular applications than others. The tool selected can have a large effect on the type of interface you design, the degree of effort required to construct the prototype, the fidelity of the prototype, the number of design iterations you can make within your schedule, whether or not you can use code from the prototype in your application, and so on. We use the following process for selecting tools:

1. Identify the available tools and review their capabilities.

2. Determine project-specific criteria.

3. Prioritize the criteria.

4. Map these criteria to the tools' capabilities.

5.1.1 Identifying Tools

Table 5-1 lists the prototyping tools we know about, followed by a short description. More extensive reviews are provided later in this chapter for the prototyping tools we have found particularly useful and are most experienced with. Since new tools are continually coming on the market and existing tools are often being improved, it pays to do a search. A literature search through a library will provide many reviews and comparisons of prototyping tools.

Product	Supplier	Environment	Type
Action!	ExperTelligence 5638 Hollister Avenue, #302 Coleta, CA 93117 (805) 967-1797	Macintosh	Code generator: Lisp
Actor	Whitewater Group 1800 Ridge Avenue Evanston, IL 60201 (800) 869-1144	Windows	Application development system
AIXWindows Interface Composer (AIC)	IBM White Plains, NY	Motif	Code generator: C
AlphaWindow	Cumulus Technology Corp. 1007 Elwell Court Palo Alto, CA 94303 (415) 960-1200	UNIX	Application development system
ATK or Andrew	Carnegie-Mellon University Information Tech. Center Pittsburgh, PA 15213 (412) 268-6108	X-Windows	Code generator: C
AppMaker	Bowers Development P.O. Box 9 Lincoln, MA 01773 (508) 369-8175	Macintosh	Code generator
Aspect	Open, Inc. 655 Southpointe Court, Suite 200 Colorado Springs, CO 80906 (719) 527-9700	OS/2, Windows, Motif, OpenLOOK	Tool kit, portable
Authorware	Authorware 8500 Normandale Lake Minneapolis, MN 55437 (800) 288-4797	Macintosh	Prototyper
Autocode	Integrated Systems 3260 Jay Street Santa Clara, CA 94054-1215 (408) 980-1500	X-Windows, VMS	User interface management system

Table 5-1. *Prototyping Tools*

Product	Supplier	Environment	Type
Builder Xcessory	Integrated Computer Solutions, Inc. 201 Broadway Cambridge, MA 02139 (617) 621-0060	Motif	Code generator: Ada, C, UIL
Chiron	Richard Taylor Computer Science Department University of California Irvine, CA 92717-3425	Motif, OpenLOOK	
Choreographer	GUIdance Technologies, Inc. 800 Vinial Street Pittsburgh, PA 15212 (412) 231-1300	OS/2, Windows	Application development system
CLIM	International Lisp Associates 114 Mount Auburn Street, 4th Floor Cambridge, MA 02138 (800) 477-CLIM		Code generator: Lisp
C-scape	Liant Software Framington, MA	OS/2, Windows, DOS, UNIX	Code generator: C and function library
Dan Bricklin's Demo II	Intersolv/Sage 1700 N.W. 167th Place Beaverton, OR 97006 (800) 547-4000	DOS	Prototyper
Data Views	V.I. Corp. 47 Pleasant Street Northampton, MA 01006 (413) 586-4144	UNIX, VMS	Code generator: C and C++
DEC Forms	Digital Equipment Corp. 146 Main Street Maynard, MA 01754-2571 (800) 343-4040	VMS	
Delphi	Borland International, Inc. Scotts Valley, CA (800) 331-0877	Windows	Code generator: Pascal

Table 5-1. *Prototyping Tools, continued*

Product	Supplier	Environment	Type
DevGuide	Sun 2550 Garcia Avenue Mountain View, CA 94043 (415) 960-1300	OpenLOOK	Code generator: C
Display Construction Set	AT&T (614) 860-4357	OpenLOOK	Code generator
Easel	V Mark 50 Washington Street Westborough, MA 01581 (508) 366-3888	OS/2, Windows, DOS	Application development system
ENFIN/2 and ENFIN/3	V Mark 25 Corporate Drive Burlington, MA 01803 (617) 221-2100	OS/2, Windows	Application development system
ExoCODE	EXOC 500 Hyacinth Place Highland Park, IL 60035 (708) 926-8500	Motif, OpenLOOK	Code generator
EZX	Sunrise Software Systems P.O. Box 329 Newport, RI 02804 (401) 847-7868	Motif	Code generator
Galaxy	Visix Software Inc. 11440 Commerce Park Drive Reston, VA 22091 (800) 832-8668	Macintosh, Windows, Motif, OpenLOOK	Tool kit, portable
Garnet	Brad Myers Carnegie-Mellon University School of Computer Science Pittsburgh, PA 15213-3891 (412) 268-5150	Macintosh, X-Windows	User interface management system
GIB	TAO Research Corp. 39812 Mission Boulevard, #205 Freemont, CA 94539 (510) 770-1344	Windows	Code generator

Table 5-1. *Prototyping Tools, continued*

Product	Supplier	Environment	Type
GMW and Guide	ASTEC Corp. Nagashimo-Daiichi Bldg. 9F Shibuya-Ku, Tokyo, Japan 00150 +81-3-476-0183		User interface management system
GUI Programming Facility (Gpf)	Gpf Systems, Inc. P.O. Box 414 30 Falls Road Moodus, CT 06469-0414	OS/2, Windows	Code generator: C, C++
Guide 2	OWL International Inc. 2800 156th Avenue, SE Bellevue, WA 98007 (206) 747-3203	DOS	Application builder: hypertext
GX Series Developer's Pak	Genus 11315 Meadow Lake Houston, TX 77077 (713) 870-0737	DOS	Tool kit
HP Interface Architech	Hewlett-Packard 4 Choke Cherry Road Rockville, MD 20850 (301) 670-4300	Motif	Code generator: C
Hypercard	Apple Computer 20525 Mariana Avenue Cupertino, CA 95014 (408) 996-1010	Macintosh	Prototyper
ICON Author	AimTech Corp. 20 Trafalgar Square Nashua, NH 03063-1973 (800) 289-2884	Windows	Prototyper: multimedia
InterMAPHics	Prior Data Sciences 240 Michael Cowpland Kanata, Ontario, Canada K2M1P6 (613) 591-7235	UNIX	User interface management system
JAM	JYACC 116 John Street New York, NY 10038 (800) 458-3313	OS/2, DOS, UNIX	Code generator

Table 5-1. Prototyping Tools, *continued*

Product	Supplier	Environment	Type
KASE:PM	KASEWORKS 1 Dunwoody Drive, Suite 130 Atlanta, GA 30338 (404) 399-6236	OS/2, Windows	Code generator: C, C++, COBOL
KEE	Intelli Corp. 125 Cambridge Park Cambridge, MA 02140 (617) 868-5611	DOS, UNIX	Tool kit: Lisp
Knowledge Pro	Knowledge Garden 473A Malden Bridge Road Nassua, NY 12123 (518) 766-3000	DOS	Prototyper
Layout	Object, Inc. 99 Rosewood Drive Danvers, MA 01923 (800) 424-6644	DOS	Application development system and code generator.
LUIS	Lockhead Austin Division 6800 Berlusen Road Austin, TX (512) 386-4171		
Macintosh Toolbox	Apple 20525 Mariani Avenue Cupertino, CA 95014 (408) 996-1010	Macintosh	Tool kit
Macromind Director	Macromind 410 Townsend, Suite 408 San Francisco, CA 94107 (415) 442-0200	Macintosh, Windows	Prototyper
Menuet	Autumn Hill Software 1145 Ithaca Drive Boulder, CO 80303 (303) 494-8865	DOS	Tool kit
Motif	Open Software Foundation (617) 621-8700	Motif	Tool kit

Table 5-1. Prototyping Tools, continued

Product	Supplier	Environment	Type
New Wave	Hewlett-Packard 19310 Pruneridge Avenue Cupertino, CA 95014 (800) 752-0900	Windows	Tool kit
NeXt Interface Builder	NeXT Inc. 900 Chesapeake Drive Redwood City, CA 94063 (800) 848-NEXT	NeXTStep	Tool kit
ObjectVision	Borland 1800 Green Hills Road Scotts Valley, CA 95067-0001 (408) 438-5300	Windows	Application development system
OLIT	Sun 2550 Garcia Avenue Mountain View, CA 94043 (800) 872-4786	OpenLOOK	Tool kit
Open Dialogue	Hewlett-Packard 330 Billerica Road Chelmsford, MA 01824 (800) 752-0900	UNIX	Application development system
Open Interface	Neuron Data, Inc. 156 University Avenue Palo Alto, CA 94301 (415) 321-4488	OS/2, Windows, UNIX, Macintosh	Code generator: C
Oracle Tools	Oracle Corp. 500 Oracle Parkway Belmont, CA 94065 (800) 633-0521		Code generator: database front end
PLUS	Spinnaker 201 Broadway Cambridge, MA 02139 (617) 494-1200	Macintosh	Prototyper
PowerBuilder	Powersoft Corporation 561 Virginia Road Concord, MA 01742-2732 (800) 395-3525	Windows	Application development system

Table 5-1. *Prototyping Tools, continued*

Product	Supplier	Environment	Type
Prograph	TGS Systems 1123 Spruce Street Boulder, CO 80302 (800) 565-1978	Macintosh	Application development system
Proteus	Genus 11315 Meadow Lake Houston, TX 77077 (713) 870-0737		Tool kit
Protofinish	Genesis Data Systems 8415 Washington Place Albuquerque, NM 87113	DOS	Prototyper
Protoscreens	Bailey and Bailey Software, Inc. 859 East 2850 North Ogden, UT 84414 (801) 782-2345	DOS	Application development system
Prototyper, Now	SmethersBarnes P.O. Box 639 Portland, OR 97207 (800) 237-3611	Macintosh	Prototyper
RIPL	Computer Technology Associates 5670 Greenwood Plaza Boulevard, Suite 200 Englewood, CO 80111 (303) 889-1200	VMS	User interface management system
SET	Caset Corp. 33751 Connemara Drive San Juan Capistrano, CA 92693 (714) 496-8670	X-Windows	User interface management system
Smalltalk/V	Digitalk, Inc. 5 Hutton Center Drive Suite 1100 Santa Ana, CA 92707 (714) 513-3000	Windows, OS/2	Application development system
SUIT	Randy Pausch University of Virginia Department of Computer Science Thornton Hall Charlottesville, VA 22903 (804) 982-2211		Interface builder

Table 5-1. *Prototyping Tools, continued*

Product	Supplier	Environment	Type
Supercard	Aldus 9770 Carroll Center San Diego, CA 92126 (206) 628-2330	Macintosh, DOS	Prototyper
TAE Plus	COSMIC UNIV Georgia 382 East Broad Street Athens, GA 30602 (404) 542-3265	X-Windows	Interface builder
Tk/Tcl	J. Ousterhout UC Berkeley Computer Science Division Berkeley, CA 94720	X-Windows	Tool kit
Teleuse	Telesoft 5959 Cornerstone Court West San Diego, CA 92121-3731 (619) 457-2700	Motif	Code generator
TIGERS	CAE Electronics CP 1800 St. Laurent Quebec, Canada H4L4X4 (514) 341-6780	Motif	
Tigre Interface Designer	Tigre Object Systems 3004 Mission Street Santa Cruz, CA 95060 (408) 427-4900	Windows, Macintosh, UNIX	Interface builder
Tool Book	Asymetrix Corp. 100 100th Avenue, NE Bellevue, WA 98004 (206) 637-1500	Windows	Prototyper
UIMX	Visual Edge Software, Ltd. 3870 Cote Vertu Montreal, Canada H4R1V4 (514) 332-6430	Motif	Code generator: C
VAPS	Virtual Prototypes 5252 deMalsonneve W. Montreal, Quebec, Canada H4A 355 (514) 483-4712	UNIX	Interface builder

Table 5-1. *Prototyping Tools, continued*

Product	Supplier	Environment	Type
Visual Age	IBM Corp. White Plains, NY (800) 426-2255	OS/2, Windows AIX	Code generator: Smalltalk, Cobol, C++
Visual Basic	Microsoft Corp. 10700 Northup Way Bellevue, WA 98004 (800) 426-9400	Windows	Prototyper, Application development system
VUIT	DEC 330 Billerica Road Chelmsford, MA 01824 (508) 256-6600	X-Windows	Interface builder
Windowcraft	Windowcraft Corp. 6 New England Executive Park Burlington, MA 01803 (617) 272-0999	DOS	Prototyper
WindowsMaker	Blue Sky Software 2375 E. Tropicana Avenue, #320 Las Vegas, NV 89119 (702) 456-6365	Windows	Code generator
Windows Development Kit	Microsoft Corp. One Microsoft Way Redmond, WA 98052-6399 (800) 426-9400	Windows	Tool kit
Xbuild	Siemens Nixdorf 4 Cambridge Center Cambridge, MA 02142 (617) 864-0066	Motif	Interface builder
XView	Sun 2550 Garcia Avenue Mountain View, CA 94043 (800) 872-4786	OpenLOOK	Tool kit
XVT	XVT Corp. P.O. Box 18750 Boulder, CO 80308 (303) 443-4223	Windows, Macintosh, Motif	Tool kit, portable

Table 5-1. *Prototyping Tools, continued*

Product	Supplier	Environment	Type
Zinc	Zinc Software Corp. 405 South 100 East, 2d Floor Pleasant Grove, UT 84062 (801) 785-8900	Windows, Macintosh, Motif	Tool kit: C++

Source: Portions of this table came from a list by Brad A. Myers, Computer Science Department, Carnegie-Mellon University, Pittsburgh, PA 15213-3891.

Table 5-1. *Prototyping Tools, continued*

Prototyping tools range from simple screen designers to sophisticated, code-generating development tools. Tools that facilitate rapid development and modification of user interfaces are desirable because they support an iterative design process. Some tools are good only for producing a throwaway prototype; others can provide the interface code for the final application. These tools run on many types of computers under several operating systems. They vary greatly in the capabilities provided, their cost, and the amount of code that must be written. The interfaces they produce range from simple character-based interfaces to sophisticated graphical and multimedia interfaces.

5.1.2 Determining Project-Specific Criteria

There are five areas to consider when determining a project's tool requirements: the goals for tool use, the intended tool user, the hardware and operating system platform for the tool, the required interface style or standard, and other application-related requirements.

5.1.2.1 Goals

When selecting a tool, the first step is to clarify and define goals for how the tool will be used. For example, when doing a proposal or during the early stages of a project, you may be interested in a quick, easy, throwaway or investigative prototype. A low-fidelity prototype such as a slide show can help you explore options or resolve issues. Alternatively, you may be interested in creating a prototype that can evolve through the life of the project to become the actual delivered interface for the system.

5.1.2.2 Tool User Profile

The next step in tool selection is identifying the intended tool user's skills. If the intended user is not a programmer, you need to select a tool that requires little programming skill. A programmer may be able to use prototyping tools that require more programming skill and concomitantly provide greater power and flexibility.

5.1.2.3 Operating System

The operating system you use limits the selection of prototyping tools available. Some tools run on more than one, but the majority are confined to a single operating system. If you want to use any code from the prototype in the interface for the product, you will need to work on the target operating system. A throwaway prototype, on the other hand, provides you more flexibility. You can for instance, prototype a Windows application on a Macintosh, but it may be more difficult to represent accurately the look and feel of the Windows application in this way.

5.1.2.4 User Interface Style or Standard

Designers usually desire to produce an interface consistent with the operating system on which the application will run. These interface styles are defined in style guides, such as CUA, the Microsoft Windows Style Guide, the Macintosh Human Interface Guidelines, and the OSF/Motif Style Guide. If you intend to follow one of these interface styles, choose a prototyping tool that will create compliant interfaces. Alternatively, you may want to create an interface that extends or deviates from the interface guidelines, so you may need to seek out a tool with the power to do this—for example, by allowing the creation of new interface controls or widgets.

5.1.2.5 Application Requirements

Each project may have a set of unique, application-specific requirements that also influence user interface tool selection. Examples of application-specific tool requirements can include dialog style, graphical capabilities, multimedia capabilities, programming language, and cost. List all these application requirements, and use them as a checklist of capabilities needed in a prototyping tool.

5.1.3 Prioritizing Project-Specific Criteria

Once you have determined the goals for using a prototyping tool, the skill level of the tool user(s), the target operating system platform, the user interface style, and application-specific requirements, it is necessary to prioritize these factors. This part of the process is important because it is unlikely you will find a prototyping tool that satisfies all the project requirements. Sometimes one or two of a project's requirements are so critical that it is quickly apparent which tools are possible candidates. At other times, many tools meet the requirements.

Trade-offs may need to be made between the defined selection criteria. For example, you may be looking for a tool that a nonprogrammer can use and produces code suitable for the final product. If a tool can't meet both these requirements, you will need to find an experienced programmer to do the prototyping or decide to make the prototype a throwaway instead of expecting to use code from it.

5.1.4 Important Features

There are a number of important characteristics to look for in a prototyping tool. Choosing a tool with the right set of characteristics will allow you to construct a prototype that has the functionality you need and can be constructed quickly and easily. Choosing the wrong tool can have a negative impact on the interface you design and reduce the number of iterations you can make. The following list of prototyping tool features is based on Hix and Hartson (1993) and Szekely (1994).

5.1.4.1 Easy to Develop and Modify Screens

Design of the visuals and layout of the interface should be quick and easy. There should be some sort of visual builder. If you have to create visuals in other tools and write code to link them into the program, it will slow you down. There should be an easy way to link actions with the visuals. Once the visuals and interactions are defined, the tool should allow you to modify the design easily.

5.1.4.2 Supports the Type of Interface You Are Developing

The interface the tool creates should run on your target platform or at least simulate that user interface style. We have seen many prototypers use a tool that is simple, like HyperCard, to prototype interfaces for other platforms such as UNIX. This is sometimes a good approach since the tools on UNIX tend to require a great deal of programming expertise, but there can also be much time wasted trying to get the visual and interaction styles to be representative. (Try prototyping an application for a three-button UNIX mouse on a Macintosh with a one-button mouse!)

In general, a tool that runs on the platform you are prototyping the application for will most easily allow you to create the correct application style without compromise or lack of fidelity. We have found ourselves switching tools frequently based on the demands of the project. It is often easier to learn a new prototyping tool than to try to force-fit an inappropriate tool just because we have experience with it. Different tools may be required for GUIs, character-based interfaces, multimedia, and so forth.

5.1.4.3 Supports a Variety of Input-Output Devices

A tool should support the hardware devices that will be supported by the target system. If you are prototyping a touch-screen application, for instance, the prototyping tool should support a touch screen. We have been involved in prototyping bank teller systems where the teller must interact with devices such as a magnetic card reader and receipt printer. It is necessary to support these in the prototype in order to accurately test usage of the combined hardware-software system.

Substitutions sometimes can be made. For example, we have used a prototyping tool and a touch panel to build simulations of printer operator panels with adequate fidelity.

5.1.4.4 Easy to Use

Some tools allow you to create screens or windows but do not provide an easy way to link them together. You may be able to create the screens in a graphical editor but need to write code to create any logic. The degree of interactivity can be very limited. Some tools allow you to create prototypes that are little more than slide shows. Look for a tool that lets you create links so that you can simulate the navigational behavior of the product. Make sure that you can also modify those links because prototypes always evolve.

Interface development is a team effort involving end users, interface designers, programmers, systems analysts, graphic artists, and others. Prototyping tools should allow any or all of these team members to participate in the prototyping process. Steep learning curves are unacceptable because many of these people do not have the time to learn complicated tools or the programming background to do difficult coding. Difficulty of use also slows the iteration cycle necessary to develop good user interfaces.

5.1.4.5 Allows Calling External Procedures and Programs

Every prototyping tool has limitations when you are trying to create a high-fidelity prototype of a complex product. The tool may lack functions you need or performance may be inadequate. You can't allow the interface you design to be handicapped by limitations in your prototyping tool. Be sure that the tool you choose is extensible. You should be able to create new functionality through either a programming language supplied with the prototyping tool or calls to external program code. Some tools, such as Visual Basic, can be extended by choosing among hundreds of routines developed by third parties.

5.1.4.6 *Allows Importing of Text, Graphics, and Other Media*

You may want to make use of graphics or other media in your prototype that you already have available rather than having to recreate them using the prototyping tool. Other tools may be better at certain tasks than your prototyping tool. You can't expect the graphics creation part of a prototyping tool to be the equal of Corel Draw, for instance. It may be necessary to export the graphics or other media and work with the external editor as you iterate on the design.

5.1.4.7 *Easy to Learn*

The quicker you can learn to use a prototyping tool, the faster you can be working on the prototype. The easier it is to use, the more pleasant and productive the work will be. Reviews are helpful, but hands-on experience with a tool is the best way to judge it. Evaluation copies are available for many prototyping tools. Try it out on a small prototype similar to the one(s) you want to create; don't just watch a sales demonstration. Prototyping tools can be very good at some things and yet very bad at others. Make sure it is good at doing what you want to do.

5.1.4.8 *Good Support from the Vendor*

Prototyping tools are often developed by small companies that may be here today and gone tomorrow. When you are feverishly trying to squash that last bug in your prototype the night before a demonstration for the big boss or an important customer, you want to know that help is available. Check out the quality of the documentation and evaluate the support before you choose your prototyping tool.

5.1.4.9 *Fits Your Design Process*

The better a prototyping tool fits into the design process at your company, the more positive impact the prototype will have. Many large companies now use CASE tools that support all phases of the development process. If your prototyping tool fits into this process, you can make use of information from earlier design phases and pass along output to the next phase. Some prototyping tools generate flowcharts or code that saves the programming team time and helps make sure their implementation matches the prototype. The usefulness of the prototype doesn't end at system deployment. The development cycle after the shipping phase can benefit from prototyping redesigns and system enhancements.

5.1.4.10 Fits Your Budget

Prototyping tools range enormously in price based on their complexity and sales volume. Popular personal computer prototyping tools such as Visual Basic and Hypercard cost less than $200. Sophisticated CASE tools for less common platforms can cost thousands of dollars. Price is often not a good indicator of quality either. Evaluate the tools for your platform carefully. If your budget is tight, you may want to consider doing your prototyping on another platform. There is no reason a PC tool, for example, can't prototype the interface for a mainframe computer product with reasonable fidelity.

5.1.4.11 Extensive Control over Interface Features

Prototyping tools should be flexible and provide extensive control over the features of the interface you are designing. One of the purposes of prototyping is to try out new ideas and the prototyping tool should facilitate this. You do not want your design to be limited by the capabilities of the tool.

5.1.4.12 Supports a Project of the Necessary Size

Some prototyping tools work well only with a particular size of prototype, while others scale over a considerable range. A tool that provides no way to structure the code, for example, may be fine for a small prototype but become quite unmanageable for a large one. Some tools encounter performance problems as the prototype grows large. A tool good at managing massive amounts of code, on the other hand, may be overkill for a small project if the learning curve is long or it produces multi-megabyte executables.

5.1.4.13 Team Development

Software products are developed by teams. Prototypes often are as well. A diverse set of skills is necessary to produce a good prototype. These skills include interface design, graphic design, knowledge of the application domain, and programming. Prototyping tools should support groups of people working together simultaneously or asynchronously, and perhaps remotely.

5.1.4.14 Data Collection Capabilities

Built-in data collection capabilities provided by the tool or programmed by the prototyper can be helpful for user testing and feedback. For example, we have added user response logs and timing features into some of our prototypes that have helped to automate usability testing and collected far more exact data than was possible through previous, manual methods. IBM sometimes builds user questionnaires into software used within the company. Questionnaires appear at a specified interval, ask users about their satisfaction with the current version of the program and suggestions for improvement, then automatically send these data to the program developers.

5.1.4.15 Distribution of the Prototype

For a prototype to be useful, you need to get it in front of the right people. This often means sending it out far and wide where you can't be around to demonstrate it. Make sure the prototyping tool generates code that can be distributed and easily installed. If it produces a single executable, that is ideal. Some tools require an expensive run time. Others require numerous support files and changes to the system configuration. Some require additional or nonstandard hardware. You can sometimes work around these distribution problems by transferring the prototype to another medium such as a videotape or a screen show.

5.1.4.16 Version Control

An important aspect of prototyping is to explore and evaluate alternative designs. Many versions of a prototype might be built while exploring alternatives. Developers might want to revisit previous designs, so keeping and managing prototype versions is important. In addition, user feedback about a prototype should be tied to the version on which it was collected to facilitate exploring designs to address issues raised during user testing.

5.2 TOOL REVIEWS

5.2.1 Smalltalk

5.2.1.1 Supported Hardware/Software Platform

Versions of Smalltalk/V (a trademark of Digitalk, Inc.) are available for both the OS/2 and Microsoft Windows environments. According to the Smalltalk/V 2.0 Tutorial and Programming Handbook, Smalltalk requires an 80386 or higher computer capable of running OS/2 Presentation Manager (Version 2.0 or beyond). In addition, it must have the following:

- the minimum RAM required by your version of OS/2 or Windows

- a hard disk and one diskette drive

The following items are optional:

- a floating-point math co-processor
- additional RAM
- a mouse

5.2.1.2 Description

Smalltalk was the first, true object-oriented language, and it remains one of the purest. It was a product of a phenomenally creative group of researchers at Xerox PARC in the early 1970s, most notably, Alan Kay, Adele Goldberg, and Dan Ingalls. Today the major dialects of Smalltalk are VisualWorks/Smalltalk-80 and Smalltalk/V, marketed by ParcPlace-Digitalk, Inc., and IBM Smalltalk, marketed by IBM. This review covers Smalltalk/VPM, the OS/2 PM version of Digitalk's Smalltalk/V.

Except for a small kernel in machine language, the Smalltalk system is written in Smalltalk and accessible to the programmer. This provides great flexibility in modifying the language and development environment. Unlike other object-oriented languages, everything in Smalltalk is an object (including characters and integers) and is capable of responding to messages.

Code is written as classes and methods. This encourages developers to write code in a modular fashion that encourages reuse. Classes inherit from those above them in the hierarchy, allowing the programmer to write large functions with small amounts of code if needed functions are already available in classes higher in the class hierarchy.

Smalltalk is more "natural" than procedural languages; that is, the syntax and metaphors are closer to the way people think and further removed from the way computers function. For instance, Smalltalk has objects like Printer and Display, you write with a pen, and these objects respond to messages like "Printer startPrintJob." It is easy to anthropomorphize and picture these objects communicating with each other, much like people holding a conversation.

Operations are easily defined in a manner that makes conceptual sense to the user and hides the underlying hardware and software dependencies. For instance, the same arithmetic operators can work with variables of multiple types. The class for each variable type can define a method with the same name, and the correct one is chosen at run time. The ability of a function (method) to work across types is called *polymorphism*. The user or programmer need not care that the implementation details are different in each class. This information hiding is called *encapsulation*.

Smalltalk is an incrementally compiled language. You can write small sections of code, then run and test them immediately. This fits very well with the iterative nature of prototyping. You can continuously try things out, see if they work the way you want, and then refine them.

5.2.1.3 Usage Scenario

We have used Smalltalk for many prototypes. For one application, we used Smalltalk to build a kiosk aimed at use in public areas such as shopping malls and bank lobbies for banking convenience functions. It can be used by bank customers to get account information or by noncustomers to get information that may encourage them to patronize the sponsor bank.

The functions provided were:

- Rate information and news headlines provided on the main screen (Figure 5-1).

- Theme music to catch the customer's attention and add a little entertainment to using the application.

- A video window that the customer may open to view the Headline News from CNN (Figure 5-2).

- A branch locator that shows the customer what cities contain branches and gives directions using a road map and color pictures of the branches (Figure 5-3 through Figure 5-5).

- An ATM instruction function that shows potential customers how an ATM works by walking them through a series of pictures and instructions (Figure 5-6).

- A balance inquiry function that shows bank customers the balances in their accounts (Figure 5-7).

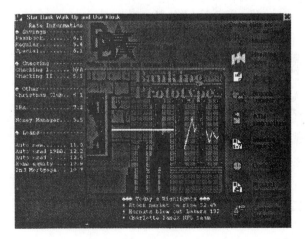

Figure 5-1. *Main Window*

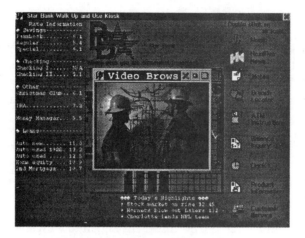

Figure 5-2. *News in Video Window*

Figure 5-3. *State Map of Bank Branches*

Figure 5-4. *Map of Charlotte Branches*

Figure 5-5. *Picture of North Tryon Branch*

Figure 5-6. ATM Instruction

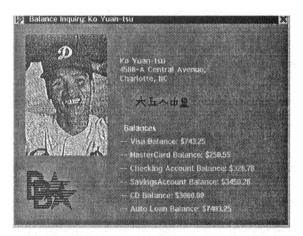

Figure 5-7. Account Balances for a Customer

- A product information function that plays a video informing the customer about products the bank offers (Figure 5-8).

- A clock function showing the time of day.

- A notes function allows the user to leave a message for the bank.

The prototype required three-person months of effort to produce approximately 1500 lines of Smalltalk code. Where Smalltalk did not provide the function we were looking for, we supplemented it by calling external EXEs to handle the video and wrote a small Easel program to play digitized audio files.

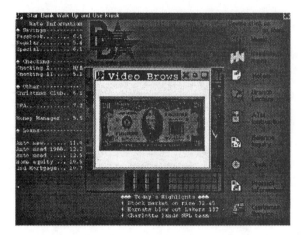

Figure 5-8. *Product Information Video*

5.1.2.4 Advantages

Functional Capabilities

- **Outstanding integrated programming environment.** The Smalltalk programming environment provides an interactive computer-supported environment for the entry, editing, linking, file management, debugging, and execution of user-generated Smalltalk source code programs and system utilities. The Smalltalk editor provides all the basic functions that most editors provide, and pop-up menus make it easy to issue editing commands quickly. Its fully integrated nature and multiwindowing format are ideal for rapidly writing code. You can run and test a program with each small increment of change. This is both helpful and rewarding. It is easy to see why so many programmers are fanatical about Smalltalk.

- **Code Reuse.** The object-oriented nature of Smalltalk promotes code reuse. Code reuse, in this sense, does not mean cutting and pasting, although Smalltalk provides a satisfactory mechanism for doing so. Rather code reuse refers to the capability to design the prototype such that classes and methods can be built that inherit behavior by subclassing from previously built applications. The ability to inherit code cuts down on code bulk and also imposes a logical structure on an application, with similar classes all in one place. As a result, inheritance allows one to build prototypes rapidly by inheriting code from previous applications.

- **Simple syntax.** The syntax of Smalltalk is simple and consistent, with a minimal number of rules and very few special characters. You won't find yourself making niggling little syntax errors so common in languages like C.

- **Incremental compile environment.** Smalltalk's incremental compile environment is a great advantage and an endearing quality. As you save each method, it is automatically compiled. This occurs quickly, and you are then ready to run the program or any part of it from within the development environment. This is a tremendous improvement over the lengthy edit-compile-link-execute sequences in so many other languages.

- **Independence.** We were able to execute instances of classes separately so that we could work more freely and had fewer dependencies on each other than if we were working on, say, a C project. The idea of a free-standing object accelerated our design and development greatly. Most software projects are group efforts, and Smalltalk lends itself well to dividing up the work without excessive amounts of required coordination.

- **Automatic garbage collection.** Objects are allocated explicitly, but there is no program construct to deallocate them. An object cannot be deallocated while any object pointer to it still exists. In Smalltalk, objects are deallocated automatically. Smalltalk uses a mechanism called "garbage collection" to deallocate objects. Through garbage collection, memory is periodically searched for accessible objects and these objects are marked. Unmarked objects are inaccessible and are deleted. The advantage of automatic garbage collection is that the programmer does not have to be concerned with keeping count of accessed objects; the system does that for him or her. This tends to be less error prone than explicit allocation, where the user must actively deallocate an object (e.g., the notion of destructors in C++).

- **Access to system primitives.** Often high-level development tools prevent programmers from accessing more primitive system function. For example many tools prevent the programmer from tailoring the user interface specifically, instead requiring the user to use the existing tool function in building an application. Smalltalk allows the programmer to access complex functions through either DLLs or through the capability to write new methods if existing methods do not provide the needed function. This is a good feature for designing next-generation software.

- **Late binding.** Late binding means that method calls are resolved at run time. This provides a number of advantages for rapid prototyping. First, fewer procedures need to be written, and code does not need to be duplicated. In addition, it is easier to run partially completed systems, because the programmer does not have to write procedures that will not be called yet. Finally, when an error is discovered at execution time, the error can be fixed and the program can be continued.

- **No run-time licensing fees.** It is a compiled language. Your EXE can be distributed freely. Compiles are done automatically when you save a method, so you don't need to request a compile explicitly and you can't forget to do it. Compiles are incremental and usually execute quickly.

- **Other support.** Smalltalk provides support for some of the newer controls such as notebooks and spin buttons. There is support built in for the Information Presentation Facility, which is the OS/2 end user help interface. Smalltalk also enables National Language Support and double byte character set support. In addition, there is a performance profiler provided that allows the developer to analyze application performance.

Tool Usability

- **Class hierarchy browser.** Allows you to view and modify code and provides basic text editor functions.

- **Sender and implementer browsers.** Provide cross-references among the methods within classes of the hierarchy.

- **Inspector.** Allows you to inspect the contents of an object.

- **Debugger.** Allows you to step through your code, inspecting the contents of objects.

These tools are all fairly easy to learn and use. Additional tools or enhancements are available from a number of companies. Source code is provided so that you can enhance the tools yourself.

Documentation/Online Help/Tutorial

- The documentation provides a combination of tutorial and reference information.

- There is no online help.

- The tutorial helps the user understand not only Smalltalk but object-oriented programming as well.

5.2.1.5 Disadvantages

Functional Capabilities

- **Punishing learning curve.** The Smalltalk learning curve is immense relative to most other rapid prototyping tools. Rosson and Carroll (1990) appropriately refer to this as "climbing the Smalltalk mountain." There are a number of reasons for this difficulty:
  - Most programmers have learned to program in a procedural rather than an object-oriented fashion. This retroactive interference serves as a major impediment to learning rapidly the Smalltalk way of doing things.
  - The code syntax is relatively easy to learn; learning the class hierarchy is another matter. Until you have a good understanding of what is in the class hierarchy and have mastered locating method information in the Smalltalk/V documentation and browsers, the amount of information in the class library seems almost overwhelming. Typically, a fundamental understanding of the class hierarchy is necessary before you can begin to write Smalltalk programs. This takes time and discipline.
  - The documentation from Digitalk is of average quality. Although it has many examples, the tutorial exercises often degenerate into nothing more than "select and do it" excursions. The documentation fails to provide the rationale for performing the exercises. As a result, there is a big difference between being able to perform the tutorial exercises and being able to design and write Smalltalk classes and methods. We were constantly running into questions the book didn't even touch on. On the other hand, we thought Volume 1 of *Inside Smalltalk* (Lelond and Pugh 1990) was very useful. Many questions that were left unanswered by the Digitalk reference were answered in *Inside Smalltalk*.
  - Lack of data typing makes it difficult to understand code, especially other people's code, since the programmer cannot tell which methods will be called unless the argument types are known. As a result, it is difficult to follow the flow of a program. This complicates the task of reading other people's code.
  - The heavy emphasis of Smalltalk on message passing yields difficulties for both novice and experienced users in following program flow since, rather than reading code in a booklike fashion like many procedural languages, code is spread throughout the system in many different classes, making it difficult sometimes to discern program control. The behavior of an object may be dependent in large part on the definition of a class in a distant part of the class hierarchy (Rosson and Carroll 1990). In addition, Smalltalk user interaction is managed under the model-view-controller paradigm (see next page).

Distributing responsibility in this way makes it more difficult for users to identify where behavioral associations between objects are taking place.

- **Lack of design guide compliant window classes.** Smalltalk/V could aid developers by providing classes of windows (primary, secondary, etc.) and other constructs that illustrate design guide compliance (CUA or Windows interface design guide). These classes would be very useful to developers not entirely familiar with developing compliant user interfaces.

- **No reference to model-view-controller.** In Smalltalk/V, user interaction is managed by a hybrid of models plus views, and controllers (MVC). The model provides the application logic, view provides a visual representation of the model's data, and the controller interprets user input so that events like mouse button clicks and menu selections initiate appropriate model actions. MVC is the major framework for building applications in Smalltalk. However, none of the documentation touches upon MVC.

- **Image management.** Image management in general can pose a serious problem. Smalltalk is the only programming environment we know of where buggy programs can both crash the system and, in effect, destroy the compiler as well. Smalltalk is one application where you must always know where the system backup disk is.

- **Change management.** Change management can be a problem. The user is frequently filing out classes in case user-specified code crashes the system. For small projects, this is not a big problem, but for large projects this could be a very time-consuming and unwanted activity. A change manager program is a necessity when developing in Smalltalk.

- **Functionality.** Much functionality that other prototyping tools have is missing in Smalltalk. These include business graphics, database support, host communications support, and a stand-alone executable generator. There are, however, many add-on tools that can be obtained from third-party vendors such as Object Share.

Tool Usability

- **Interface layout tool.** Most modern prototyping tools provide an interface layout facility, which lets you create windows and add controls in a WYSIWYG fashion. You can purchase interface builders for Smalltalk such as Window Builder Pro (a trademark of Object Share Int.) from Object Share, or you can use the visual window builder included in the Digitalk offering.

- **Change manager.** Change managers let you save your work incrementally and add code created by other members of a team. A change manager called Envy is available from Object Technology Int., and Digitalk has a change management tool called Team/V.

Documentation/Online Help/Tutorial

- **Documentation.** The documentation is, generally, fairly good but too brief and incomplete to learn Smalltalk or to serve as a robust programmer's reference. Much of the class hierarchy and the fine points of Smalltalk programming are learned by browsing the hierarchy or by trial and error.

- **Tutorials.** The tutorials are helpful, but not sufficient to learn Smalltalk completely.

5.2.1.6 Recommendation

Smalltalk is a difficult programming language to learn. Even experienced programmers struggle with it because the object-oriented principles underlying the tool are so different from procedural languages like C or Pascal. But once you learn the tool, it is relatively quick and easy to write programs in Smalltalk. As a result, Smalltalk/V is one of our tools of choice for prototyping.

There are two roles we believe Smalltalk fills well in the world of a prototyping. First, if your product will be developed in Smalltalk, it is a good choice as prototyping tool because some or all of the code may be used in the product. Second, if you need to include functions in your prototype that require the power of a programming language and are beyond the scope of other prototyping tools, Smalltalk may be the answer. For instance, the developers of CUA '91 were able to use Smalltalk to create controls that were not yet in OS/2 Presentation Manager.

5.2.2 KASE:VIP

KASE:VIP is a CASE tool for generating graphical user interfaces (KASE:VIP and KASE are trademarks of KASEWORKS, Inc.).

5.2.2.1 Supported Hardware/Software Platform

KASE:VIP runs under and generates code for Microsoft Windows or OS/2 Presentation Manager. This review concentrates on the OS/2 version.

KASE:VIP requires:

- 3 megabytes of disk space

- 6 megabytes or more of RAM is recommended

- 386 or higher PC running OS/2 2.x

To compile the code generated by KASE:VIP, you need the IBM C Set/2 compiler and OS/2 2.x Toolkit.

5.2.2.2 Description

The KASE:VIP Workbench is used to define the appearance and behavior of an application using a collection of designers. After using these designers to create the interface, an intelligent code generator produces source code for the application; supporting files include resource, module definition, link response, and help files.

KASEWORKS provides knowledge bases for generating C, C++, COBOL, FORTRAN, and OS/2 Presentation Manager, Windows, and XVT, in various combinations.

Features are provided for team development and reuse of application parts. The tool can be extended through the use of "snap-on" designers and by adding knowledge bases that generate code for different languages.

There is no run-time component required. The code generated by KASE:VIP can be provided to a compiler for the appropriate language to generate an executable.

5.2.2.3 Usage Scenario

The KASE:VIP Workbench is divided into Designer, Tool, and WorkSet components. The Designers folder contains all the design tools. The Tool palette holds the font editor, text editor, icon editor, dialog editor, and other user-defined tools. The WorkSets folder holds objects that have been built by the various designers.

The Designers are tools that allow the developer to specify interactively the appearance, behavior, and connections for various components of the user interface. These Designers are:

- **Application Designer.** Specifies global characteristics of the application, such as the compile and link options.

- **DLL Designer.** Essentially the same as the Application Designer, except that it builds a dynamic link library instead of a stand-alone executable program.

- **Container Designer.** Defines the styles, views, contents, and drag and drop behavior for a container control.

- **Notebook Designer.** Defines the styles, tabs, fonts, and colors of a notebook control. The contents of the pages are designed with the Panel Designer. This Designer visually shows what the notebook will look like as you choose style settings.

- **Window Designer.** Defines the attributes of a window, including style, location, size, icon, and menu. A test mode animates the window, including opening other windows and dialogs that are reached through menu items. The client area of a window can be filled with dialog-type controls (like entry fields and list boxes), a container, or a notebook.

- **Panel Designer.** For designing the pages of a notebook or dialog boxes. By specifying actions for push buttons, dialogs can be connected to other objects produced by the KASE:VIP Designers including windows, other dialogs, and user-defined code.

- **Menu Designer.** For building reusable menu components. Optionally, it will validate the spelling, mnemonics, shortcut keys, and other syntactic aspects of these menus for conformance with CUA guidelines. Shortcut keys are defined visually, by choosing the key combinations from a graphical rendering of the keyboard. Items on the menu pull-down can be connected to objects produced by other Designers, including containers, notebooks, dialogs, processes, user-defined code, windows, functions in DLLs, and executables.

- **Process Designer.** Defines a sequential process that can be connected to objects produced by other Designers. The steps may include containers, notebooks, dialogs, user-defined code, functions in DLLs, and executables. The entire process may be run in a separate thread of execution.

- **Data Object Designer.** Defines data structures for the application. The source code generator will include these definitions and the necessary memory management code.

- **User-Defined Code Designer.** Invokes a text editor and allows arbitrary code blocks to be included in the application. It is configurable so the developer may use his or her favorite editor. User-defined code blocks can be connected to objects produced by other designers.

The information produced by each of these Designers is stored in individual files that the KASE:VIP literature calls "requirements databases." The contents of these files are used by the knowledge base to produce source code.

Icons are created using the IBM OS/2 Icon Editor and dialogs using the IBM OS/2 Toolkit Dialog Editor; icons for calling them are in the KASE:VIP tool palette. These can be replaced by other tools if the user desires.

Applications are built by creating application objects using the Designers or by assembling existing objects from the WorkSets folder. Using the C language knowledge base, KASE:VIP will generate the C, H, make, RC, IPF, DEF, and LNK files for the application. The compile, link, and execution steps can all be called from within KASE:VIP.

5.2.2.4 Advantages

Functional Capabilities

- **32 bit.** KASE:VIP is a 32-bit application and generates 32-bit application code.

- **Memory optimization.** The DLL Designer lets the application developer demand-load parts of the application, helping to optimize the application's use of memory.

- **Drag and drop.** Applications can be designed to exploit drag and drop features, primarily through containers.

- **Threads.** Multiple threads of execution are supported, and thread management code is generated automatically. This is useful, for example, to maintain responsiveness of the user interface while other processing occurs in the background.

- **Extensibility.** The architecture is open, allowing the use of snap-on Designers and knowledge bases, which add new functions to KASE:VIP or allow it to generate code for additional target environments.

- **Code generation.** KASE:VIP generates source code that can be used for the application as well as a prototype.

- **Regeneration.** User-defined code is preserved when the interface is changed and the code regenerated.

- **Size.** There are no intrinsic limits on size of an application, number of windows, or other application elements. The code is efficient and clean. There is no run-time layer and no unusual memory requirements for the completed application.

- **Reliability.** The source code generated appears to be reliable and of high quality. KASE:PM may be an aid to creating reliable applications.

- **Maintenance features.** Maintaining an application built with KASE:VIP is easier than an application coded from scratch because of the support for reusable objects and the coded regeneration capabilities.

Tool Usability

- **Compliance checking.** Automatic checks are made for some aspects of CUA compliance, making it easier for the developer to create CUA-compliant interfaces.

- **Easy to use.** The user interface is consistent and easy to learn.

- **WYSIWYG.** The Designers allow interfaces to be designed and laid out in an easy WYSIWYG fashion. No code is necessary to create most visual components of the interface.

- **Code reuse.** Reusable components can be created. This allows applications to be constructed quickly from code generated on previous projects or by other users.

- **Logic separation.** KASE:VIP encourages a clean split between the application's user interface and the business logic. This makes it easier to change the interface or to split the work between application designers and business logic programmers.

- **Shortcuts.** Shortcuts and other fast-path options are provided for expert users. There is also extensive customization capability.

- **Team development.** This product is well suited for team development and large applications. Because components can be built and stored as objects, several developers can work together and keep the code in a common repository.

Documentation/Online Help/Tutorial

- **Help generation.** Templates can be generated for the help files that include entries for all dialogs, controls, and so forth.

- **Documentation.** The information provided by the documentation is adequate. After becoming familiar with KASE:VIP, users should seldom need to refer to the documentation.

- **Code.** The code generated is well laid out and commented. It can serve as an aid to learning Presentation Manager programming.

5.2.2.5 Disadvantages

Functional Capabilities

- **No WPS classes.** KASE:VIP does not generate code to use or build Workplace Shell classes.

- **Animation errors.** When animating the interface, dialogs sometimes do not display their contained controls correctly.

- **Incomplete team support.** There is no versioning or change control capability to support team development.

Tool Usability

- **Programming skill required.** Significant OS/2 Presentation Manager programming skill is required to build all but the most trivial prototypes or applications.

- **Test.** Test and animation facilities are available to review the interface as it is being developed, but these features are limited, and it is necessary to generate source code and compile it accurately to see how the interface will work. This can be a negative point for prototyping since the compile-edit-link cycle is often lengthy.

- **Speed.** Regeneration times can be extremely slow, although this has improved greatly over previous versions.

- **Source control.** There is no explicit source control. In a team programming environment, this puts a burden on the team members to track code changes and provide their own check-out mechanisms.

- **Installation.** The installation process is partly manual. The user must copy some files and update the config.sys file.

Documentation/Online Help/Tutorial

- **Help generation.** Although KASE:VIP can generate help templates, the developer must use a text editor to create the help text and must be knowledgeable about the IPF help format.

- **Documentation quality.** The documentation is in one very large looseleaf binder. It would be more convenient divided into two or more smaller books. There are many typographic errors, and the screen captures are of low quality.

- **Tutorial.** The tutorial is overly long and goes into greater depth than most users are likely to want in the beginning stages of using the product.

5.2.2.6 Recommendation

KASE:VIP is a good third-generation language case tool. It is suited to laying out an interface, but adding behavior to it requires significant programming. The lengthy edit-compile-link cycle makes it tedious to use for iterative prototyping. This tool is best used when the prototyper is a skilled programmer and source code generation is important for the project.

5.2.3 XVT

The Extensible Virtual Toolkit (XVT) is a set of portable, high-level application programming interfaces for graphical user interfaces.

5.2.3.1 Supported Hardware/Software Platform

XVT can be used to create GUIs that are portable across OS/2, Windows, Macintosh, Motif, OpenLOOK, and Windows NT. The XVT APIs call the underlying tool kit APIs so that applications created with XVT have the look and feel of native applications. This review will concentrate on the OS/2 version of XVT.

XVT for OS/2 PM requires 2.7 MB of disk space, 6 MB of RAM, and a 386 or higher PC. Supporting software required is OS/2 and the IBM C Set/2 compiler.

5.2.3.2 Description

XVT is a CASE tool that allows a developer to write a single version of an application and compile it for multiple platforms.

XVT provides its own proprietary set of APIs that are common across a variety of platforms. These APIs abstract system services for the user interface, addressing events, windows, fonts, graphics, and online help. The XVT APIs are then translated into those of each native platform.

The XVT APIs follow a common-denominator approach. They provide the degree of function common across all target platforms. This limits the features the interface designer can put in the application but makes the code easily portable. No source code changes are necessary to port an application; you just recompile and relink.

Run-time libraries are required to support an application on each platform.

5.2.3.3 Usage Scenario

The XVT Designer allows WYSIWYG layout of the windows and controls for an interface. The Designer generates user interface definitions in universal resource language (URL), plus a skeleton of the application's code. A utility called CURL converts URL into the native resource file syntax for each platform. The code is organized into event-handling procedures that should be familiar to programmers who have worked with event-driven windowing systems.

The Designer is an optional (separately purchased) component of XVT. Applications can be created by writing code entirely by hand using the tool kit services.

XVT provides APIs and services in the following areas:

- **Events.** XVT applications follow the event-driven programming model used by many modern GUI systems. Events are notifications of user actions (such as clicks on a push button) or system events (such as redrawing a window).

- **Windows, menus, and controls.** XVT provides window types that are more specific than provided by many other window managers, including document windows, child windows, dialogs, print windows, and task windows. Some windows automatically provide certain types of support—for example PostScript output from print windows. The common controls are provided.

- **Graphics.** XVT uses a pen-and-brush graphics model that is implemented on top of various graphics engines. Twenty-four-bit color, various shapes, and encapsulated pictures are supported.

- **Fonts.** A font mapper matches the font style, point size, and metrics to the closest font available on the target platform.

- **Help.** XVT provides its own portable help system. A help compiler is provided to transform plain text into the help database that is shipped with the application.

XVT generates one source file for every window in the application.

5.2.3.4 Advantages

Functional Capabilities

- Supports a wide variety of compilers and platforms.

- Provides portable graphics services.

- Provides a portable help system.

- Supports C and C++ on a variety of platforms, including Windows, OS/2 PM, Macintosh, Motif, and OpenLOOK.

Tool Usability

- Layout editor offers adequate function.

- Predefined dialogs are provided to save development time and increase consistency.

- Installation is easy except that the user must manually update the config.sys file.

Documentation/Online Help/Tutorial

- Documentation is in two three-ring-binder books, which include installation instructions, a tutorial, a user's guide, and a reference. The documentation is of average quality.

5.2.3.5 Disadvantages

Functional Capabilities

- Does not support widgets that are available on one of the supported platforms but not others.
- Does not generate any code for the application's business logic.

Tool Usability

- Procedures for defining mnemonics and accelerator keys are cumbersome.
- The help system does not allow the creation of context-sensitive help. The look and feel of the help generated by XVT is unlike any of the target platforms.
- When the code is regenerated, it wipes out any changes the programmer has made.
- The interactive test facility allows navigation between windows and dialogs, but to see accurately how the application will work, the developer must go through a lengthy compile-link-debug cycle.
- Significant programming skill on the part of the prototyper is required to use XVT.
- There is a high learning curve for the XVT API set. These are different enough from other platforms that experienced programmers can find it difficult to switch to XVT.
- Code generation is very fast compared with other CASE tools.

Documentation/Online Help/Tutorial

- The documentation provides almost no information on how to compile code for other environments.

5.2.3.6 Recommendation

XVT is the best of the small crop of cross-platform GUI builders. It is appropriate for projects where portability and code generation are primary concerns. Lengthy compile cycles and a high requirement for programming skills make this an appropriate prototyping tool only when the prototyping will be done by a skilled programmer and the prototype code must be used for the final application.

5.2.4 Visual Basic

Visual Basic is a fourth-generation language for designing and building applications with GUIs. It is based on an enhanced version of the Basic language. It is a product of Microsoft Corp.

5.2.4.1 Supported Hardware/Software Platform

There are versions of Visual Basic for DOS and for Microsoft Windows. This review looks at the Windows version.

Visual Basic version 3.0 for Windows runs on 80386 or higher PCs running Microsoft Windows version 3.0 or higher. It requires 1 meg of memory (2 meg recommended) above that required by Windows.

A professional version is available, providing a wider collection of controls, the ability to build your own controls, and database connectivity.

5.2.4.2 Description

Visual Basic has proved to be a very popular tool for prototyping and construction of small applications. It is based on Basic, probably the most widely understood programming language and one of the easiest to learn. It provides a visual development environment for layout of the user interface of an application. All components of the development environment are well integrated. It follows an event-driven programming model.

There are two main functional areas in Visual Basic: the *designer,* for laying out the visual elements of the interface, defining event procedures, and creating the program logic, and the *debugger,* which allows the program to be executed and debugged.

5.2.4.3 Usage Scenario

Application design typically begins by laying out the visual components of an application's user interface using the Designer. Windows, dialogs, and other components are referred to as *forms* in Visual Basic (Figure 5-9). Controls are dragged from the tool palette into these forms.

Menus for the application are created using the menu design window (Figure 5-10). Each form may have a set of pull-down menus. A properties window lists the properties that may be set for each control and shows the current values of each property (Figure 5-11). These properties allow the programmer to define the appearance and some aspects of behavior of each control.

Each interface object may have event procedures associated with it. Visual Basic creates a skeleton of a subroutine associated with each control. An editor is used to add code to these subroutines specifying what the program is to do when the control receives a specified event (Figure 5-12).

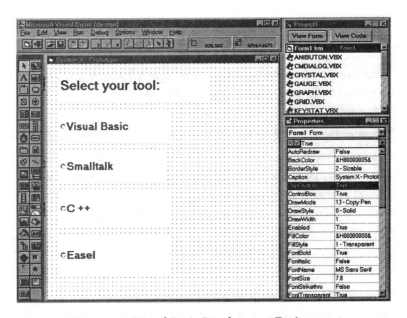

Figure 5-9. *Visual Basic Development Environment*

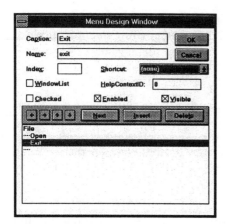

Figure 5-10. *Menu Design Window*   **Figure 5-11.** *Properties Window*

A project window allows you to group the forms, variables, and basic modules comprising an application (Figure 5-13).

Applications can be compiled to create an EXE, but they require a DLL to be distributed with them in order to run.

5.2.4.4 Advantages

Functional Capabilities

- **Complete set of controls.** All the common Windows application controls are provided (push buttons, radio buttons, list boxes, combo boxes, scroll bars, etc.).

- **Extensibility.** Many third-party tools are available to extend Visual Basic.

- **Links to other languages.** You may link Visual Basic applications to DLLs created in other languages such as C or FORTRAN, particularly useful if you want to create a user interface using Visual Basic and create the business logic in another language.

- **Database connectivity.** Support for connection to external databases is provided in the professional edition. This can facilitate the creation of client-server applications.

- **Flexibility.** Visual Basic will let you prototype almost any Windows application. Some things may be harder to do than others, but you should find few

Figure 5-12. *Code Editor*   *Figure 5-13.* *Make File*

real roadblocks. This is not a tool that will force you to design around the limitations of the prototyping tool.

Tool Usability

- **Good integrated programming environment.** There are a variety of editors in Visual Basic; all are called from the designer and work well together.

- **Easy to learn.** Basic is an easy language to learn. The commands are English-like, and the syntax is simple.

- **Interactivity.** That programs can be created in an incremental manner and tested as you go along fits well with the iterative nature of prototyping.

Documentation/Online Help/Tutorial

- **Good documentation.** The hard-copy documentation and the online help are very good relative to that provided with other prototyping tools.

- **More documentation available.** The computer section of any large bookstore is likely to have several titles on using Visual Basic. It should be no problem finding supplemental information when you need a clearer explanation or a clue on how to perform one of the more difficult programming feats.

- **Samples.** Tutorial and several sample applications are provided. The documentation walks you through creating an application.

5.2.4.5 Disadvantages

Functional Capabilities

- **It's Basic.** The Basic programming language is a curse as well as an advantage. It lacks the structure and power of other languages such as C and Smalltalk.

- **It's a programming language.** Make no mistake about it: you have to program to do a useful prototype in Visual Basic. After drawing a few windows, you must write code to get the application to do anything. The code you must write is Basic, which still looks much like it did thirty years ago. There are no visual tools to create a program by drawing flowcharts or connecting objects.

- **Not appropriate for large prototypes.** There are no tools provided to support development in a team environment. As the prototype increases in size, it will become progressively harder to maintain, and performance may suffer.

- **Not a CASE tool.** There are no facilities for generating code in other languages. Unless the product you are prototyping will be coded in Visual Basic, you will be creating a throwaway prototype.

- **Creating help.** There are no facilities for creating help files in the standard edition.

Tool Usability

- **Event-driven model.** Many programmers are unfamiliar with the event-driven programming model, and it can take some time to catch on to. Event-driven code can be hard to debug.

Documentation/Online Help/Tutorial

- **Always needed.** The documentation and help will be needed frequently, even after you have some experience with Visual Basic. There are many objects, functions, and properties to remember that must be provided with parameters in the proper syntax.

5.2.4.6 Recommendation

Visual Basic is one of the best prototyping tools available for Windows applications. It is easy to learn, and you can quickly construct prototypes of great detail and fidelity. It does, however, require programming ability to do anything more than screen layout.

5.2.5 PowerBuilder

PowerBuilder is a fourth-generation tool for prototyping or building client-server applications that run under Microsoft Windows. It is designed for use by professional programmers.

5.2.5.1 Supported Hardware/Software Platform

PowerBuilder version 2.0 for Windows runs on 80386 or higher PCs running Microsoft Windows version 3.0 or higher. It requires 2 meg of memory above that required by Windows.

5.2.5.2 Description

PowerBuilder applications consist of windows containing controls and menus, functions, data structures, and user-defined objects. Tools called painters are provided for defining and maintaining these components.

PowerBuilder largely shields the programmer from the Windows event logic. This reduces the learning curve but also makes it difficult to get a sense of the total application flow and the linkages and dependencies between window objects. The development environment allows applications to be debugged interactively and iteratively.

PowerBuilder applications are written in a proprietary fourth-generation language called PowerScript. It supports calls to external C functions in DLLs.

PowerBuilder applications are stored in libraries during development and compiled to an EXE for distribution. Support files may accompany this EXE, including the PowerBuilder run-time libraries, INI files, DLLs, and help files.

5.2.5.3 Usage Scenario

Work starts from the **Power Panel**, which holds each of the tools and painters used to create PowerBuilder applications. The painters and tools include the following:

- **Application Painter.** Specifies overall default information about the application, such as its name, icon, and the location of compiled objects and scripts.

- **Window Painter.** Used to lay out window controls and define their scripts. Scripts for controls handle Windows events such as defining the application's responses to drag and drop events, list selection events, and entry field modification events.

- **Menu Painter.** Builds menus that can be attached to windows. Menu items have scripts that define what happens when the menu item is selected.

- **DataWindow Painter.** Defines structures much like records in other programming languages. Structures can contain elements of standard data types such as Boolean, string, and date, as well as elements that are window controls, such as radio buttons, bitmaps, and drop-down lists.

- **Database Painter.** Defines and maintains database definitions and contents. PowerBuilder supports several popular database interfaces. The Database Painter is used to create and modify database definitions and perform other database administrator functions.

- **Function Painter.** Used to build functions containing application logic. These functions are written in the PowerScript language.

- **Library Painter.** Used to create and maintain libraries of PowerBuilder objects and to create run-time libraries.

- **User Object Painter.** Used to build custom objects or new controls.

Other tools on the Power Panel include the following:

- **Preferences Tool.** Sets PowerBuilder options and lets you customize the development environment.

- **Online-help.** Displays help for the PowerBuilder development environment.

- **Picture Tool.** Starts an external paint program (of the user's choice) for drawing bitmaps.

- **Run Tool.** Executes the current application.

- **Debug Tool.** Executes the current application in interactive debug mode.

PowerBuilder has a proprietary fourth-generation extension language called PowerScript. It has a traditional language grammar with standard constructs, parameters, functions, and syntax. The language is primarily procedural, with some support for PowerBuilder unique object-based characteristics.

5.2.5.4 Advantages

Functional Capabilities

- **Access to OS features.** PowerBuilder provides a high degree of access to operating system features and services.

- **Drag and drop.** Drag and drop can be implemented easily. In many competing tools, drag and drop is either not supported or is very difficult to implement.

- **Hooks.** User hooks allow application developers access to functions that are not directly supported by PowerBuilder.

- **Control support.** PowerBuilder supports all of the standard Windows controls. In addition, it includes the powerful DataWindow control, which provides a tabular, spreadsheet, or free-form display of data from a database query.

- **Extensible.** PowerBuilder objects can be extended by modifying or grouping existing controls or by making calls to external DLLs.

- **Client-server.** It is well suited to producing client-server applications.

- **Library.** Library facilities allow developers to partition an application for both performance and packaging benefits.

Tool Usability

- **Easy to program.** PowerScript is easy for programmers. Even less skilled programmers can produce significant applications with it.

- **Supports iterative development.** PowerBuilder is well suited to the iterative development process, which works well for prototyping.

- **Easy to learn.** The user interface is consistent and easy to learn.

- **WYSIWYG.** The painters and tools generally work in a WYSIWYG fashion, allowing you to see how the application will look throughout development.

- **Fast paths.** There are a number of fast-path features provided. For example, the Window Painter resizes controls automatically as you type text into them, each tool bar has a backtrack icon that takes you to the previous tool, and a search feature will look for a text string in any object.

- **High productivity.** Productivity is very high using PowerBuilder.

- **Error checking.** Scripts are compiled immediately after editing so that syntax errors are caught immediately.

Documentation/Online Help/Tutorial

- **English language.** PowerBuilder is an English-only product, although the documentation has been translated into some other languages.

- **Clear documentation.** Documentation is generally clear and complete, with few errors.

- **Good online help.** Online help often equals the printed help in terms of clarity, completeness, and appearance. Hypertext links and graphical cues are extensive.

- **Good tutorial.** A good online tutorial is provided.

5.2.5.5 Disadvantages

Functional Capabilities

- **Lags OS changes.** As with any other fourth-generation language, changes to the operating system may not always be reflected immediately in PowerScript functions.

- **Incomplete drag and drop support.** Drag and drop is supported only within a single PowerBuilder application, not between PowerBuilder applications or between a PowerBuilder application and another Windows program.

- **Reliability problems.** There are occasionally reliability problems, such as screen repaint problems and programming errors the compiler does not check for, which are not caught until run time.

- **Run time required.** A run time component must be distributed with the EXE.

- **Poor team development support.** The library support and check-in/check-out procedures are inadequate to support team development.

Tool Usability

- **Many tools to learn.** It can be difficult at first to understand the many painters and tools.

- **Piecemeal development.** Programs are developed in small pieces, which can make it difficult to understand flow of control.

- **Programming skills required.** You must be a programmer to produce significant applications or prototypes with PowerBuilder. There is no notion of visual programming in the product.

Documentation/Online Help/Tutorial

- **Difficult to create help.** Creating help files is difficult. They must be created in rich text format using an external editor and then compiled using the Windows SDK. Time, skill, and care are required to synchronize context ids.

5.2.5.6 Recommendation

PowerBuilder is an excellent tool for prototyping Windows applications (particularly client-server applications) provided the prototyper has programming experience. It will produce code suitable for the final product, but only if that product is to be created with PowerBuilder.

5.2.6 EASEL

Easel is a set of programs for developing and executing graphical applications on OS/2 and Windows. Its use is specifically aimed at:

- Graphical end user interfaces for existing terminal-based host applications.

- Client-server application development.

- GUI front ends for database applications.

- Stand-alone or LAN-based applications.

- The workstation portion of a cooperative processing application.

5.2.6.1 Supported Hardware/Software Platform

Easel requires a machine that can run IBM OS/2 2.X or Windows 3.X.

To run effectively, the development environment requires approximately 12 MB fixed disk capacity and approximately 8 MB of main storage.

Easel supports the following:

- Support for most GUI widgets and a set of specialized tools for creating customized user interfaces.

- Database access via Microsoft's Open Database Connectivity, Microsoft and Sybase SQL Server, Oracle, DEC, and UNIX servers, static and dynamic access to DB2/2, DB2, SQL/400, and Informix.

- Audio capture and playback.

- 3270, 5250, CICS OS/2, and peer-to-peer protocols for data communications.

- Business graphics.

- Dynamic data exchange (DDE) protocol to allow communication between EASEL and other Presentation Manager programs.

- National Language Support for single-byte, left-to-right language applications. It meets the requirements for selection of keyboards and code pages for languages in Europe, Canada, and Latin America.

5.2.6.2 Description

Easel has a relatively advanced suite of visual tools for GUI construction. These tools include the Layout Editor, which is a WYSIWYG user interface definition facility that allows the user to construct and test prototype windows, dialog boxes, and interface flows. The Menu Editor provides an easy-to-use method for creating and modifying menus, and the Drawing Editor gives the user a number of tools for creating graphics.

The ESL Wizard is a visual programming tool that provides reusable code libraries and dynamic code generation. It provides sample Easel code libraries that can be added through an easy-to-use point-and-click interface. It is a good set of tools for jump-starting a novice Easel prototyper.

Easel applications can utilize most standard GUI controls in OS/2 Warp and Windows, including:

- cascading menus

- multiline entry fields

- notebooks

- combination boxes, drop-down combination boxes, and drop-down lists

- nondisplay password entry fields.

The source code generator will also optionally generate separate source files for graphical object definitions and application processing logic.

The developer tool kit for OS/2 or Windows is recommended for developers who want to design their own icons or fonts, write their own DLLs, or otherwise extend the capabilities of Easel. A paint tool such as CorelDraw or PhotoShop and a tool to convert these output formats to OS/2 bitmaps are also highly recommended for applications that will require highly detailed color bitmapped graphics.

5.2.6.3 *Usage Scenario*

We have used Easel for prototyping and usability testing efforts for branch banking applications. Prototypes have been developed for:

- Transaction sets for use by financial service representatives and tellers.

- A transaction definition enabler, which allows banks to customize existing transactions or build entirely new transaction sets to fit individual branch needs.

- An advanced function banking workplace that integrates existing bank automation tools.

Figure 5-14 shows a sample of the user interface for completing customer check orders. In support of the development effort, we use the prototypes in an iterative fashion to solicit field feedback from bankers and marketing specialists through off-site prototype focus groups. We then use this feedback to improve the prototypes. We distribute the prototypes and Easel Runtime with the functional specifications to supplement the specification material (Rudd, Isensee, and Beechler 1990). Using Easel to develop prototypes rapidly in this fashion has allowed us to:

- Develop a much better understanding of market requirements.

- Prototype advanced functions not currently in branch products and give management important early market feedback for the viability and acceptance of new features that may not have been previously considered.

- Get early customer input so that product design and architecture can be modified in the requirements phase while changes are still easy to make.

- Help customers plan their long-range strategies by giving them an early look at the prototypes of new product offerings.

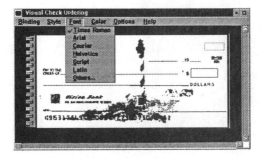

Figure 5-14. *Check Ordering*

- Provide developers with a prototype so that they can gain hands-on experience to allow them to hit the ground running when they start on the project. It has allowed them to concentrate on how to implement a function rather than what functions to provide and how they should look and feel.

- Give reviewers a better picture of how the product works and therefore put them in a position to provide more accurate and complete design input.

5.2.6.4 Ease of Use

Easel provides the Layout Editor tool, which allows the user to create user interfaces that conform to CUA and Windows user interface guidelines. The Layout Editor is a WYSIWYG editor that allows the user to create the visual layout of the user interface through the use of a direct manipulation tool palette. Once the visual appearance of the interface has been specified, the interface can be converted directly into Easel code that is compiled and run. Figure 5-15 shows the opening screen of the Layout Editor window.

The user creates windows and dialog boxes by selecting items on the Project pull-down. GUI controls are added to windows and dialog boxes by selecting objects from the tools palette. The user can use clipboard options to cut, copy, and paste GUI controls. The user can also align controls and create selection fields by selecting items from the Arrange and Options pull-downs. The Layout Editor provides extensive help.

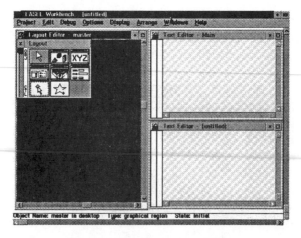

Figure 5-15. The Layout Editor

Once the windows and dialog boxes have been developed by the user, they can be converted to Easel source code. Subroutines are generated and responses added for any pull-down choices that are to bring up windows.

After the Layout Editor source is converted, like most other rapid prototyping tools, the user will need to modify and add to the generated Easel code by using the Text Editor or a self-supplied editor. Depending on the type of application that is being developed, user-provided code may represent 50 percent or more of the total lines of code once the prototype is finished.

After the code is modified by the user, it is compiled, and the user can then use the Interactive Debugger and the Trace facility to debug and incrementally refine the code. Despite being event driven in nature (i.e., responses to events launch procedures and functions), the Easel coding language uses familiar procedural control structure (if-then-else, do-loops, etc.). Most experienced programmers will have little trouble picking up the language. VMark calls the language "object based."

Most users will find the Layout Editor to be very easy to use, comparable to most of today's fourth-generation languages. The Easel tool has been around longer than most of the other leading prototyping tools, such as Visual Basic or Visual Age, and most of its rough edges have long since disappeared.

5.2.6.5 Advantages

- The WYSIWYG Layout Editor is a very good layout tool, superior to most others currently available.

- The coding language is relatively easy to learn, especially when compared to object-oriented languages such as Smalltalk and C++.

- It provides superior support for graphics, bitmaps, and business graphics.

- It provides good integration with other applications, such as word processing, spreadsheets, and Lotus Notes.

- It provides an integrated compiler-editor development environment. This allows the user to develop prototypes incrementally.

5.2.6.6 Disadvantages

- It does not generate C and PM language like some other popular fourth-generation languages.

- Because it is aimed at enterprise-wide computing, it has a host of tools that most prototypers will not need. It has a hefty price tag to go along with it.

5.2.6.7 Recommendation

Easel is a good tool for creating prototypes quickly without requiring a great deal of programming expertise on the part of the prototyper. If you are creating a client-server application, you may be able to use Easel to create the front end for the actual application.

Chapter

6

PROTOTYPING EXAMPLES

This, then, is the test we must set for ourselves; not to march alone but to march in such a way that others will wish to join us.

Hubert H. Humphrey

It is often said that a picture is worth a thousand words. Just as pictures help to clarify written descriptions, examples help greatly to clarify concepts. From our experience we have chosen a variety of prototypes, representing a variety of types of applications and tools, to help illustrate the concepts presented in the earlier chapters of this book.

We provide descriptions of how the prototypes work and pictures to show the user interface. Code samples demonstrate differences between the programming languages in each tool. These examples will help you to see what real-world prototypes look like, although there is no substitute for hands-on experience. The best way to learn to prototype is to pick up one of the tools for your computing platform and give it a try.

6.1 MULTIMEDIA KIOSK

As multimedia becomes more common and interfaces are designed to make effective use of images, video, and sound, user interface designers must develop new skills. They must be artists and media production specialists. From television and movies, users are accustomed to slick productions. They expect that software will also be presented in a manner that is professional and aesthetically pleasing.

We put our multimedia ideas into practice by prototyping a banking kiosk. The kiosk would be located in some public place such as a shopping center or mall, where it would provide customers with information regarding account information and product offerings, as well as serve as advertising for the bank. We have created a fictitious bank, called Our Bank, with samples of the sorts of functions a bank provides. The purpose of the prototype was to gauge customer interest in the use of multimedia for kiosk operations. The main window contains a series of touch-sensitive buttons that provide various functions to the end user.

6.1.1 Branch Locator

By selecting the top button (Figure 6-1), the user is assisted in finding a branch to do business. The customer selects the city on a state map (Figure 6-2) and selects the part of town where a branch is located on a city map. The customer is then presented with a digitized video and audio of detailed instructions from a customer service representative. After the video and audio presentation, the customer is presented with an image of the bank branch. A push button is available so that the customer may choose to print instructions on locating the branch.

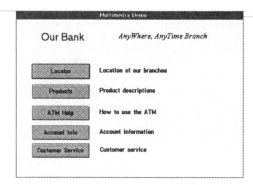

Figure 6-1. Opening Screen

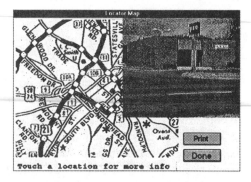

Figure 6-2. Branch Locator

6.1.2 Product Information

Product information can be obtained by selecting the Products button on the screen. Upon selecting this button, the customer is presented with a multimedia demonstration of product advantages and comparisons (Figure 6-3). The customer can also perform a number of what-if calculations to determine whether the product meets certain financial goals. If customer service is needed at this point, the customer can press a button on the screen and, using existing long-distance videoconferencing hardware and software, be connected with a customer service representative. This information is provided through the use of digitized video utilizing digital video interactive (DVI) technology.

6.1.3 Automated Teller Machine (ATM) Instructions

The ATM instruction feature provides a series of images and audio describing how to use an automated teller machine (Figure 6-4). It is intended to show the user that it is easy to operate an ATM. This function is provided by displaying digitized video in 9-bit compressed video (RTV) or through 8-bit, 256-color bit maps.

6.1.4 Account Information

The account information feature allows existing customers to query their account balances (Figure 6-5). To use this feature, the customer selects the Account Information button and is prompted to enter a personal identification number. At this point, the customer's balances are shown numerically and graphically.

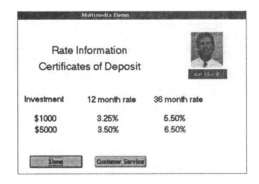

Figure 6-3. *Product Information*

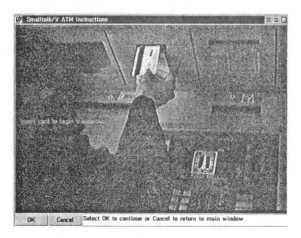

Figure 6-4. *ATM Instructions*

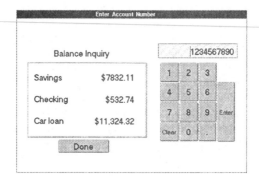

Figure 6-5. *Account Information*

6.1.5 Customer Service

At any time, the customer can select the Customer Service Representative button and be connected with a live customer service representative. In Figure 6-6, a customer service representative is reconciling a problem with a customer's checking account by showing recent account activity and displaying an image of a check that may be in question.

6.1.6 Implementation of Kiosk

The initial prototype of the kiosk was implemented in SmalltalkV for Presentation Manager. Smalltalk is a general-purpose, workstation-based, object-oriented language. Object-oriented

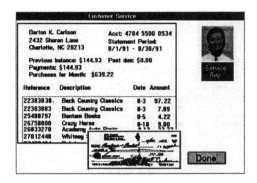

Figure 6-6. *Customer Service*

languages have properties that make them distinct from procedural languages. Smalltalk has characteristics that make it more "natural" than procedural languages. The syntax and metaphors are closer to the way people think and further removed from the way computers function. For instance, Smalltalk has objects like Printer and Display, and these objects respond to messages like "Printer startPrintJob." It is easy to anthropomorphize and picture these object's communicating with each other, much as people hold conversations.

Operations are easily defined in a manner that makes conceptual sense to the user and hides the underlying hardware and software dependencies. For instance, the same arithmetic operators can work with variables of multiple types. The class for each variable type can define a method with the same name, and the correct one is chosen at run time. The ability of a function (method) to work across types is called *polymorphism*. The user or programmer need not care that the implementation details are different in each class. This information hiding is called *encapsulation*.

Smalltalk is an incrementally compiled language. You can write small sections of code (methods), then run and test them immediately. This fits very well with the iterative nature of prototyping. You can continuously try things out, see if they work the way you want, and then refine them.

Smalltalk was chosen as a prototyping language for the multimedia kiosk because it provides a powerful set of tools for rapidly developing and validating the features of the prototype. Using Smalltalk, we created classes of multimedia objects and wrappers.

There were, however, a number of shortcomings with Smalltalk that resulted in our reconsidering the selection of prototyping tools when we decided to improve the prototype. The major drawback of Smalltalk was that multimedia support was not integrated into it, so we had to write extensions to integrate and call DVI modules. Not only did this make the code more complex, but it also resulted in performance decrements that we considered unacceptable. Finally, not having an authoring system for multimedia integrated into Smalltalk caused us to take longer than was desirable when constructing the multimedia objects for the prototype.

When we later decided to improve the prototype, the multimedia programming environment MediaScript (a trademark of Network Technologies Corp.) was available, and it proved to be a fast and easy way to construct multimedia applications. We were able to recode our application completely in a couple of weeks. Support for digital video and audio is built into the product as well as a number of powerful screen construction tools. Following is an example of the style of code required to implement the bank branch locator function in both Smalltalk and MediaScript.

6.1.6.1 Smalltalk Code for Branch Locator

```
ApplicationWindow subclass: #JRRBranchLocator
 instanceVariableNames:
   'bitMapID mapText '
   classVariableNames: ''
 poolDictionaries:
  'PMConstants ' !
```

```
getDirections: aKey
 "JRR - 11-12-91 - This class method determines
 what directions should be taken from a flat file based
 on the map being viewed by the user. Once a match has
 been found, the dictionary entry is answered as aString."

 | aCustomer inFile fullRecord aPrintRecord id |

 inFile := (Directory current) file: 'DIRECT.TXT'.

 id :=String new.
 ^[inFile atEnd]
  whileFalse:
    [fullRecord := inFile nextLine asArrayOfSubstrings.
    (fullRecord size = 0 or: + fullRecord = ' ' ])
        ifFalse:
          [id := (fullRecord at: 1 ).
          (id asInteger = aKey)
            ifTrue:
              [aPrintRecord := Dictionary new.
              aPrintRecord := (fullRecord at: 2).
              inFile close.
              (aPrintRecord) ]. "if a match has occurred."
              ]. "If end of entry"
        ]. "EOF"! !
```

```
!JRRBranchLocator instance methods !
```

```
bitMapID
    " JRR 11-4-91 Answer my bitmap id number"

    ^bitMapID!

 bitMapID: anInteger
    "JRR 11-15-91 Set my bitmap identification number"

    ^bitMapID := anInteger.!

 buildMenuBar
    "JRR 11/11/91   override so no menu bar will be created"!

 close: aGraphPane
    "JRR 11-12-91 Close the branch locator"

    self close.!

 defaultFrameStyle
    " JRR—11-12-91 Override and answer the default PM
    frame style for the receiver."

    ^FcfSysmenu | FcfTitlebar | FcfIcon | FcfSizeborder!

nextMap: aGraphPane
 " 11/12/91—The purpose of this method is to
  display the appropriate map depending
  upon where the user clicked. It displays a bitmap
  and puts some explanatory text over the top.
  "
  | window font bitmap location bMapId|
  location := (aGraphPane mouseLocation) x.

    bMapId := self selectMap: aGraphPane.

    font := Font face: 'Tms Rmn'
     size: 13@26 fixedWidth:  false attributes: FaceSize.

    aGraphPane stretch: 0.

    bitmap := Bitmap fromModule: 'CSC691J' id: bMapId.
    window := 0@0 extent: 391@334.

    aGraphPane pen drawRetainPicture:
     [aGraphPane pen
        copyBitmap: bitmap from: window at: 0@0;
        foreColor:ClrBlue;
```

```
        backColor: ClrDarkgray;
        font: font; displayText: mapText at:10@10]

openIt
 "JRR 11-15-91 Open an instance of JRRBranchLocator"

 | font |

 font := Font face: 'Courier' size:6@18
  fixedWidth: false attributes: FaceSize.

 self
   owner: self;
   label: 'Branch Locator';
   bitMapID: 2001;
   yourself.

 "This holds the maps and the branch pictures"
 self addSubpane:
   (GraphPane new
    owner: self;
    when: #getContents perform: #showMap: ;
    when: #button1DoubleClick perform: #nextMap:;
    framingRatio: ((0)@(1/8) extent:(1)@(7/8));
    style: (GraphPane noScrollbarsFrameStyle)).

 "This button pane allows the user to print
 directions to the branch"
 self addSubpane:
   (ButtonPane new pushButton
    owner: self;
    contents: 'Print Directions';
    when: #clicked perform: #printDirections:;
    framingRatio: (0@0 extent: (1/3)@(1/8))).

 "Cancel push button"
 self addSubpane:
   (ButtonPane new pushButton
    owner: self;
    contents: 'Cancel';
    when: #clicked perform: #close:;
    framingRatio: (1/3@0 extent: (1/6)@(1/8))).

 "User explanatory text in a graph pane"
 self addSubpane:
   (GraphPane new
    owner: self;
```

```
    textFont: SysFont;
    when: #getContents perform: #windowText: ;
    style: (GraphPane noScrollbarsFrameStyle);
    framingRatio: (1/2@0 extent: (1/2)@(1/8))).

self openWindow.!

showMap: aGraphPane
  "JRR—11-2-91—Called by openIt, this displays the initial
  contents of the Branch Locator"

|bitmap window font|

font := Font face: 'Tms Rmn' size:15@13
  fixedWidth: false attributes: FaceSize.

aGraphPane stretch: 0.

bitmap :=  Bitmap fromModule: 'CSC691J' id: bitMapID.

window  := 0@0 extent: 319@278.

aGraphPane pen drawRetainPicture:
   [aGraphPane pen
    copyBitmap: bitmap from: window at: 40@40;
    foreColor:ClrBlue;font: font].!
```

Clearly this source code is much different than one would find with a procedurally oriented language such as C or Pascal. Methods are written to respond to objects. Very specific
code is required to initialize and set up the Presentation Manager controls. Once the ini-
tialization has occurred, however, the selection of maps to display is contained in the
methods showMap and nextMap.

Although Smalltalk is object oriented in its logical design of application objects, the user
interface portion of the environment provides a text editor interface where one adds and mod-
ifies code. This approach is considerably different from the one provided by MediaScript.

6.1.6.2 MediaScript Code for Branch Locator

Figure 6-7 shows the MediaScript code for the branch locator portion of the prototype. It
consists of a series of icons that represent various functions to be performed by the
MediaScript run-time environment. For example, win(6) Locator Map initializes the window that will hold the locator map. The nine commands that follow set up bit maps or
video clips, which will be displayed in the window. Depending on the user's selection, the

contents of a backup window, win(10), are transferred to the locator window for display to the user. Win(6)-2 Items draws two bit maps to the window. Clicking on this particular icon will open a dialog box that allows the programmer to assign actions to these controls. The object called 7 Items responds to user touch or mouse input to select which images will be presented.

In general, the code is visually oriented, with little actual text entry writing and editing of code. All "code writing" is done by selecting multimedia and presentation format objects on a tools menu. That the tool is geared to nonprogrammers can be frustrating for programmers. On the other hand, a visually oriented multimedia construction set is ideal for multimedia designers who are not programmers and are more interested in having tools available to improve the quality of their multimedia presentations.

In summary, developing for multimedia requires a reevaluation of how one develops a prototype. Languages that are well suited for the development of graphical user interface prototypes may not be the tool of choice for multimedia prototypes. Language comparisons are important because of the impact tools have on the design process. A good tool speeds the coding process, provides the capability to implement more and better features, and allows the programmer to make sufficient design iterations to evolve the design to a state where it fully meets the needs of the users.

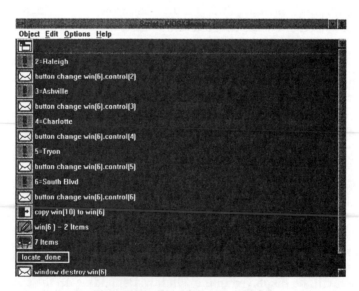

Figure 6-7. Branch Locator Code

6.2 POWER COMPANY CUSTOMER SERVICE SYSTEM

The prototype described in this report was developed to support a bid by an IBM branch office for a contract designed to develop a power company customer service application. The goals of the prototype were to show to the power company IBM's ideas for the user interface, integrate existing applications along with new ones into a single program, and demonstrate competence with the language that the customer wanted the application developed in—Smalltalk. The request for support was made very late. Thus, the prototype was developed in three days, so it could be demonstrated at the proposal meeting.

6.2.1 Operational Description

6.2.1.1 Logo

The program opens displaying the power company's logo (Figure 6-8). The user clicks on the OK push button to remove the logo and advance to the primary application window.

6.2.1.2 Primary Window

The primary window contains icons for customer information, the equipment database, the service response system, the maintenance system, electronic mail, and meter orders (Figure 6-9). These represent either new functions for the customer service representatives (CSRs) or new interfaces to existing functions.

Figure 6-8. *Power Company Logo*

6.2.1.3 *Customer Information*

Customer information is accessed by double clicking on the Customer icon. This opens a window, and the CSR enters information to initiate a search of the customer files (Figure 6-10). Searches can be performed based on any of the three fields: name, address, or phone number.

In the example, we search for customer "Owen, C." There is only one match in the database, so the record for that customer is brought up immediately. The information is organized in two notebook controls, with the top notebook containing information about the customer and the bottom notebook containing information about the location (Figure 6-11). This dual notebook design was chosen to minimize page flipping. In most instances, all the information the CSR needs to answer a query will be on the screen when the notebook first appears.

Pages may be turned by clicking on the tabs. The pages on each notebook can be turned independently. Letters, memos, and maps pertaining to the customer are stored on the

Figure 6-9. Primary Window

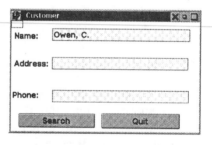

Figure 6-10. Search Window

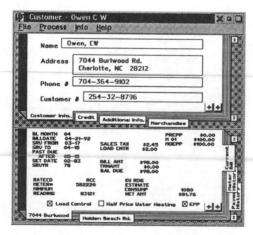

Figure 6-11. Notebook: Customer Information and Current Bill

additional information page of the notebook (Figures 6-12 and 6-13). Clicking on any of these objects opens them in a new window.

The CSR can call up information from the procedures manual by clicking on the information pull down. Figure 6-14 shows the effect of selecting one of the information pull-down options. BookManager is called and opened to the proper page in the procedures manual.

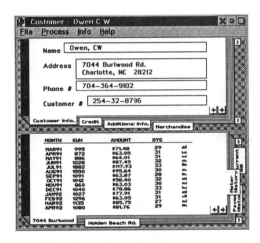

Figure 6-12. *Notebook: Additional Information and Meter History*

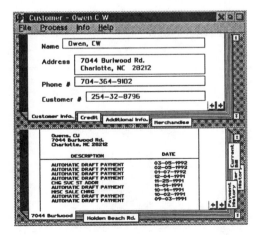

Figure 6-13. *Notebook: Additional Information and Payment History*

6.2.1.4 E-Mail

By double clicking on the E-Mail icon, the CSR can initiate a videoconference with an adviser (Figure 6-15). The CSR can see the adviser in a video window, send notes back and forth, exchange bit maps or screen images, and draw on a clipboard.

6.2.1.5 Service Response

The Service Response icon calls up a service training video, which plays in a window (Figure 6-16).

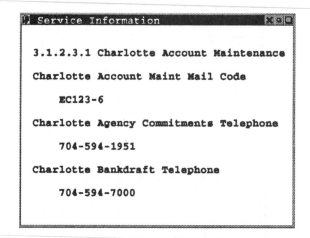

Figure 6-14. *Service Information*

Figure 6-15. *Videoconferencing*

6.2.1.6 Radar

The radar application is a program to display a recent weather map obtained from the U.S. Weather Service (Figure 6-17). The CSRs use this map to make a judgment about whether repair times will be affected by storms. The application was placed on the OS/2 desktop to show that it can be called at any time while the customer service system is running.

6.2.1.7 Alerts

Alerts is a late-breaking news function to inform the CSRs of any information they need to keep up on (Figure 6-18). It is another existing application placed on the OS/2 desktop to show it can work alongside the new customer service system.

6.2.2 Program Logic

6.2.2.1 Logo

The logo window is implemented by the PowerLogo class. It builds a window without the default menu bar, creates a graphpane to which the logo is written, and provides an OK button to dismiss the window.

Figure 6-16. Video Message

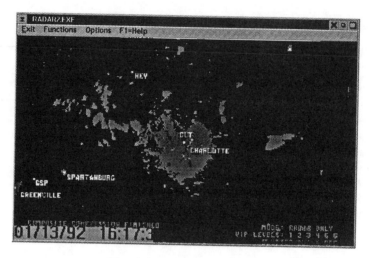

Figure 6-17. Weather Radar

```
ALERTS.EXE                                               X □ ■
*********************************************
THERE  ARE APPX 60 RESIDENTIAL CUSTS IN THE STERLING
AREA THAT ARE BEING TRANSFERRED FROM PINEVILLE ELEC TO
POWER CO. WE EXPECT TO CONVERT AROUND 10 TO 15 CUSTS A
DAY UNTIL WE GET THEM ALL. ON THE DAY OF CONVERSION, A
DOOR HANGER WILL BE LEFT STATING THAT THEY ARE NOW
SERVED BY DPC AND IF THEY HAVE ANY QUESTIONS TO CALL
373-8050..***THESE CUSTOMERS WILL NOT SHOW UP WITH ACCTS
ON OUR SYSTEM FOR SEVERAL DAYS!***
***************************TUXEDO
HYDRO*********************************
              ESTIMATED GREEN RIVER RELEASE

DATE          UNIT              HOURS OF OPERATION

4-28   TUESDAY       1                24 HRS
4-29   WEDNESDAY     1                24 HRS
4-30   THURSDAY      1                24 HRS
5-1    FRIDAY        1                24 HRS

****************************************************
************
```

Figure 6-18. Alerts

6.2.2.2 Primary Window

The primary window was originally implemented by class PowerMain as a full-screen window. Partway through the coding, new requirements came in, and we decided to change to a smaller window. One of the benefits of object-oriented programming is the ability to make changes such as this easily. We created a subclass of PowerMain that inherited all the function of PowerMain, and then overrode the method that sized the window, thereby creating two versions of the prototype with minimal effort.

The bit maps are loaded from a DLL when the window is created in the open method. The method SelectSomething: controls which applications are launched by testing the *x* and *y* coordinates when a mouse click is detected.

6.2.2.3 Customer Information

The customer information is implemented by class PowerNote, which loads the notebook images into the window from a DLL. The selectTop: and selectBottom: methods detect selection of the notebook tabs. This is an example of using smoke and mirrors in a prototype. Implementing a real notebook would have taken more time than was available for completing the prototype. Displaying bit maps that appeared to be a notebook showed the customer the design just as effectively.

6.2.2.4 E-Mail

Videoconferencing and other executables called from Smalltalk use class PowerStartEXE, which provides the basic code for calls to initiate OS/2 programs. PowerP2P is a subclass of PowerStartEXE, which provides the name of the program to be called—in this case, Person-2-Person, a program to provide videoconferencing over a local area network.

6.2.2.5 Service Response

The PowerServiceResponse class calls a windowed video player from the AVK tool kit.

6.2.2.6 Radar and Alerts

The radar and alerts programs were existing programs. We created icons for them and placed them on the OS/2 2.0 desktop for the demonstration.

6.2.3 Code Listings

The following code is owned by IBM. Copyright © 1992 International Business Machines Corporation.

6.2.3.1 PowerCustomer Class

```
ViewManager subclass: #PowerCustomer
 instanceVariableNames: ''
 classVariableNames: ''
 poolDictionaries:
   'WBConstants '  !

!PowerCustomer class methods !

wbCreated

        ^true! !

!PowerCustomer methods !

close: aPane

 "Generated by WindowBuilder for a pane callback."
       ^self close.!

drag: aGraphPane
"Changes pointer icon for drag and drop"
" SI 4/29/92 "
 CursorManager moveHand change.
     self clearTextModified.!

notebook: aPane

 "Generated by WindowBuilder for a pane callback."
     self close.
 PowerNote new open.!

open

 "WARNING!! This method was automatically generated by
 WindowBuilder. Code you add here which does not conform
 to the WindowBuilder API will probably be lost the next time
 you save your layout definition."

   | v |

 self addView: (
   v := self topPaneClass new
    owner: self;
    labelWithoutPrefix: 'Customer';
    noSmalltalkMenuBar;
```

```
      viewName: 'mainView';
      framingBlock: ( FramingParameters new iDUE: 880 @ 444; lDU: 659 r: #left;
tDU: 244 r: #top; cRDU: (11 @ 398 rightBottom: 869 @ 8));
       pStyle: #(sysmenu minimize maximize sizable titlebar);
       addSubpane: (
          Button new
             owner: self;
             framingBlock: ( FramingParameters new iDUE: 363 @ 56; lDU: 416 r: #left;
rDU: 779   r: #left; tDU: 328 r: #top; bDU: 384 r: #top);
             startGroup;
             when: #clicked perform: #close:;
             contents: 'Quit';
             yourself
       );
       addSubpane: (
          Button new
             owner: self;
             framingBlock:( FramingParameters new iDUE: 355 @ 52; lDU: 35 r: #left;
rDU: 389   r: #left; tDU: 330 r: #top; bDU: 382 r: #top);
             startGroup;
             when: #clicked perform: #notebook:;
             contents: 'Search';
             yourself
       );
       addSubpane: (
          StaticText new
             owner: self;
             framingBlock:( FramingParameters new iDUE: 125 @ 34; lDU: 16 r: #left;
rDU: 141   r: #left; tDU: 36 r: #top; bDU: 70 r: #top);
             startGroup;
             contents: 'Name:';
             yourself
       );
       addSubpane: (
          StaticText new
             owner: self;
             framingBlock:( FramingParameters new iDUE: 171 @ 36; lDU: 13 r: #left;
rDU: 184   r: #left; tDU: 136 r: #top; bDU: 172 r: #top);
             startGroup;
             contents: 'Address:';
             yourself
       );
       addSubpane: (
          StaticText new
             owner: self;
             framingBlock:( FramingParameters new iDUE: 141 @ 30; lDU: 8 r: #left;
```

```
rDU: 149    r: #left; tDU: 248 r: #top; bDU: 278 r: #top);
            startGroup;
            contents: 'Phone:';
            yourself
        );
        addSubpane: (
          EntryField new
            owner: self;
            framingBlock:( FramingParameters new iDUE: 616 @ 40; lDU: 192 r: #left;
rDU: 819    r: #left; tDU: 244 r: #top; bDU: 292 r: #top; indent: 3 @ 4);
            startGroup;
            tabStop;
            yourself
        );
        addSubpane: (
          EntryField new
            owner: self;
            framingBlock:( FramingParameters new iDUE: 616 @ 40; lDU: 189 r: #left;
rDU: 816    r: #left; tDU: 128 r: #top; bDU: 176 r: #top; indent: 3 @ 4);
            startGroup;
            tabStop;
            yourself
        );
        addSubpane: (
          EntryField new
            owner: self;
            framingBlock:( FramingParameters new iDUE: 624 @ 40; lDU: 189 r: #left;
rDU: 824    r: #left; tDU: 26 r: #top; bDU: 74 r: #top; indent: 3 @ 4);
            startGroup;
            tabStop;
            yourself
        );
        addSubpane:
                ( GraphPane new
                    owner: self;
                    when: #button1Down perform: #drag:;
                    framingRatio: (0@(15/16) extent: (1/16)@(1/16));
                    style: (GraphPane noScrollBarsFrameStyle));

    yourself
    ).


 self openWindow!

textModifiedIn: paneSymbol
    "Answer true if any pane with the name paneSymbol was
    modified and the user does not want to save it or
```

```
    throw it away. Else answer false."
| answer panes |

panes := self modifiedPanes: paneSymbol.
^panes size > 1
! !
```

6.2.3.2 *PowerLogo Class*

```
ViewManager subclass: #PowerLogo
 instanceVariableNames:
    'bitMapID label handle parent '
 classVariableNames: ''
 poolDictionaries:
    'PMConstants '    !

!PowerLogo class methods ! !

!PowerLogo methods !

bitMapID: anInteger
    "Sets bitmap ID to retrieve bitmap from DLL"
        "SI 4-27-92"

     ^ bitMapID := anInteger.!

buildMenuBar
    "No menu bar"
        " SI 4-27-92"!

buildMenuBar: topPane
    "No menu bar"
        " SI 4-27-92"
     | mw |
     mw := topPane menuWindow.
     mw removeMenu: (mw menuTitled: 'File').!

closeDown: anItem
    "close this window"
    " SI 4-27-92"

    self close.!

initWindowSize
    "Makes window full screen (VGA)"
        "SI 4-27-92"
```

```
^ (0@0 extent: 640@480).!

label: aString
    "Set the window label of the receiver to aString
    without Smalltalk prefix."

 label := aString.
 label size > 500
     ifTrue:
         [label := label copyFrom: 1 to: 500].

    "Experimentally determined that labels more than 500 bytes
    cause PM to mess up the title bar."

 handle isNil ifTrue: [^self].
 handle = NullHandle
     ifFalse: [parent handle setWindowText: label].!

logo: aGraphPane
    "Writes logo bitmap to logo window"
        "SI 4-27-92"

    | bitmap window |
    self bitMapID: 1002.
    bitmap := Bitmap fromModule: 'duke' id: bitMapID.
    window := 0@0 extent: 640@480.

    aGraphPane pen drawRetainPicture:
        [aGraphPane pen copyBitmap: bitmap from: window at: 0@0].!

open
    "About box. Displays at application startup"
    "SI 4-27-92"
    | graphPane |

    PowerMainSmall new open.
    self
       owner: self;
       labelWithoutPrefix: 'Power Co. Customer Service System'
       yourself.
    self when: #menuBuilt perform: #buildMenuBar:.

    self addSubpane:
       (graphPane := GraphPane new
          owner: self;
          when: #getContents perform: #logo:;
          framingRatio: (0@0 extent: 1@1);
```

```
                style: (GraphPane noScrollBarsFrameStyle)).

        self addSubpane:
          (ButtonPane new pushButton
            owner: self;
            contents: 'OK';
            when: #clicked perform: #closeDown:;
            framingRatio: (3/8@0 extent: (1/6)@(1/16))).

            self openWindow.! !
```

6.2.3.3 PowerMain Class

```
PowerLogo subclass: #PowerMain
 instanceVariableNames:  'locationX locationY '
 classVariableNames: ''
 poolDictionaries:  'PMConstants '   !

!PowerMain class methods ! !

!PowerMain methods !

buildMenuBar
    "Creates the menu bar"
        " SI 4-27-92"
 self menuWindow addMenu: (self fileMenu) owner: self.
 self menuWindow removeMenu: (self menuWindow menuTitled: '~File').
 self menuWindow addMenu: (self processMenu) owner: self.
 self menuWindow addMenu: (self infoMenu) owner: self.
 self menuWindow addMenu: (self helpMenu) owner: self.!

buildMenuBar: topPane
    "Creates the menu bar"
        " SI 4-27-92"
| mw |
 mw := topPane menuWindow.
 mw removeMenu: (mw menuTitled: 'File');
    addMenu: (self fileMenu) owner: self;
    addMenu: (self processMenu) owner: self;
    addMenu: (self infoMenu) owner: self;
    addMenu: (self helpMenu)  owner: self.!

close
    "Private—Close the receiver"
    " SI 4/27/92"
    Smalltalk isRunTime
```

```
          ifTrue:
            [(MessageBox confirm:
            'Are you sure you want to exit?')]
              ifTrue: [^Smalltalk exit]
              ifFalse: [^self]
            ifFalse: [^super close]!

desktop: aGraphPane
    "Writes the desktop bitmap to the main window"
    "SI 4-27-92"

    | bitmap window |
    self bitMapID: 1001.
    bitmap := Bitmap fromModule: 'duke' id: bitMapID.
    window := 0@0 extent: 640@480.

    aGraphPane pen drawRetainPicture:
      [aGraphPane pen copyBitmap: bitmap from: window at: 0@0].!

equalPay
    "calls equal payment class"
    " SI 4/28/92"

    CursorManager execute change.
    PowerEqualPay new open.
    CursorManager normal change.!

fileMenu
    "SI 4/27/92 Answer the File menu ."
    | ctrlBits |
    ctrlBits := AfChar ] AfControl.
    ^Menu new
      appendItem: '~Open                       Ctrl+O'
        selector: #notimplemented
        accelKey: $o accelBits: ctrlBits;
      appendItem: '~Close                      Ctrl+C'
        selector: #notImplemented
        accelKey: $c accelBits: ctrlBits;
      appendSeparator;
      appendItem: '~Search... Ctrl+S'
        selector: #notImplemented
        accelKey: $w accelBits: ctrlBits;
      appendSeparator;
      appendItem: 'E~xit                        F3'
        selector: #close
        accelKey: VkF3 accelBits: AfVirtualkey ;
      title: '~File'.!
```

```
helpMenu
    "SI 4/28/92 Answer the help menu ."
    | ctrlBits|
    ctrlBits := AfChar ] AfControl.

    ^Menu new
      appendItem: 'Help ~index'
        selector: #notimplemented
        accelKey: $o accelBits: ctrlBits;
      appendItem: '~General help'
        selector: #notImplemented
        accelKey: $c accelBits: ctrlBits;
      appendItem: '~Using help'
        selector: #notImplemented
        accelKey: $w accelBits: ctrlBits;
      appendItem: '~Tutorial'
        selector: #notImplemented
        accelKey: VkF3 accelBits: AfVirtualkey ;
      appendItem: '~Product information'
        selector: #notImplemented
        accelKey: VkF3 accelBits: AfVirtualkey ;
      title: '~Help'.!

infoMenu
    "SI 4/28/92 Answer the info menu ."
    | ctrlBits |
    ctrlBits := AfChar ] AfControl.

    ^Menu new
      appendItem: '~Load control'
        selector: #loadControl
        accelKey: $o accelBits: ctrlBits;
      appendItem: '~Half price water heating'
        selector: #waterHeating
        accelKey: $c accelBits: ctrlBits;
      appendItem: '~Equal payment plan'
        selector: #equalPay
        accelKey: $w accelBits: ctrlBits;
      appendItem: '~Library'
        selector: #library
        accelKey: VkF3 accelBits: AfVirtualkey ;
      title: '~Info'.!

library
    "calls library class"
    " SI 4/28/92"
```

```
        CursorManager execute change.
        PowerLibrary new open.
        CursorManager normal change.!

loadControl
        "calls load control class"
        " SI 4/28/92"

        CursorManager execute change.
        PowerLoadControl new open.
        CursorManager normal change.!

notImplemented
        "no-op method for functions not yet implemented"
                " SI 4/28/92 "
        ^ self.!

open
        "Main application window"
                "SI 4-27-92"
        | graphPane |

        self
          owner: self;
          labelWithoutPrefix: 'Power Power Customer Service System'
          yourself.

          self when: #menuBuilt perform: #buildMenuBar:.

          self addSubpane:
            (graphPane := GraphPane new
            owner: self;
            when: #getContents perform: #desktop:;
            when: #button1DoubleClick perform: #selectSomething:;
            framingRatio: (0@0 extent: 1@1);
            style: (GraphPane noScrollBarsFrameStyle)).
            self openWindow.!

processMenu
        "SI 4/28/92 Answer the process menu ."
        | ctrlBits |
        ctrlBits := AfChar | AfControl.

     ^Menu new
          appendItem: '~Add service'
            selector: #notimplemented
            accelKey: $o accelBits: ctrlBits;
```

```
        appendItem: '~Cut-off service'
          selector: #notImplemented
          accelKey: $c accelBits: ctrlBits;
        appendItem: 'C~hange address'
          selector: #notImplemented
          accelKey: $w accelBits: ctrlBits;
        appendItem: '~Report outage'
          selector: #notImplemented
          accelKey: VkF3 accelBits: AfVirtualkey ;
        appendItem: '~Deferred payment calc'
          selector: #notImplemented
          accelKey: VkF3 accelBits: AfVirtualkey ;
        title: '~Process'.!

selectSomething: aGraphPane
    "Instantiates a class when an icon is selected"

    locationX := (aGraphPane mouseLocation) x.
    locationY := (aGraphPane mouseLocation) y.

    "instantiate the meter
    ((locationX < 284) and: [locationY > 342])
      ifTrue:[PowerMeter new open]."

    "instantiate the database
    ((locationX < 284) and: [locationY < 342 and: [locationY > 269]])
      ifTrue:[PowerNotebook new openOn: 'dukenote.dat' ]."

    "instantiate the customer"
    ((locationX < 284) and: [locationY < 269 and: [locationY > 186]])
      ifTrue:[PowerCustomer new open].

    "instantiate the SSG"
    ((locationX < 284) and: [locationY < 186 and: [locationY > 104]])
      ifTrue:[PowerSSG new open].

    "instantiate the Service Response"
    ((locationX < 284) and: [locationY < 104 and: [locationY > 0]])
      ifTrue:
        [CursorManager execute change.
        PowerServiceResponse new open.
        CursorManager normal change].

    "instantiate the weather"
    ((locationX > 284) and: [locationY > 342])
      ifTrue:
        [CursorManager execute change.
```

```
          PowerWeather new open.
          CursorManager normal change].

    "instantiate the Alerts"
    ((locationX > 284) and: [locationY < 342 and: [locationY > 269]])
       ifTrue:[PowerAlerts new open].

    "instantiate the MAIDS
    ((locationX > 284) and: [locationY < 269 and: [locationY > 186]])
       ifTrue:[PowerAMIDS new open].

    "instantiate the EMail"
    ((locationX > 284) and: [locationY < 186 and: [locationY > 104]])
       ifTrue:
          [CursorManager execute change.
          PowerP2P new open.
          CursorManager normal change].

    "instantiate the CSC Library
    ((locationX > 284) and: [locationY < 104 and: [locationY > 0]])
       ifTrue:[PowerCSCLibrary new open]."!

showLocation: aGraphPane
    "Shows cursor location to test where icons are located"
    " SI 4/27/92 "

    locationX := (aGraphPane mouseLocation) x.
    locationX inspect.!

waterHeating
    "calls water heating class"
    " SI 4/28/92"

    CursorManager execute change.
    PowerWaterHeating new open.
    CursorManager normal change.! !
```

6.2.3.4 PowerMainSmall Class

```
PowerMain subclass: #PowerMainSmall
 instanceVariableNames: ''
 classVariableNames: ''
 poolDictionaries: 'PMConstants ' !

!PowerMainSmall class methods ! !
```

```
!PowerMainSmall methods !

close
 "Private—Close the receiver"
 " SI 4/27/92"

 ^Smalltalk isRunTime
   ifTrue:
     [(MessageBox confirm:
     'Are you sure you want to exit?')]
       ifTrue: [Smalltalk exit]
       ifFalse:[self].
   ifFalse: [^super close]!

desktop: aGraphPane
   "Writes the desktop bitmap to the main window"
   "SI 4-29-92"

   | bitmap window |

   self bitMapID: 1004.
   bitmap := Bitmap fromModule: 'duke' id: bitMapID.
   window := 0@0 extent: 640@480.

   aGraphPane pen drawRetainPicture:
     [aGraphPane pen copyBitmap: bitmap from: window at: 0@0]!

drop: aGraphPane
   "Instantiates a class when an icon is selected"
   locationX := (aGraphPane mouseLocation) x.
   locationY := (aGraphPane mouseLocation) y.

   "instantiate the database"
   ((locationX < 102) and: [locationY < 83 ]])
   ifTrue:
     [CursorManager normal change.
     DK clearTextModified.
     DK close.
     PowerNote new open]!

initWindowSize
   "Makes 1/2 screen (VGA)"
   "SI 4-29-92"

   ^ (0@0 extent: 377@210).!

open
```

```
     "Main application window"
          "SI 4-27-92"

  | graphPane |

self
    owner: self;
    labelWithoutPrefix: 'Power Co. Customer Service System'
    yourself.
    self when: #menuBuilt perform: #buildMenuBar:.

    self addSubpane:
    (graphPane := GraphPane new
      owner: self;
      when: #getContents perform: #desktop:;
      when: #button1Up perform: #drop:;
      when: #button1DoubleClick perform: #selectSomething:;
      framingRatio: (0@0 extent: 1@1);
      style: (GraphPane noScrollBarsFrameStyle)).

    self openWindow.!

selectSomething: aGraphPane
    "Instantiates a class when an icon is selected"

    locationX := (aGraphPane mouseLocation) x.
    locationY := (aGraphPane mouseLocation) y.

    "instantiate the meter"
    ((locationX < 284) and: [locationY > 342])
      ifTrue:[PowerMeter new open].

    "instantiate the database"
    ((locationX < 102) and: [locationY < 83 ])
      ifTrue:
        [CursorManager normal change.
         PowerNote new open.].

    "instantiate the customer"
    ((locationX < 102) and: [locationY > 83 ])
      ifTrue:[DK := PowerCustomer new open].

    "instantiate the SSG"
    ((locationX > 102) and: [locationX < 188 and: [locationY > 83]])
      ifTrue:[PowerSSG new open].

    "instantiate the Service Response"
```

```
((locationX > 102) and: [locationX < 188 and: [locationY < 83]])
  ifTrue:
     [CursorManager execute change.
      PowerServiceResponse new open.
      CursorManager normal change].

"instantiate the weather"
((locationX > 284) and: [locationY > 342])
  ifTrue:
     [CursorManager execute change.
      PowerWeather new open.
      CursorManager normal change]

"instantiate the Alerts"
((locationX > 284) and: [locationY < 342 and: [locationY > 269]])
  ifTrue:[PowerAlerts new open].

"instantiate the MAIDS"
((locationX > 284) and: [locationY < 269 and: [locationY > 186]])
 ifTrue:[PowerAMIDS new open].

"instantiate the EMail"
((locationX > 188) and: [locationX < 2786 and: [locationY < 83]])
  ifTrue:
     [CursorManager execute change.
      PowerP2P new open.
      CursorManager normal change].

"instantiate the CSC Library"
((locationX > 284) and: [locationY < 104 and: [locationY > 0]])
   ifTrue:[PowerCSCLibrary new open].!

showLocation: aGraphPane
   "Shows cursor location to test where icons are located"
   " SI 4/27/92 "

   locationY := (aGraphPane mouseLocation) y.
   locationX := (aGraphPane mouseLocation) x! !
```

6.2.3.5 PowerNote Class

```
PowerLogo subclass: #PowerNote
 instanceVariableNames:
   'locationY locationX topNotebook bottomNotebook '
 classVariableNames: ''
 poolDictionaries:
```

```
   'PMConstants '    !

!PowerNote class methods ! !

!PowerNote methods !

addInfo: aGraphPane
    "Writes bitmap for the top notebook to the graphpane"
    "SI 4-29-92"

    | bitmap window |
    self bitMapID: 1007.
    bitmap := Bitmap fromModule: 'duke' id: bitMapID.
    window := 0@0 extent: 540@230.

    aGraphPane pen drawRetainPicture:
       [aGraphPane pen copyBitmap: bitmap from: window at: 0@0]!

bottomNotebook: aGraphPane
    "Writes bitmap for the bottom notebook to the graphpane"
    "SI 4-29-92"

    | bitmap window |

    self bitMapID: 1006.
    bitmap := Bitmap fromModule: 'duke' id: bitMapID.
    window := 0@0 extent: 540@230.

    aGraphPane pen drawRetainPicture:
       [aGraphPane pen copyBitmap: bitmap from: window at: 0@0]!

buildMenuBar: topPane
    "Creates the menu bar"
    " SI 4-27-92"

    | mw |
    mw := topPane menuWindow.
    mw removeMenu: (mw menuTitled: 'File');
       addMenu: (self fileMenu) owner: self;
       addMenu: (self processMenu) owner: self;
       addMenu: (self infoMenu) owner: self;
       addMenu: (self helpMenu) owner: self!

currentBill: aGraphPane
    "Writes current bill bitmap for the bottom notebook to the graphpane"
    "SI 4-29-92"
```

```
    | bitmap window |
    self bitMapID: 1006.
    bitmap := Bitmap fromModule: 'duke' id: bitMapID.
    window := 0@0 extent: 540@230.

    aGraphPane pen drawRetainPicture:
        [aGraphPane pen copyBitmap: bitmap from: window at: 0@0]!

custInfo: aGraphPane
    "Writes customer info bitmap for the bottom notebook to the graphpane"
    "SI 4-29-92"

    | bitmap window |
    self bitMapID: 1005.
    bitmap := Bitmap fromModule: 'duke' id: bitMapID.
    window := 0@0 extent: 540@230.

    aGraphPane pen drawRetainPicture:
        [aGraphPane pen copyBitmap: bitmap from: window at: 0@0]!

equalPay
    "calls equal payment class"
    " SI 4/28/92"
    CursorManager execute change.
    PowerEqualPay new open.
    CursorManager normal change!

fileMenu
    "SI 4/27/92 Answer the File menu ."
    | ctrlBits |

    ctrlBits := AfChar ] AfControl.
    ^Menu new
        appendItem: '~Open                    Ctrl+O'
            selector: #notimplemented
            accelKey: $o accelBits: ctrlBits;
        appendItem: '~Close                   Ctrl+C'
            selector: #notImplemented
            accelKey: $c accelBits: ctrlBits;
        appendSeparator;
        appendItem: '~Search... Ctrl+S'
            selector: #notImplemented
            accelKey: $w accelBits: ctrlBits;
        appendSeparator;
        appendItem: 'E~xit                     F3'
            selector: #close
            accelKey: VkF3 accelBits: AfVirtualkey ;
```

```
        title: '~File'.!

helpMenu
    "SI 4/28/92 Answer the help menu ."
    | ctrlBits |

    ctrlBits := AfChar | AfControl.
    ^Menu new
      appendItem: 'Help ~index'
        selector: #notimplemented
        accelKey: $o accelBits: ctrlBits;
      appendItem: '~General help'
        selector: #notImplemented
        accelKey: $c accelBits: ctrlBits;
      appendItem: '~Using help'
        selector: #notImplemented
        accelKey: $w accelBits: ctrlBits;
      appendItem: '~Tutorial'
        selector: #notImplemented
        accelKey: VkF3 accelBits: AfVirtualkey ;
      appendItem: '~Product information'
        selector: #notImplemented
        accelKey: VkF3 accelBits: AfVirtualkey ;
    title: '~Help'!

infoMenu
    "SI 4/28/92 Answer the info menu ."
    | ctrlBits |
    ctrlBits := AfChar | AfControl.

    ^Menu new
      appendItem: '~Load control'
        selector: #loadControl
        accelKey: $o accelBits: ctrlBits;
      appendItem: '~Half price water heating'
        selector: #waterHeating
        accelKey: $c accelBits: ctrlBits;
      appendItem: '~Equal payment plan'
        selector: #equalPay
        accelKey: $w accelBits: ctrlBits;
      appendItem: '~Library'
        selector: #library
        accelKey: VkF3 accelBits: AfVirtualkey ;
    title: '~Info'.!

initWindowSize
    "SI 4-29-92"
```

```
    ^ (100@0 extent: 540@480)!

library
    "calls library class"
    " SI 4/28/92"

    CursorManager execute change.
    PowerLibrary new open.
    CursorManager normal change.!

loadControl
    "calls load control class"
    " SI 4/28/92"

    CursorManager execute change.
    PowerLoadControl new open.
    CursorManager normal change.!

meterHistory: aGraphPane
    "Writes meter history bitmap for the bottom notebook to the graphpane"
    "SI 4-29-92"

    | bitmap window |
    self bitMapID: 1009.
    bitmap := Bitmap fromModule: 'duke' id: bitMapID.
    window := 0@0 extent: 540@230.
    aGraphPane
      pen drawRetainPicture:
        [aGraphPane pen copyBitmap: bitmap from: window at: 0@0]!

open
    "opens a notebook"
    "SI 4-28-92"

    self
      owner: self;
      labelWithoutPrefix: 'Customer—Owen C W'
      yourself.
    self when: #menuBuilt perform: #buildMenuBar:.

    self addSubpane:
      (topNotebook := GraphPane new
        owner: self;
        when: #getContents perform: #topNotebook:;
        when: #button1Up perform: #selectTop:;
        framingRatio: (0@(1/2) extent: 1@(1/2));
          style: (GraphPane noScrollBarsFrameStyle)).
```

```
    self addSubpane:
      (bottomNotebook := GraphPane new
        owner: self;
        when: #getContents perform: #bottomNotebook:;
        when: #button1Up perform: #selectBottom:;
        framingRatio: (0@0 extent: 1@(1/2));
        style: (GraphPane noScrollBarsFrameStyle)).

    self openWindow!

paymentHistory: aGraphPane
    "Writes meter history bitmap for the bottom notebook to the graphpane"
    "SI 4-29-92"

    | bitmap window |
    self bitMapID: 1008.
    bitmap := Bitmap fromModule: 'duke' id: bitMapID.
    window := 0@0 extent: 540@230.

    aGraphPane
      pen drawRetainPicture:
        [aGraphPane pen copyBitmap: bitmap from: window at: 0@0]!

processMenu
    "SI 4/28/92 Answer the process menu ."
    | ctrlBits |
    ctrlBits := AfChar | AfControl.

    ^Menu new
      appendItem: '~Add service'
        selector: #notimplemented
        accelKey: $o accelBits: ctrlBits;
      appendItem: '~Cut-off service'
        selector: #notImplemented
        accelKey: $c accelBits: ctrlBits;
      appendItem: 'C~hange address'
        selector: #notImplemented
        accelKey: $w accelBits: ctrlBits;
      appendItem: '~Report outage'
        selector: #notImplemented
        accelKey: VkF3 accelBits: AfVirtualkey ;
      appendItem: '~Deferred payment calc'
        selector: #notImplemented
        accelKey: VkF3 accelBits: AfVirtualkey ;
      title: '~Process'.!
```

```
selectBottom: aGraphPane
    "Instantiates a class when an icon is selected"
    " SI 4/29/92"

    locationX := (aGraphPane mouseLocation) x.
    locationY := (aGraphPane mouseLocation) y.

    "respond to additional info tab"
    ((locationY < 134) and: [locationY > 81])
      ifTrue:[self meterHistory: aGraphPane].

    "respond to payment history tab"
    (locationY < 81)
      ifTrue:[self paymentHistory: aGraphPane].

    "respond to current bill tab"
    (locationY > 134)
      ifTrue:[self currentBill: aGraphPane]!

selectTop: aGraphPane
    "changes bitmaps when a notebook tab is selected"
    " SI 4/29/92"

    locationX := (aGraphPane mouseLocation) x.
    locationY := (aGraphPane mouseLocation) y.

    "respond to additional info tab"
    (locationX > 186 and: [locationY < 91 ])
      ifTrue:
        [CursorManager execute change.
        self addInfo: aGraphPane.
        CursorManager normal change].

    "respond to customer info tab"
    (locationX < 186 and: [locationY < 91 ])
      ifTrue:
        [CursorManager execute change.
        self custInfo: aGraphPane.
        CursorManager normal change].

    "respond to letter icon"
    (locationX < 132 and: [locationY > 91 ])
      ifTrue:
        [CursorManager execute change.
        PowerLetter new open.
        CursorManager normal change].
```

```
    "respond to memo1 icon"
    (locationX < 226 and: [locationX > 132 and: [locationY > 83]])
       ifTrue:
          [CursorManager execute change.
          PowerMemo1 new open.
          CursorManager normal change]

    "respond to memo2 icon"
    (locationX < 326 and: [locationX > 226 and: [locationY > 83]])
       ifTrue:
          [CursorManager execute change.
          PowerMemo2 new open.
          CursorManager normal change]

    "respond to memo2 icon"(locationX > 226 and: [locationY > 83])
       ifTrue:
          [CursorManager execute change.
          PowerMap new open.
          CursorManager normal change]!

showLocation: aGraphPane
    "Shows cursor location to test where icons are located"
    " SI 4/27/92 "

    locationY := (aGraphPane mouseLocation) y.
    locationX := (aGraphPane mouseLocation) x.

topNotebook: aGraphPane
    "Writes bitmap for the top notebook to the graphpane"
          "SI 4-29-92"
    | bitmap window |

    self bitMapID: 1005.
    bitmap := Bitmap fromModule: 'duke' id: bitMapID.
    window := 0@0 extent: 540@230.

    aGraphPane pen
       drawRetainPicture:
          [aGraphPane pen copyBitmap: bitmap from: window at: 0@0]!

waterHeating
    "calls water heating class"
    " SI 4/28/92"

    CursorManager execute change.
    PowerWaterHeating new open.
    CursorManager normal change! !
```

6.2.3.6 *PowerStartEXE Class*

```
Object subclass: #PowerStartEXE
  instanceVariableNames:
    'pid'
    classVariableNames: ''
    poolDictionaries: '' !

!PowerStartEXE class methods !

endProgram: pid
    " Terminate a program that was started thru execProgram:parameters: "

    DosLibrary killProcess: 0 pid: pid!

    execProgram: aString1  parameters: aString2

    " Input: 'aString1' = Fully qualified name of program to execute.
    'aString2' = Paramter string to pass to the program. "

    " Answers anInteger = DosExecProgram return code. "

    |objNameBuffer programName parameters resultCodes rc |

    programName := aString1 asAsciiZ.
    aString2 isNil
      ifTrue: [parameters := '']
      ifFalse: [parameters := aString2 asAsciiZ].

    objNameBuffer := String new: 100.
    rc := DosLibrary execPgm: objNameBuffer
      objNameBuf1: objNameBuffer size
      exeFlags: 1 "Start as async process—don't care when it terminates"
      argPointer: (programName, parameters) asAsciiZ
      envPointer: 0 "Inherit environment from Smalltalk process"
          returnCodes: (resultCodes := ByteArray new: 4)
          pgmPointer: programName.

    ^(rc = 0)
      ifTrue: [PMStructure fromBytes: (resultCodes copyFrom: 1 to: 2))
       uShortAtOffset: 0 ]
      ifFalse: [rc]!

killProcess: actionCode  pid: processID
    " Call to DosKillProcess. "

    <api: '#10' ushort ushort ushort>
```

```
    ^self! !

!PowerStartEXE methods !

example
    "demonstrates starting an EXE—the M-Motion video browser"
    " To run an example, evaluate the following: "

    pid := PowerStartEXE
        execProgram: 'p2p.exe'
        parameters: ''.

    " To kill the program, evaluate the following:"
    " PowerStartEXE endProgram: pid "! !
```

6.2.3.7 PowerAlerts Class

```
PowerStartEXE subclass: #PowerAlerts
  instanceVariableNames: ''
  classVariableNames: ''
  poolDictionaries: '' !

!PowerAlerts class methods ! !

!PowerAlerts methods !

open

    "Calls alerts program "
    " SI 4/28/92 "

    pid := PowerAlerts
        execProgram: 'e.exe'
        parameters: 'alerts.dat'.! !
```

6.2.3.8 execPgm and killProcess Methods for DosDLL Class

```
!DosDLL methods !

execPgm: pobjNameBuf
    objNameBufl: anIntl
    exeFlags: anInt2
    argPointer: aStringl
    envPointer: aString2
```

```
    returnCodes: pReturnCodes
    pgmPointer: aString3

    " Call to DosExecPgm.  Added for named pipes support. "

    <api: '#144' struct short ushort struct ulong struct struct ushort>
    ^self invalidArgument! !

killProcess: actionCode
    pid: processID

    " Call to DosKillProcess. "

    <api: '#10' ushort ushort ushort>
    ^self! !
```

6.2.3.9 *PowerEqualPay Class*

```
PowerStartEXE subclass: #PowerEqualPay
    instanceVariableNames: ''
    classVariableNames: ''
    poolDictionaries: '' !

!PowerEqualPay class methods ! !

!PowerEqualPay methods !

open
    "Calls Bookmanager equal payment section "
    " SI 4/28/92 "

    pid := PowerEqualPay
      execProgram: 'bookmgr.exe'
      parameters: 'ref /b 16.0'.! !
```

6.2.3.10 *PowerLetter Class*

```
PowerStartEXE subclass: #PowerLetter
    instanceVariableNames: ''
    classVariableNames: ''
    poolDictionaries: '' !

!PowerLetter class methods ! !
```

```
!PowerLetter methods !

open
    "Calls letter cmd "
    " SI 4/30/92 "

    pid := PowerLetter
      execProgram: ''
      parameters: ''! !
```

6.2.3.11 PowerLibrary Class

```
PowerStartEXE subclass: #PowerLibrary
    instanceVariableNames: ''
    classVariableNames: ''
    poolDictionaries: '' !

!PowerLibrary class methods ! !

!PowerLibrary methods !

open
    "Calls Bookmanager library section "
    " SI 4/28/92 "

    pid := PowerLibrary
      execProgram: 'bookmgr.exe'
      parameters: 'csc_bks /s'! !
```

6.2.3.12 PowerLoadControl Class

```
PowerStartEXE subclass: #PowerLoadControl
    instanceVariableNames: ''
    classVariableNames: ''
    poolDictionaries: '' !

!PowerLoadControl class methods ! !

!PowerLoadControl methods !

open
    "Calls Bookmanager load control section "
    " SI 4/28/92 "
```

```
pid := PowerLoadControl
   execProgram: 'bookmgr.exe'
   parameters: 'central /b to 3.1.2.3.1'! !
```

6.2.3.13 PowerMap Class

```
PowerStartEXE subclass: #PowerMap
   instanceVariableNames: ''
   classVariableNames: ''
   poolDictionaries: '' !

!PowerMap class methods ! !

!PowerMap methods !

open
   "Calls memo1 cmd "
   " SI 4/30/92 "

   pid := PowerMap
      execProgram: ''
      parameters: ''! !
```

6.2.3.14 PowerMemo1 Class

```
PowerStartEXE subclass: #PowerMemo1
   instanceVariableNames: ''
   classVariableNames: ''
   poolDictionaries: '' !

!PowerMemo1 class methods ! !

!PowerMemo1 methods !

open
   "Calls memo1 cmd "
   " SI 4/30/92 "

   pid := PowerMemo1
      execProgram: ''
      parameters: ''! !
```

6.2.3.15 PowerMemo2 Class

```
PowerStartEXE subclass: #PowerMemo2
    instanceVariableNames: ''
    classVariableNames: ''
    poolDictionaries: '' !

!PowerMemo2 class methods ! !

!PowerMemo2 methods !

open
    "Calls memo1 cmd "
    " SI 4/30/92 "

    pid := PowerMemo2
    execProgram: ''
    parameters: ''! !
```

6.2.3.16 PowerP2P Class

```
PowerStartEXE subclass: #PowerP2P
    instanceVariableNames: ''
    classVariableNames: ''
    poolDictionaries: '' !

!PowerP2P class methods ! !

!PowerP2P methods !

open
    "Calls P2P "
    " SI 4/28/92 "

    pid := PowerP2P
    execProgram: 'P2P.exe'
    parameters: ''! !
```

6.2.3.17 PowerServiceResponse Class

```
PowerStartEXE subclass: #PowerServiceResponse
    instanceVariableNames: ''
    classVariableNames: ''
    poolDictionaries: '' !
```

```
!PowerServiceResponse class methods ! !

!PowerServiceResponse methods !

open
    "Calls the AVS player "
    " SI 4/28/92 "

    pid := PowerServiceResponse
      execProgram: 'splayer.exe'
      parameters: ''! !
```

6.2.3.18 PowerWeather Class

```
PowerStartEXE subclass: #PowerWeather
    instanceVariableNames: ''
    classVariableNames: ''
    poolDictionaries: '' !

!PowerWeather class methods ! !

!PowerWeather methods !

open
    "Calls the weather program "
    " SI 4/28/92 "

    pid := PowerWeather
      execProgram: 'radar2.exe'
      parameters: ''! !
```

6.2.4 Supporting OS/2 Files

6.2.4.1 POWER DLL

Binary file.

6.2.4.2 POWER.DEF

```
;-------------------------------------------------------------------------------
; POWER.DEF module definition file
;-------------------------------------------------------------------------------

LIBRARY POWER
```

6.2.4.3 POWER.RC

```
#define INCL_PM
#include <os2.h>
BITMAP 1001 power03.bmp /* main window */
BITMAP 1002 logo.bmp /* logo */
BITMAP 1003 notebook.bmp /* notebook */
BITMAP 1004 power05.bmp /* .5 size main window */
BITMAP 1005 note01a.bmp /* notebook 1 top */
BITMAP 1006 note01b.bmp /* notebook 1 bottom */
BITMAP 1007 note02a.bmp /* notebook 1 bottom */
BITMAP 1008 note03b.bmp /* notebook 1 bottom */
BITMAP 1009 note02b.bmp /* notebook 1 bottom */
```

6.2.4.4 POWER.CMD

```
rc -r power.rc
link power, power.dll /align:16, NUL,,power
rc power.res power.dll
```

6.3 BANKING KIOSK

This section describes a prototype developed to support a bid by an IBM branch office to produce a banking kiosk. The bank wanted to provide functions not currently available through its ATMs. It wanted these new functions to be delivered in a manner that was appealing to customers and easy to use. It especially wanted to see how multimedia could be used to serve bank customers better.

IBM used this prototype to show the bank our ideas for how the system could be implemented and to differentiate our proposal from those of competing vendors. Limited time and funds were available, so we implemented the prototype with a two person–week effort.

The language we chose was IBM's Ultimedia Audio Visual Connection (AVC) because it provided the multimedia support we needed and allowed us to make very fast progress. Hardware was a PS/2 model 80 with an ActionMedia II digital video card, an M-Audio Adapter, two stereo speakers, and an IBM 8516 touch display.

6.3.1 Operational Description

The program begins by displaying the name of the prototype and playing background music via the audio adapter (Figure 6-19). This would not be part of the actual kiosk but provides an opportunity for the marketing representative to introduce the prototype.

When a customer walks up to the kiosk, he or she will see the screen, which requests the person to insert his or her ATM card (Figure 6-20). The user is prompted by text across the bottom of the screen, a video of a card being inserted, which repeats across the upper right quadrant of the screen, and an audio request to insert the card. The bank logo and a picture of the headquarters building customize this screen for the bank. Card reader hardware was not available for the prototype, so card entry was simulated with a key press.

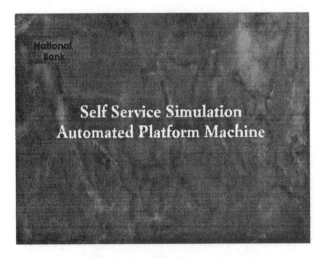

Figure 6-19. Introductory Screen

Figure 6-20. Insert Card Request

After inserting the card, the customer must enter his or her personal identification number (PIN). A video window provides instructions (Figure 6-21). The customer enters the PIN via a keypad on the touch panel. Then the main menu provides a list of the services offered by the kiosk (Figure 6-22). The customer selects a service by pressing a key on the touch screen. If the customer selects the rate information service, a screen appears showing current rates for each type of account the bank offers (Figure 6-23). The customer presses the Return button when done viewing the rates.

Figure 6-21. *Personal Identification Number Entry*

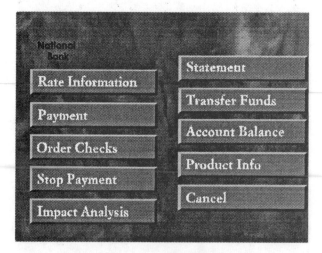

Figure 6-22. *Main Menu*

The rate information service, along with many of the other services provided by the kiosk, requires a host inquiry to obtain current information. While the host inquiry is in progress, a message box appears with a clock and the message "Working..." (Figure 6-24). The prototype is self-contained, but provides this message and time delay to simulate accurately the way the final product will work.

This prototype implemented a subset of the functions the bank would like to see in a real kiosk in order to demonstrate feasibility. When the user hits a key for a function that

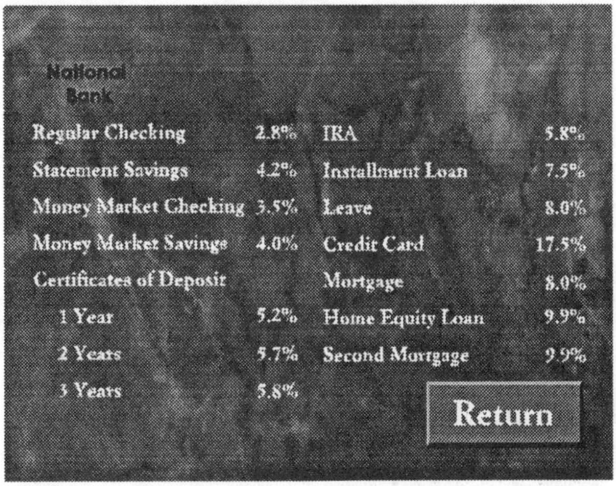

Figure 6-23. Rate Information

Figure 6-24. Working Screen

is not in the prototype, a "function not available" message appears on the screen (Figure 6-25).

The check ordering function allows the user to request a new batch of checks, which will be shipped to the person's home. The first screen in this function displays to the customer a copy of the person's current check and allows him or her to reorder more of the same or choose a new style (Figure 6-26). A customer who hits the Order More Checks button is given the option of ordering one, two, or three boxes (Figure 6-27) and receives an acknowl-

Figure 6-25. *Function Not Available Screen*

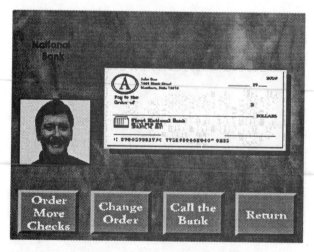

Figure 6-26. *Check Ordering Function: Initial Screen*

edgment via the video window. By hitting the Change Order button, the customer is presented with a new check style. Keys along the bottom of this screen allow the person to change the style of the check, the color of the check, or the font (Figure 6-28). Hitting the Change Design button changes the check background from a mill to a seashore scene (Figure 6-29). Hitting the Change Design button again changes the check background to a tropical scene (Figure 6-30).

Figure 6-27. *Check Ordering Function: Selecting Size of Order*

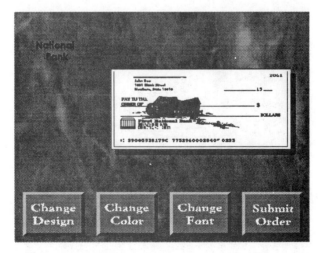

Figure 6-28. *Check Ordering Function: Changing the Check Order*

When the customer has found a suitable check background, he or she presses the Submit Order key. This brings up a screen with thanks for the order and a promise that the checks will arrive shortly (Figure 6-31). The customer can then press the Another Transaction button to go back to the main menu or the Get Card button to end the transaction.

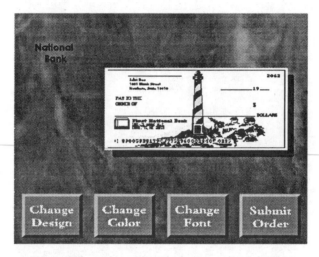

Figure 6-29. *Check Ordering Function: Changing the Check Design*

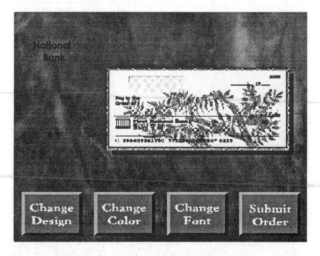

Figure 6-30. *Check Ordering Function: Seashore Scenic Check*

If the customer selects the Account Balance function on the main menu, a bar graph is displayed showing each of the customer's accounts and balances in each (Figure 6-32). Instructions are given via a video window.

Selecting the Product Information function on the main menu brings up a screen with push buttons for each of the bank products (Figure 6-33). Selecting a product plays a video commercial for that product.

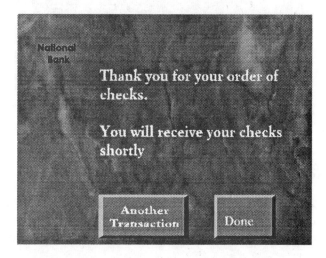

Figure 6-31. *Thanks for the Check Order Screen*

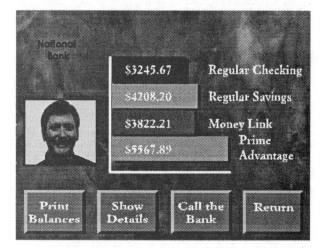

Figure 6-32. *Account Balance Screen*

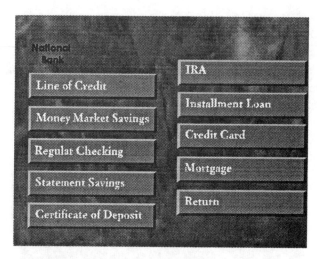

Figure 6-33. *Product Information Screen*

6.3.2 Conclusion

We found that AVC worked well for a quick prototype. It has the multimedia graphics, sound, and video functions that we needed. It does not, however, provide the power that a general-purpose programming language usually provides and does not create CUA interface controls.

The bank was impressed with the functions provided in the prototype, and the IBM branch office was pleased with the speed at which we were able to create it.

6.3.3 Code Listings

The code examples that follow will be helpful to those interested in creating multimedia applications with Ultimedia AVC.

```
/*AVC*/ /* Text file created from SOCIETY on Tue Sep 29 16:07:06 1992 */
/*=======================================================================
/* Kiosk for Society Bank
/* Scott Isensee and Jim Rudd, IBM Charlotte, September, 1992
/*=======================================================================
@NOFAIL = 1
DCONFIG ERS YES
CURSOR = NO
@cursorx = 0;@cursory=0;
load pin1a keep
```

```
load pin1b keep
load pin1c keep
load pin1d keep

OpeningScreen:
play "d:\society.!ap\mozart" {FADEIN ,A ,100 ,10 ,
    , , , }
show chart1a {REPLACE,DOWN ,NONE ,0.5 ,
    5.0 ,FULL, , , , , , }
paste chart2a /*Self-Serv Simulation{REPLACE,RIGHT ,NONE ,0.5 ,
    A 10 ,PART, 5.0, 6.0,86.6,19.7,5.0 ,6.0 }
paste chart2a /*Self-Serv Simulation{REPLACE,RIGHT ,NONE ,0.5 ,
    A 12 ,PART, 3.6,36.0,86.6,19.7,3.6 ,36.0 }
paste chart2a /*Self-Serv Simulation{REPLACE,RIGHT ,NONE ,0.5 ,
    KEY ,PART,19.4,75.0,48.6,17.0,19.4 ,75.0 }
beep(1000,200)
play stop /* Stop the music { ,A , ,04 ,0 , , , }

LogoScreen:
dconfig ers yes
show chart3a {REPLACE,DOWN ,NONE ,0 ,
    0 ,FULL, , , , , , }
do forever until @keycode=317
    dconfig A_V av
call PerformPrint
dlocate S 0 0 100 100
dlocate T 72.7 3.9 24.1 30.2
DPLAY "d:\society.!ap\insert.avs"
clear black    { , , , ,
        ,PART,72.7, 3.9,24.1,30.2, 71.6, 3.9}
wait 10 /* Adjust this to match video
play insert /* audio file { ,A ,100 ,10 ,
        , , , }
wait 8
paste chart3a { , , , ,
        ,PART,62.7, 1.6,33.3,34.5, 63.6, 0}
DLOCATE T 0 0 0 0
/* wait 10
end

dconfig A_V none
DLOCATE T 0 0 0 0

/******** Enter PIN ********************
/* Enter PIN
call PINSetup
show 'PIN1' /* no PIN yet {REPLACE,DOWN ,NONE ,0.5 ,
```

```
      .FULL, , , , , , }
dconfig A_V av
dpause
clear black {EXPLODE,OUT_V , , ,
      ,PART, 3.6,37.5,27.5,32.2,3.6 ,37.0 }
wait key
beep(1000,200)
show 'PIN1A' /* 1st PIN {REPLACE,DOWN ,NONE ,FAST ,
    KEY ,PART,38.8,21.2, 5.5, 5.8,38.8 ,21.2 }
beep(1000,200)
show 'PIN1B' /* 2nd PIN {REPLACE,DOWN ,NONE ,FAST ,
    KEY ,PART,43.6,21.2, 5.2, 5.6,43.6 ,21.2 }
beep(1000,200)
show 'PIN1C' /* 3rd PIN {REPLACE,DOWN ,NONE ,FAST ,
    KEY ,PART,48.6,21.6, 5.0, 5.4,48.6 ,21.6 }
beep(1000,200)
show 'PIN1D' /* 4th PIN {REPLACE,DOWN ,NONE ,FAST ,
    KEY ,PART,53.3,21.8, 5.0, 5.0,53.3 ,21.8 }
beep(1000,200)
dlocate T 0 0 0


/********Transaction Selection Menu ********************
TransactionMenu:
@cursorx = 50; @cursory = 50
dconfig A_V none
dlocate T 0 0 0
DO FOREVER
show 'SELECT1' /* Transaction menu {REPLACE,DOWN ,NONE ,FAST ,
    TRIGGER,FULL, , , , , , }
beep(1000,200)
IF @TF = "RateInformation" THEN CALL RateInformation
ELSE IF @TF = "Payment" THEN CALL TransactionNotImplemented
ELSE IF @TF = "OrderChecks" THEN CALL CheckOrdering
ELSE IF @TF = "StopPayment" THEN CALL TransactionNotImplemented
ELSE IF @TF = "ImpactAnalysis" THEN CALL TransactionNotImplemented
ELSE IF @TF = "Statement" THEN CALL TransactionNotImplemented
ELSE IF @TF = "TransferFunds" THEN CALL TransactionNotImplemented
ELSE IF @TF = "AccountBalance" THEN CALL AccountBalances
ELSE IF @TF = "ProductInformation" THEN CALL ProductInformation
ELSE IF @TF = "CancelSelectionMenu" THEN CALL LogoScreen
END


/***************************** Account Balances *********************
AccountBalances:
    call BalancesSetup
    show chart5a/* balances chart {REPLACE,DOWN , , ,
      ,FULL, , , , , , }
```

```
    dconfig A_V av
    dpause
    clear black   {EXPLODE,OUT_V , , ,
       ,PART, 1.1,34.5,23.4,32.2,SAME , SAME}

BalanceTriggers:
    wait trigger
beep(1000,200)
    do until @tf="Return"
       if @TF = "PrintBalances" then signal AccountPrint
       if @TF = "ShowDetails" then signal NotImplemented
       if @TF = "CalltheBank" then signal NotImplemented
    end

dlocate T 0 0 0 0
signal TransactionMenu

AccountPrint:
 print=1
 paste chart7 /* Print balances MB{REPLACE,DOWN , , ,
    2 ,PART,31.1,38.9,36.1,24.5, 31.1, 39.5}
 paste chart5a {REPLACE,DOWN , , ,
    0 ,PART,27.7,11.0,72.2,63.9,27.7 ,11.0 }
    signal BalanceTriggers

BalancesSetup:
    call PleaseWait
    dconfig A_V none
    dlocate S 8 0 100 100
    dlocate T 1.1 34.5 32.2 32.2
    DPLAY "d:\society.!AP\bal.avs"
    wait D 0
    dpause
return

/************** Check Ordering ***************************
CheckOrdering:
    call OrderSetup
    show chart9a /* Ordering ch {REPLACE,DOWN , , ,
       ,FULL, , , , , }
    paste check2 {REPLACE,DOWN , , ,
       ,PART,0 ,0 ,62.2,37.7,30.0 ,25.2 }
    dconfig A_V av
    dpause
    clear black {EXPLODE,OUT_V , , ,
       ,PART, 1.1,34.5,23.4,32.2,SAME , SAME}
```

```
OrderTriggers:
    wait trigger
beep(1000,200)
    do until @tf="Return"
       if @TF = "OrderMore" then do
          signal BoxesofChecks
       end
       if @TF = "ChangeOrder" then signal ChangeOrder
       if @TF = "CalltheBank" then signal CallBankNotImplemented
    end

OrderSetup:
    Order=5
    call PleaseWait
    dconfig A_V none
    dlocate S 8 0 100 100
    dlocate T 1.1 34.5 32.2 32.2
    DPLAY "d:\society.!AP\checko.avs"
    wait D 0
    dpause
  return

ChangeOrder:
    call ChangeOrderSetup
    paste chart16a /* No. of B {REPLACE,DOWN , ,FAST ,
       0 ,FULL, , , , , }
    dconfig A_V av
    dpause
    clear black {EXPLODE,OUT_V , , ,
          ,PART, 1.1,34.5,23.4,32.2,SAME , SAME}

ChangeOrderTriggers:
    wait trigger
    beep(1000,200)
    do until @tf="return"
       if @TF = "changedesign" then signal ChangeDesign
       if @TF = "changecolor" then signal ChangeColor
       if @TF = "changefont" then signal ChangeOrderNotImplemented
    end
    signal OrderThankYou

ChangeDesign:
    if Order=8 then Order=5
    if Order<5 then Order=5
    if Order=5 then do
       paste check5              {    ,    ,    ,    ,
          ,PART, 0, 0,62.2,37.7, 28.0, 25.2}
```

```
      end
    if Order=6 then do
      paste check6            {    ,    ,    ,    .
         ,PART, 0, 0,62.2,37.6, 28.0, 25.2}
      end
    if Order=7 then do
      paste check7            {    ,    ,    ,    .
         ,PART, 0, 0,62.2,37.6, 28.0, 25.2}
      end
    Order=Order+1
signal ChangeOrderTriggers

ChangeColor:
    if Order>4 then Order=2
    if Order=2 then do
      paste check2            {    ,    ,    ,    .
         ,PART, 0, 0,62.2,37.7, 28.0, 25.2}
      end
    if Order=3 then do
      paste check3            {    ,    ,    ,    .
         ,PART, 0, 0,62.2,37.6, 28.0, 25.2}
      end
    if Order=4 then do
      paste check4            {    ,    ,    ,    .
         ,PART, 0, 0,62.2,37.6, 28.0, 25.2}
      end
    Order=Order+1
signal ChangeOrderTriggers

BoxesofChecks:
    call BoxesSetup
      paste chart10a {  , , , .
         , , , , , , }
      dconfig A_V av
      dpause
      clear black {EXPLODE,OUT_V , , .
         ,PART, 1.1,34.5,23.4,32.2,SAME , SAME}


BoxTrigger:
      wait trigger
beep(1000,200)
  do until @tf="return"
    if @TF = "OneBox" then signal HowManyChecks
    if @TF = "TwoBox" then signal HowManyChecks
    if @TF = "ThreeBox" then signal HowManyChecks
end
```

```
OrderThankYou:
    dconfig A_V none
    paste CHART11A {REPLACE,DOWN , , ,
       TRIGGER,FULL,36.1,38.9,36.1,24.5, 31.1, 39.3}
beep(1000,200)
    if @TF = "anothertransaction" then signal TransactionMenu
    if @TF = "getcard" then signal LogoScreen

ChangeOrderSetup:
    call PleaseWait
    dconfig A_V none
    dlocate S 8 0 100 100
    dlocate T 1.1 34.5 32.2 32.2
    DPLAY "d:\society.!AP\checkd1.avs"
    wait D 0
    dpause
return

BoxesSetup:
    call PleaseWait
    dconfig A_V none
    dlocate S 8 0 100 100
    dlocate T 1.1 34.5 32.2 32.2
    DPLAY "d:\society.!AP\checkr1.avs"
    wait D 0
    dpause
return

PINSetup:
/* call PleaseWait
    dconfig A_V none
    dlocate S 8 0 100 100
    dlocate T 3.6 37.5 32.2 32.2
    DPLAY "d:\society.!AP\pinv.avs"
    wait D 0
    dpause
return

/************** How many checks have been ordered***********
HowManyChecks:
    if @TF = "OneBox" then do
    dlocate S 8 0 100 100
    dlocate T 1.1 34.5 32.2 32.2
    DPLAY "d:\society.!AP\box1.avs"
      end
      else if @TF = "TwoBox" then do
    dlocate S 8 0 100 100
```

```
    dlocate T 1.1 34.5 32.2 32.2
    DPLAY "d:\society.!AP\box2.avs"
      end
      else if @TF = "ThreeBox" then do
    dlocate S 8 0 100 100
    dlocate T 1.1 34.5 32.2 32.2
    DPLAY "d:\society.!AP\box3.avs"
      end
      signal BoxTrigger

/************** Utilities *********************************
NotImplemented:
    dconfig A_V none
    clear black {EXPLODE,OUT_H , ,FAST ,
      0 ,FULL, , , , , }
    paste sorry {REPLACE,DOWN , ,2 ,
      2 ,FULL,31.1,38.9,36.1,24.5, 31.1, 39.5}
    paste chart5a {REPLACE,DOWN , , .
      0 ,FULL,27.7,11.0,72.2,63.9,27.7 ,11.0 }
    signal BalanceTriggers

CallBankNotImplemented:
    dconfig A_V none
    clear black {REPLACE,DOWN , ,FAST ,
      0 ,FULL, , , , , }
    paste sorry {REPLACE,DOWN , ,2 ,
      2 ,FULL,31.1,38.9,36.1,24.5, 31.1, 39.5}
    paste chart9a {REPLACE,DOWN , , .
      0 ,FULL,27.7,11.0,72.2,63.9,27.7 ,11.0 }
    signal OrderTriggers

TransactionNotImplemented:
    dconfig A_V none
    clear black {REPLACE,DOWN , ,FAST ,
      0 ,FULL, , , , , }
    paste sorry {REPLACE,DOWN , ,2 ,
      2 ,FULL,31.1,38.9,36.1,24.5, 31.1, 39.5}
    signal TransactionMenu

ProductNotImplemented:
    dconfig A_V none
    clear black {REPLACE,DOWN , ,FAST ,
      0 ,FULL, , , , , }
    paste sorry {REPLACE,DOWN , ,2 ,
      2 ,FULL,31.1,38.9,36.1,24.5, 31.1, 39.5}
    signal ProductInformation
```

```
ChangeOrderNotImplemented:
    dconfig A_V none
    clear black {EXPLODE,OUT_H , ,FAST ,
        0 ,FULL, , , , , }
    paste sorry {REPLACE,DOWN , ,2 ,
        2 ,FULL,31.1,38.9,36.1,24.5, 31.1, 39.5}
    paste chart16a {REPLACE,DOWN , ,FAST ,
        2 ,FULL,31.1,38.9,36.1,24.5, 31.1, 38.9}
    signal ChangeOrderTriggers

PleaseWait:
    clear black            {REPLACE,DOWN ,   ,FAST ,
        0 ,FULL, , , , , }
    paste plswait {REPLACE,DOWN , ,FAST ,
        0 ,FULL,36.1,38.9,36.1,24.5, 31.1, 39.3}
    return

/************** Printing***********
PerformPrint:
    if print=1 then do
    avcprint "d:\SOCIETY.!AP\CHART5A._IM" "PRINTER" "LASER" "NEG"
        "LANDSCAPE"
    print=0
end
return

/************** Rate Information***********
RateInformation: /* Display rates for all products
show 'RTINFO1' {REPLACE,DOWN ,NONE ,FAST ,
    TRIGGER,FULL, , , , , }
beep(1000,200)
@cursorx = 50; @cursory = 50
IF @TF = "ReturnRateInfo" THEN CALL TransactionMenu
RETURN

/************** Product Information***********
ProductInformation: /* Select a product for which information is want
show 'Product1' {REPLACE,DOWN ,NONE ,FAST ,
    TRIGGER,FULL, , , , , }
beep(1000,200)
@cursorx = 50; @cursory = 50
IF @TF = "MMChecking" THEN CALL ProdVid
IF @TF = "MMSav" THEN CALL ProductNotImplemented
IF @TF = "RegularChecking" THEN CALL ProductNotImplemented
IF @TF = "StatementSavings" THEN CALL ProductNotImplemented
IF @TF = "CD" THEN CALL ProductNotImplemented
IF @TF = "IRA" THEN CALL ProductNotImplemented
```

```
IF @TF = "InstallmentLoan" THEN CALL ProductNotImplemented
IF @TF = "CreditCard" THEN CALL ProductNotImplemented
IF @TF = "Mortgage" THEN CALL ProductNotImplemented
IF @TF = "ReturnProdInfo" THEN CALL TransactionMenu
RETURN

ProdVid: /* Show product video for money market checking
  dconfig A_V av
dlocate S 0 0 100 100
dlocate T 0 0 100 100
clear black { , , , ,
    0 , , , , , , , }
DPLAY "d:\SOCIETY.!AP\loc.avs" S
wait 4
show 'ProdVid' {REPLACE,DOWN ,NONE ,FAST ,
    KEY ,PART, 3.8,85.6,96.1,13.3, 1.3, 90.2}
beep(1000,200)
dlocate T 0 0 0 0
signal ProductInformation
RETURN
```

6.4 CREDIT CARD WORKSTATION

Prototyping has many strengths; one of them is as a communication vehicle for selling new ideas. The prototype described in this section was conceived to show how an object-oriented user interface might be used in the credit card industry. The goal of the prototype was to show industry executives the value of a user interface based on objects and how an object-oriented user interface is especially well suited to many users in the credit card industry who are engaged in analysis tasks, such as selling services and assessing customer worth.

This prototype was shown throughout the world: in Europe, the United States, Asia, Africa, and Australia. Because it was a different approach to user interfaces at the time, it received a lot of attention at trade shows and in some banking trade journals. It served so well in communicating the goals of objects that it contributed to the launch of a large development effort to bring the power of objects to the finance industry.

In this example, Barton Carlson, a good customer of the bank, had sent a letter to his personal banker indicating that he would like to meet with the banker to straighten out a billing problem with his Visa credit card. Unfortunately, his banker was going to be out of the office, so the banker sent an audio mail to one of his assistants to meet with Carlson.

6.4.1 Operational Description

The first screen capture shows the state of the user interface when the customer service representative (CSR) first logs on in the morning. As with all other good prototyping efforts, potential users of the product were brought in to help design the interface. Users told us that for this sort of task, they wanted their desktop to initialize in a very organized-looking fashion. Hence, icons were lined up on the left-hand side of the screen (Figure 6-34). The icons represent objects that are most important to a credit card CSR. For example, icons were available on the screen that allowed the user to select an individual or corporate cardholder and to access other product offerings easily. A Calendar icon was available to allow the user to access frequently used calendar functions. There are many lost cards in this business, so users wanted a way to schedule the air express of replacement cards easily. Acceptance of automatic teller machines was still below expectations, so CSRs often try to steer customers to ATMs for simple withdrawal and deposit activity. An icon on the CSR's desktop provided an easy mechanism for locating ATMs for the customer. The News Flash icon allowed the user to read up-to-the-minute mail. The last two icons, Collections and Dispute Processing, scheduled mainframe transaction processing activities.

The first thing the CSR does after signing on in the morning is read the mail. She double-clicks on the News Flash icon and is presented with a list of new mail (Figure 6-35). She notices a news flash from her boss, Bill Stern. By double clicking on Letter from B. Carlson, she is presented with an audio mail advising the CSR that Bill Stern will be out of the office and that Bart Carlson will be coming in to discuss a billing problem with his credit card account (Figure 6-36). The audio clip includes Carlson's account number.

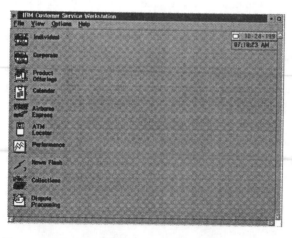

Figure 6-34. *Customer Service Representative Desktop*

The CSR looks up Carlson in the bank's customer information database by clicking on the icon labeled Individual. She is presented with a window that allows her to conduct searches of the database (Figure 6-37). She types in "Ca" in the name field and a fragment of Carlson's account number, "3253," in the account number field to perform a fuzzy search. Upon pressing the Search button, the user is presented with the results of the search: four clients match the criteria of the search, one of whom is, of course, Barton Carlson (Figure 6-38). From this

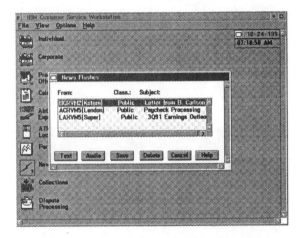

Figure 6-35. *News Flashes*

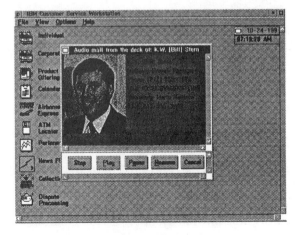

Figure 6-36. *Audio Mail*

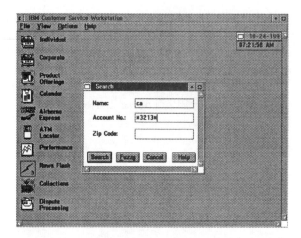

Figure 6-37. *Search*

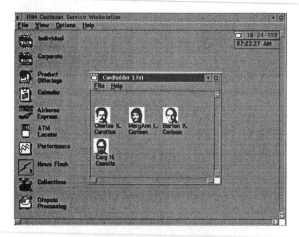

Figure 6-38. *Cardholders*

window, the CSR can select and drag Bart Carlson from the Cardholder List window and drop him on the desktop (Figure 6-39).

The CSR can now double-click on Bart Carlson. This action opens up Bart Carlson's work area, a container for holding all information about a certain segment of work. When the user opens a work area, the items that are in the work area are restored to the state they were in when the user left the work area previously. In Figure 6-40, Barton Carlson's work area has been opened (the window directly below the icon of Barton) along with a window that

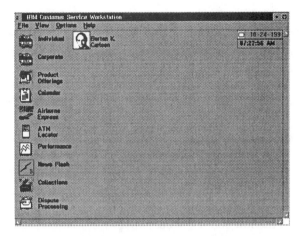

Figure 6-39. *Customer Icon*

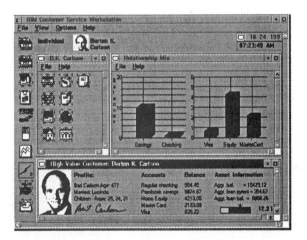

Figure 6-40. *Customer Information*

shows Carlson's asset-to-liability relationship mix (to the left of the work area). The bottom window shows a summary of the bank's relationship with Carlson and characterizes him as a high-value customer.

The work area contains icons that represent each of the relationships Carlson has with the bank (Figure 6-41). This window contains icons representing (from left to right, top to bottom) a Visa account, a savings account, a set of correspondence (the "1" represents the number of correspondence items in Carlson's folder), a MasterCard account, notes regarding Carlson's account, a checking account, a graph showing the customer's relationship mix (opened), a home mortgage, and a summary of Carlson's relationship with the bank. The user can obtain icon text through a bubble help feature, activated by holding the mouse pointer steady over the icon of interest for a period of time. Double-clicking on any of these icons opens the view associated with the icon. In this case, two icons have been double-clicked and their respective views opened: the Relationship Mix window and the Customer Summary window.

The Relationship Mix window graphically shows the customer's mix of assets and liabilities (Figure 6-42). The user can readily see at a glance the financial standing of the customer. The Customer Summary window, High-Value Customer: Barton K. Carlson, shows at a glance the value of the customer to the CSR (Figure 6-43), information that helps the CSR in making decisions about how to handle the customer's problems. The window shows background information about the customer (age, marital status, children), the customer's signature, account and balance information, and known asset information. The multicolored graphic in the lower-right-hand corner is an indicator that, when double-clicked, shows on a scale of 1 to 20 the customer's relative value to the bank. A high score (between 10 and 20) indicates to the CSR that the customer requires special handling. A low score (between 0 and 2) indicates that the customer has not been a good credit risk, does not have many assets associated with the bank, is a relatively new customer, or all three.

The next step the CSR takes is to check any correspondence between the bank and its customer. The CSR selects the Correspondence icon, which opens the window that contains Barton Carlson's recent correspondence (Figure 6-44). B. Carlson has only one piece of mail

Figure 6-41. *Relationship Window*

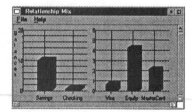

Figure 6-42. *Relationship Mix Window*

Figure 6-43. *Customer Summary Window*

in his folder. By double-clicking on the icon associated with that piece of mail, the CSR can read the correspondence (Figure 6-45). This note indicates that Carlson has indeed encountered a problem with his account, one serious enough to require a visit to the bank. The CSR notes the problem, closes the window, and opens the work area associated with Carlson's Visa account. Perhaps the CSR can find the account problem by examining Carlson's Visa activity.

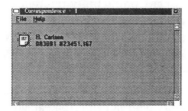

Figure 6-44. *Correspondence Window*

Figure 6-45. *Letter in Folder*

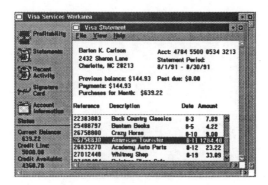

Figure 6-46. *Visa Work Area*

The Visa work area contains all information associated with Carlson's Visa account (Figure 6-46). From this work area, the user can access a number of informational displays about the user. The bottom left portion of the window shows the current state of Carlson's account: current balance, credit line, and credit available. This includes a Visa profitability index, the customer's statements for the past twelve months, recent account activity, the customer's signature card, and account details.

Figure 6-47 shows Carlson's card profitability quotient as indicated by the exploded block. The left axis (Heavy User–Light User) shows that Carlson is a heavy Visa card user (he charges around $4,000 a month), and the top axis shows that he is halfway between an extender (one who maintains a balance from month to month) and a convenience user (one who pays off his balances each month). The dollar amount indicates how much his Visa account generates for the bank each month ($103). The percentage value indicates, on average, the percentage of cardholders who fall into the category. The user can also view the cardholder's signature card to help verify identity (Figure 6-48). Additionally, the user can

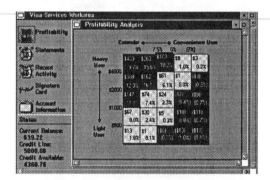

Figure 6-47. Profitability Analysis

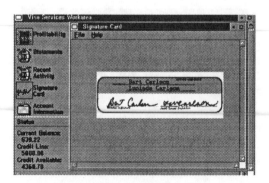

Figure 6-48. Signature Card

obtain graphical displays of previous monthly statements, recent account activity, and account background information, such as security password, address information, additional cardholders, and any special handling information for the cardholder.

Since Carlson has a problem with his previous statement, the CSR selects the Statements icon, which opens a view on that statement, for August 1991 (Figure 6-49). As the CSR is reviewing the account information, Carlson arrives at the bank. It turns out his concern is with the $1,284.40 charge to American Tourister: The charge was not for $1,284.40, he says, but instead for $128.44. The CSR can double-click on that statement entry to get an image of the charge slip submitted by the merchant (Figure 6-50). As the charge slip shows, the charge was indeed for $128.44. The CSR apologizes to Carlson and takes immediate action to rectify the error. To do this, she selects Adjust from the Visa statement menu bar (Figure 6-51). This launches a window to adjust the account (Figure 6-52). On the Adjust window, the Account Number, Item Number, and From Amount fields are prefilled, since they reflect data already shown to the CSR. To make the adjustment, she types the changed amount and then selects from a drop-down combination box the reason for the error—in

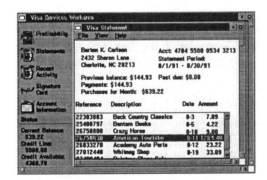

Figure 6-49. Last Statement

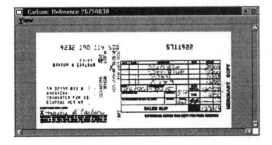

Figure 6-50. Charge Receipt Image

Figure 6-51. Menu Selection

Figure 6-52. *Adjust Window*

Figure 6-53. *Adjustment Notice*

this case, probably a keying error, and the CSR enters it as such. When the CSR selects Adjust, a message box appears that contains scripted information about when the adjustment will appear in the cardholder's account (Figure 6-53).

Carlson acknowledges the change and wishes the CSR a good day.

6.4.2 Code Listings

Here is a partial code listing from our Easel prototype, to give you the flavor of the syntax and design. Easel has a proprietary language that is procedural and event driven.

```
###### BV.EAL
# Generated by Layout/CUA
# (Layout/CUA COPYRIGHT (C) EASEL 1990. ALL RIGHTS RESERVED)
# Code generated on WEDNESDAY APRIL 4, 1990 at TIME 09:28:41
#
screen size 640 480
module BGraph
#include bga.inc
#include wincall.inc
#include eslhelp.inc
include accel.inc
include datelib.inc ### Easel date/time include library
include esldde.inc ### Easel DDE include include library
include pmptr.inc ### Easel pointer include library
#include message.inc ### Easel message box library

function ReplyToMessage(string: MixedCaseString,
        string: MixedCaseString,
        integer: Integer_1,
        integer: Integer_2,
        integer: Integer_3) returns string
library "reply"
```

```
stimulus DDE "esldde"              # DDE stimulus declaration

integer variable      ConvID is 0   # conversation ID, supplied by DDE DLL
        TempID    # for terminating extra convs
        Status    # conversation status flags
        ErrorID   # ID of last error which occurred
        DataLength  # for DDEDataString call

boolean variable WildCard is true    # for DDERegisterServer

string variable      AppName is "Easel"    # local (server) application name
        Topic is "CDdata"  # conversation topic   LLG
        ItemName  # item name for data exchange
        Format  # format requested by client
        DataString  # buffer for data

include "fileio.inc"
fileid FileID # declarations for input file
string FileName is "c:\\locdata.txt" # that contains LOC data from
string Read is "read-only" # the Excel spreadsheet
float Lines[10] # LOCVSCD.XLS using macro
integer Counter is 1 # DDE2LLG.XLM

record InputLine is
    Lines[Counter] 10
end record

#subroutine CHANGECOLORS()
#library "wincall"

#################################################################################
# TIRS VARIABLES
#

application TIRSKB

string variable TIRSMessageSV # Holds latest line sent from TIRS
string variable TIRSReturnSV # Holds first word of latest line sent from TIRS
string variable TIRSQuestionSV # Holds TIRS parameter/slot name
integer variable KBSMessageLineCounterIV is 0 # Number of lines in msg region
string variable TIRSClientTimeSV is "none\n" # Holds client time response
string variable TIRSClientIncomeSV is "decreasing\n" # Holds client income
  response
string variable TIRSClientNetWorthSV is "high\n" # Holds client net worth
  response
string variable TIRSBankIndexSV is "1\n" # Holds bank index response
string variable TIRSClientObjectiveSV is "cash\n" # Holds client objective
```

```
response

##################################################################

#WINSETSYSCOLORS(HWND_DESKTOP,LCOL_RESET,LCOLF_CONSECRGB,SYSCLR_ACTIVETITLE,
boolean variable DidOKCUA
boolean variable PermLogoffFlag is (false)
        ResetPasswordFlag is (false)
        ControlPanelFlag is (false)
        Off
        On
        OnOffCheckReg is (false)
        RegCheckProductsFlag is (false)
        SpCheckProductsFlag is (false)
        PassbookPFlag is (false)
        CNGOFlag is (false)
        CIGOFlag is (false)
        CD6MOFlag is (false)
        SavingsStatementPFlag is (false)
        SavingsMMPFlag is (false)
        OnOffSavingsPW is (false)
        PointerFlag is (false)
        DMixFlag is (false)
        CertificateFlag is (false)
        TelephoneFlag is (false)
        VisaFlag is (false)
        IRAFlag is (false)
        SpecialCheckingFlag is (false)
        BIFlag is (true)
        SupervisorFlag is (false)
        CalculatorFlag is (false)
        TicklerFlag is (false)
        MailFlag is (false)
        DotFlag is (true)
        LaserFlag is (true)
        NotesFlag is (false)
        BalanceInquiryFlag is (false)
        PhotographFlag is (false)
        RecentActivityFlag is (false)
        BiographyFlag is (false)
        DepositMixFlag is (false)
        LastStatementFlag is (false)
        SpecialOpenedFlag is (false)
        LOCFlag is (false) # tells us that a LOC
                # has been selected in the
                # products palette
        BartLOCFlag is (false)# tells us that Barton's LOC
```

```
              # has been selected in
              # Bartons CIF
      LOCSoldFlag is (false) # tells us that a LOC appears in
              # Barton's container
      BartonCDFlag is (false) # Flag for Barton's 5 yr. CD

      CustomerFlag is (false)
      VIPFlag is (false)
      ProductsFlag is (false)
      AddedNotes is (false)
      CIFFlagLoaded is (false)
      NewCIFFlagLoaded is (false)
      CIFFlagSelected is (false)
      NewCIFFlagSelected is (false)
      NewBioFlag is (false)
      BartFlag is (false) # Flag that is set when "bart" is
            # the customer search criteria
      LassiterBVFlag is (false) #Flag for LassiterBVKey
      BartonBVFlag is (false) # Flag for BartonBVKey

#   New CIF Flags for Products

      NewSavingsFlag is (false)
      NewCertificateFlag is (false)
      NewIRAFlag is (false)
      NewBankCardFlag is (false)
      NewNotesFlag is (false)
      Success
      CheckingLSFlag is (false)
      SummaryLSFlag is (false)
      RecentLSFlag is (false)
      SigCardLSFlag is (false)
      WorthFlag is (false)
      BartWorthFlag is (false)

global variable PrimaryColor is 25
global variable WINDOW_BACKGROUND is 19 #25
variable PayToCustomer
#string variable CurrentGraphPart
integer variable Special_Counter is 0
integer variable LOC_Counter is 0
integer variable TimePeriod is 0
integer variable UALevel is 0
integer variable Lassiter_Counter is 0
integer variable Barton_Counter is 0

font NewFont is facename "Tms Rmn" size 12 16
```

```
font LittleFont is facename "Courier" size 8 10
# I have changed all LittleFont to system to use the system font
# To change it back I have to type c/"system"/LittleFont/* *
font ItalicFont is facename "Helv" size 8 15 italic bold
font TinyFont is facename "Tms Rmn" size 5 10 bold
font ItalicFont2 is facename "Tms Rmn" size 8 15 bold
font TinyFont2 is facename "Helv" size 5 10

string Message is ""
string variable Userid is ""
        Password is ""
        EditMaskString is "********"
        CustomerTitle is ""
        Title is ""
        SW4_Title is "Checking Statements"
float variable RegularSavingsBalance is 9874.67
        BartCDBalance is 4496.20# 5017.60 #was 5874.67
        SpecialCheckingBalance is 0.00
        RegularCheckingBalance is 554.45
        BartRegularCheckingBalance is 1246.21
        IRABalance is 4213.05
        CDBalance is 2133.99 #This is car loan
        HoldTo is 0.00
        HoldFrom is 0.00
        HoldTransferAmount is 0.00
        VisaCreditLine is 4360.78
        VisaBalance is 639.22
        BartVisaBalance is 2133.99
        TelephoneBalance is 87.63
        Total_Deposit is 14642.17
        BartTotal_Deposit is 5742.41 #6263.81 #was 7120.88
        BartLoanBalance is 2133.99
        RM_Holder is 0.00
        Establish_Holder is 0.00

integer variable BICounter is 0
        Elements is 0
        Years is 0
        Holder is 0
        TypeSet is 0
        YearsElement is 0
        A is 5
        ColumnX is 1
        DefaultPlaceKey is 760
        DefaultPlaceImage is 800

## Forward declarations for subroutines
```

```
subroutine ProcessLastStatementSW(boolean :DidOKCUA)
subroutine ProcessCheckingStatementSW(boolean :DidOKCUA)
subroutine ProcessSecondaryWindow4(boolean :DidOKCUA)
subroutine ProcessRecentStatementSW(boolean :DidOKCUA)
subroutine ProcessUpdateAccountDB(boolean: DidOKCUA)
subroutine ProcessSignatureCard(boolean: DidOKCUA)
subroutine ProcessSecondaryWindow1(boolean: DidOKCUA)
subroutine ProcessCIFWindow(boolean: DidOKCUA)
subroutine ProcessEstablishLOC( boolean : DidOKCUA )
subroutine ProcessTIRSWindow( boolean : DidOKCUA )


#
# Action Bar Template Definition(s)
#

#action bar PrimaryWindowContextABCUA is
#  pulldown Choice1 text " "
#    choice Choice6 text "Mo~ve"
#    choice Choice7 text "Co~py"
#    choice Choice8 text "Co~nnect"
#    separator
#    choice Open text "~Open customer file..."
#    choice Choice3 text "~New file..."
#    choice ChoiceCopy text "~Copy customer file..."
#    choice Choice5 text "~Mark customer file"
#    choice Close text "~Close customer file"
#  end pulldown
#end action bar

action bar PrimaryWindowABCUA is
    pulldown Welcome text "~File"
       choice ExistingCustomer text "~Open..."
       choice NewCustomer text "~New Account..."
       choice SearchPD text "~Search..."
       choice Close text "~Close customer file..."
       separator
       choice Promote text "~Promote..."
       separator
       choice LogoffPD text "Logoff..."
    end pulldown
    pulldown View text "~View"
       choice NamesPD text "~Names"
       checked choice IconsPD text "~Icons"
       separator
       choice ProfileAllPD text "Profile ~All"
       choice ProfileSomePD text "Profile ~Some..."
       separator
```

```
          choice PromoteAllPD text "Promote ~All"
          choice PromoteSomePD text "Promote ~Some..."
          choice PromoteByPD text "Promote ~By..."
          choice RefreshPD text "~Refresh"
       end pulldown
       pulldown OptionsPD text "~Options"
       choice ShowSystemPD text "~Show status..."
       #  choice ShowApplicationPD text "Show ~application status..."
       #  choice ControlPanelPD text "~Control panel..."
       #  choice CalculatorPD text "Show ~calculator..."
       #  checked choice ToolsPD text "~Tools..."
       #  separator
          disabled choice GoModePD text "~GoMode..."
       end pulldown
       pulldown HelpPD text "~Help"
          choice HelpforHelpPD text "~Help for help..."
          choice ExtendedHelpPD text "~Extended help..."
          choice KeysHelpPD text "~Keys help..."
          choice HelpIndexPD text "Help ~index..."
          choice BankBookPD text "Banking ~guidelines..."
          separator
          choice About text "About..."
       end pulldown
       end action bar

##############################################################################
action bar NotesABCUA is
       pulldown Choice1 text "~File"
          choice ExitNotes text "~Exit"
       end pulldown
end action bar

#
# Primary Window Graphical Region Definition
#
enabled visible color PrimaryColor primary graphical region PrimaryWindow
    size 620 440
# size 524 176
    at position 22 255
# size 353 176 #706
#at position 68 201
       color green foreground
       size border
       title bar "IBM Customer Workstation"
       system menu
       horizontal scroll bar scroll by 8
       vertical scroll bar scroll by 20
```

```
    no scale
    action bar PrimaryWindowABCUA
    minimize button using "bv.ico"
    maximize button

#
# Icons for Client area of workplace
#
visible color PrimaryColor image region CustomerI size 32 32
 at position 10 395 in PrimaryWindow
 no scale
 file "cc0003.bmp"

visible enabled color PrimaryColor key CustomerKey
    at position 10 393 in PrimaryWindow
    move to 0 0
    box 34 34
    move to 34 16
    font "system" white text "Individual"
#  move to 24 2
#  font "system" white text "Accounts"

visible color PrimaryColor image region VIPI size 32 32
    at position 10 395 in PrimaryWindow
    no scale
    file "cc0003.bmp"

visible enabled color PrimaryColor key VIPKey
    at position 10 393 in PrimaryWindow
    move to 0 0
    box 34 34
    move to 34 16
    font "system" white text "Corporate"
#  move to 24 2
#  font "system" white text "Accounts"

#we often leave previous code in our prototypes to show iteration changes
#visible color PrimaryColor image region CustomerI size 32 32
#  at position 10 130 in PrimaryWindow
#  no scale

#visible enabled color PrimaryColor key CustomerKey
#at position 7 95 in PrimaryWindow
#  move to 0 36
#  box 38 38
#  move to 2 16
```

```
# font "system" white text "Individual"
# move to 2 2
# font "system" white text "Accounts"
#
#
#
invisible color PrimaryColor image region LassiterBVI size 36 36
at position 10 50 in PrimaryWindow #was 608 668
   no scale
 file "pack.bmp"

invisible enabled color 1 key LassiterBVKey at position 7 15 in PrimaryWindow
 #was 573 613
    move to 0 36
    box 38 38
    move to 2 16
    move to 66 62
    font "system" white text "William F."
    move to 2 2
    font "system" white text "Lassiter "

invisible color PrimaryColor image region BartonBVI size 46 46 at position 10 50
 in PrimaryWindow #was 608 668
    no scale
# file "jim.bmp"

invisible enabled color 1 key BartonBVKey at position 7 12 in PrimaryWindow #was
 573 613
    move to 0 36
    box 48 48
    move to 2 14
    move to 66 62
    font "system" white text "John G."
    move to 2 2
    font "system" white text "Barton"

#
visible enabled color PrimaryColor key Clear_Pointer_Key at position 87 15 in
 PrimaryWindow #was 573 613
    move to 0 36
    box 35 35

# Lassiter DDKey is used as an anchor for dropping the person icon

visible enabled color PrimaryColor key LassiterDDKey at position 7 15 in
 PrimaryWindow #was 573 613
    move to 0 36
```

```
     box 35 35

#visible color PrimaryColor image region VIPI size 32 32 at position 90 130 in
 PrimaryWindow #was 608 668
# no scale
# file "files.bmp"
#
#visible enabled color PrimaryColor key VIPKey at position 87 95 in
 PrimaryWindow #was 573 613
# move to 0 36
# box 38 38
# move to 2 16
## move to 66 62
# font "system" white text "Business"
# move to 2 2
# font "system" white text "Accounts"
#
#visible color PrimaryColor image region PrintBVI size 32 32 at position 464 130
 in PrimaryWindow #was 608 668
# no scale
# file "printbv.bmp"
#
#visible enabled color PrimaryColor key PrintBVKey at position 461 95 in
 PrimaryWindow #was 573 613
# move to 0 36
# box 35 35
# move to 2 16
## move to 66 62
# font "system" white text "Printer"
#
#visible color PrimaryColor image region InBVI size 32 34 at position 384 130 in
 PrimaryWindow #was 608 668
# no scale
# file "inbv.bmp"
#
#visible enabled color PrimaryColor key InBVKey at position 381 95 in
 PrimaryWindow #was 573 613
# move to 0 36
# box 35 35
# move to 2 16
## move to 66 62
# font "system" white text "In basket"
#
#visible color PrimaryColor image region OutBVI size 32 34 at position 384 50 in
 PrimaryWindow #was 608 668
# no scale
# file "outbv.bmp"
```

```
#
#visible enabled color PrimaryColor key OutBVKey at position 381 15 in
 PrimaryWindow #was 573 613
# move to 0 36
# box 35 35
# move to 2 16
## move to 66 62
# font "system" white text "Out basket"
#
#
#visible color PrimaryColor image region ShredBVI size 32 32 at position 464 50
 in PrimaryWindow #was 608 668
# no scale
# file "shredbv.bmp"
#
#visible enabled color PrimaryColor key ShredBVKey at position 461 15 in
 PrimaryWindow #was 573 613
# move to 0 36
# box 35 35
# move to 2 16
## move to 66 62
# font "system" white text "Shredder"

##########################################################################
#
Secondary Window Graphical Region Definition(s)
#

##########################################################################
#SetUpContext menus
#
Context menu for files folder in main window
#

enabled invisible dialog region PrimaryWindowCM
  size 93 43 #was 46 #was 37
  at position 32 42 # .65 and .40
  in PrimaryWindow
enabled visible list box Control1
  size 115 45 #was 36
  at position 0 -3
  in PrimaryWindowCM
    insert "Open customer file..."
    insert "New file..."
    insert "Copy files..."
    insert "Mark files..."
```

```
      insert "Transfer files..."

##############################################################
#
#
# Context menu for the customer file that has been dragged to
# main window.

enabled invisible dialog region PrimaryWindowCIFCM
  size 60 32 #was 46 #was 37
  at position 42 9 # .65 and .40
  in PrimaryWindow

enabled visible list box Control1
  size 70 36 #
  at position 0 -3
  in PrimaryWindowCIFCM
     insert "Open..."
     insert "Transfer..."
     insert "Consult..."
     insert "Close..."

##############################################################
enabled invisible color 25 graphical region Notes
  size 480 328
  at position 65 86
  in desktop
# in PrimaryWindow
  color 27 foreground
  size border
  title bar "Customer Notes"
  system menu
#priority is 1
  maximize button
  minimize button
#horizontal scroll bar scroll by 8
  vertical scroll bar scroll by 20
# no scale
  action bar NotesABCUA

  color PrimaryColor textual region NotesRegion size 480 328
     at position 0 0 in Notes
  font LittleFont

###############################################################
# Data Collection Textual Region Definition
enabled invisible textual region Collection window size 50 columns
```

```
    35 lines at default position

#enabled invisible color 25 graphical region ApplicationStatusSW
# size 220 42
# at position 4 93
# in desktop
# color 27 foreground
# title bar "Application Status"
# system menu
# black border
## horizontal scroll bar scroll by 8
## vertical scroll bar scroll by 20
# no scale
## minimize button
## action bar ApplicationStatusSWABCUA

enabled invisible color 18 graphical region SystemStatusSW
# size 220 42
  size 135 107
  at position 2 5 #was 4 7
#at position 4 152 #183
#in desktop
  in PrimaryWindow
  color 27 foreground
  title bar "Status"
  system menu
  color 23 border
# no scale
# minimize button
# action bar SystemStatusSWABCUA

#enabled visible color 25 graphical region TempSW
# size 220 42
# size 135 131
# at position 4 7
# at position 4 152 #183
# in desktop
# color 27 foreground
# title bar "Status"
# system menu
# color 23 border
# no scale
# minimize button
# action bar SystemStatusSWABCUA

visible color 18 image region HostStatusImage size 64 64
    at position 10 0
```

```
    in SystemStatusSW
    no scale
    file "host.bmp"

visible color 18 image region DeviceStatusImage size 64 64
    at position 62 0
    in SystemStatusSW
    no scale
    file "dstatus.bmp"

visible color 18 image region TrainingModeImage size 64 64
    at position 10 48 #was 50
    in SystemStatusSW
    no scale
    file "super.bmp" #This should always be greyed out

visible color 18 image region PrintersStatusImage size 64 64
    at position 62 48 #was 50
    in SystemStatusSW
    no scale
    file "printer.bmp"

#visible color 18 image region GoModeImage size 40 40
# at position 62 57
# in SystemStatusSW
# file "gomode.bmp"

#visible color 25 image region TimerModeImage size 40 40
# at position 112 57
# in SystemStatusSW
# file "timer.bmp"

#visible color 25 image region ForcedOfflineImage size 40 40
# at position 62 57
# in SystemStatusSW
# file "offline.bmp"
#
#visible color 25 image region TraceModeImage size 40 40
# at position 114 57
# in SystemStatusSW
# file "trace.bmp"
#
#
################################################################
#
#       SYSTEM ROUTINES
```

```
action Wait is
    set pointer to 3
    wait 3
    set pointer to 1

subroutine Wait_Some(integer : Periods) is
    set pointer to 3
    wait Periods
    set pointer to 1

subroutine TransactionComplete( string : Title) is
    if (ReplyToMessage(Title,"Transaction Complete",0,1,48) = "ok") then
    end if

#
# Dialog Box Object Definition(s)
#

enabled invisible modal dialog box ResetPasswordDB
    size 200 110
    at position 152 78
    dialog border
    title bar "Reset Password"
    system menu

enabled visible static text Control1
    size 63 12
    at position 37 74
    in ResetPasswordDB
    left align
    vertical center align
    text "Old Password:"

enabled visible entry field Control2
    size 57 12
    at position 101 73
    in ResetPasswordDB
    text size 30 columns
    left align

enabled visible static text Control6
  size 63 12
  at position 37 59
  in ResetPasswordDB
  left align
  vertical center align
  text "New Password:"
```

```
enabled visible entry field Control5
 size 57 12
 at position 101 58
 in ResetPasswordDB
 text size 30 columns
 left align

enabled visible static text Control8
 size 63 12
 at position 37 44
 in ResetPasswordDB
 left align
 vertical center align
 text "New Password:"

enabled visible entry field Control7
 size 57 12
 at position 101 43
 in ResetPasswordDB
 text size 30 columns
 left align

enabled visible default push button OK
 size 38 12
 at position 6 4
 in ResetPasswordDB
 group is Actions
 text "OK"

enabled visible cancel push button Cancel
 size 38 12
 at position 56 4
 in ResetPasswordDB
 group is Actions
 text "Cancel"

enabled visible push button Control4
 size 38 12
 at position 6 4
 in ResetPasswordDB
 text "OK"

enabled visible push button Control3
 size 38 12
 at position 6 4
 in ResetPasswordDB
 text "OK"
```

```
enabled visible push button Control9
  size 38 12
  at position 99 4
  in ResetPasswordDB
  text "Help"

#
# Subroutine Definition(s)
#

#subroutine ChangeColors()
# library "wincall"
#subroutine RESETWIN(Success)
# library "resetwin"

subroutine ProcessResetPasswordDB( boolean : DidOKCUA ) is
  begin resumable
    response to start
      make ResetPasswordDB visible
    response to OK in ResetPasswordDB
      copy true to DidOKCUA
      copy "Reset Password" to Title
      call TransactionComplete(Title)
      make ResetPasswordDB invisible
      make DialogBox1 invisible
      uncheck Control8 in DialogBox1
      copy false to ResetPasswordFlag
    response to Cancel in ResetPasswordDB
      copy false to DidOKCUA
      make ResetPasswordDB invisible

  end

##################### INCLUDE FILES #########################
#include super_ed.inc
#include control1.inc
#include sell_bv.inc

##################### Responses to Icons #########################
#
# Lassiter key
#
#
response to LassiterBVKey
  if (LassiterBVFlag = true) then
    copy false to LassiterBVFlag
  else
```

```
      copy true to LassiterBVFlag
  end if

if (eventnumber=17) then
 copy false to LassiterBVFlag
 make PrimaryWindowCIFCM invisible
 make LassiterBVKey color PrimaryColor
 call ProcessCIFWindow(DidOKCUA)
end if

if (LassiterBVFlag = true) then
 make LassiterBVKey color 1
 make PrimaryWindowCIFCM visible #Context menu
else
 make LassiterBVKey color PrimaryColor
 make PrimaryWindowCIFCM invisible #context menu
end if

###################################################################
#
# Barton key
#
#
response to BartonBVKey
if (BartonBVFlag = true) then
    copy false to BartonBVFlag
 else
    copy true to BartonBVFlag
 end if

 if (eventnumber=17) then
    copy false to BartonBVFlag
    make PrimaryWindowCIFCM invisible
    make BartonBVKey color PrimaryColor
    call ProcessCIFWindow(DidOKCUA)
 end if

 if (BartonBVFlag = true) then
    make BartonBVKey color 1
    make PrimaryWindowCIFCM visible #Context menu
 else
    make BartonBVKey color PrimaryColor
    make PrimaryWindowCIFCM invisible #context menu
 end if
```

```
##################################################################

response to ControlPanelKey
 if (ControlPanelFlag = true) then
    copy false to ControlPanelFlag
 else
    copy true to ControlPanelFlag
 end if

 if (eventnumber=17) then
    if (ControlPanelFlag = true) then
       copy false to ControlPanelFlag
    else
       copy true to ControlPanelFlag
    end if
end if

 if (ControlPanelFlag = true) then
 make ControlPanelKey color 7##
else
 make ControlPanelKey color 25
end if

##################################################

response to CalculatorKey
 if (CalculatorFlag = true) then
    copy false to CalculatorFlag
 else
    copy true to CalculatorFlag
 end if

 if (eventnumber=17) then
    if (CalculatorFlag = true) then
       copy false to CalculatorFlag
    else
       copy true to CalculatorFlag
    end if

    invoke "pmcalc.exe"
    end if

       if (CalculatorFlag = true) then
       make CalculatorKey color 7##
    else
       make CalculatorKey color 18
    end if
```

```
##################################################

response to TicklerKey
 if (TicklerFlag = true) then
   copy false to TicklerFlag
 else
   copy true to TicklerFlag
 end if

 if (eventnumber=17) then
   if (TicklerFlag = true) then
     copy false to TicklerFlag
   else
     copy true to TicklerFlag
   end if
# call ProcessTickler(DidOKCUA)
 end if

 if (TicklerFlag = true) then
   make TicklerKey color 7##
 else
   make TicklerKey color 18
 end if

##################################################

response to ProductsKey
 if (ProductsFlag = true) then
   copy false to ProductsFlag
 else
   copy true to ProductsFlag
 end if

 if (eventnumber=17) then
   if (ProductsFlag = true) then
     copy false to ProductsFlag
   else
     copy true to ProductsFlag
   end if
 call ProcessSecondaryWindow1(DidOKCUA)
 end if

 if (ProductsFlag = true) then
   make ProductsKey color 1##
 else
   make ProductsKey color PrimaryColor #18
 end if
```

```
####### Customer Key ########################

response to CustomerKey
  if (CustomerFlag = true) then
    copy false to CustomerFlag
  else
    copy true to CustomerFlag
  end if

  if (eventnumber=17) then
    copy false to CustomerFlag
    make PrimaryWindowCM invisible
    make CustomerKey color PrimaryColor
    call ProcessFuzzySearchDB(DidOKCUA)
    # call ProcessSearchBox(DidOKCUA)
    # call ProcessCustomer(DidOKCUA)
  end if
```

BIBLIOGRAPHY

Aaram, J. (1984). The BOP prototyping concept. In *Approaches to Prototyping*. Edited by R. Budde, K. Kuhlenkamp, L. Mathiassen, and H. Zullighoven. Berlin: Springer-Verlag.

Adler, M. (1991). Shoot-out at the OK button corral: Comparing application generators. *Microsoft Systems Journal* (November): 87–111.

Alavi, M. (1984). An assessment of the prototyping approach to information systems development. *Communications of the ACM* 27 (6) (June): 556–563.

Alavi, M., and Wetherbe, J. C. (1991). Mixing prototyping and data modeling for information-system design. *IEEE Software* 8(4): 86–92.

Alexander, H., and Potter, B. (1989). Case study: the use of formal specification and rapid prototyping to establish product feasibility. *Information and Software Technology* 29(7): 388–394.

Alford, M. (1977). A requirements engineering methodology for real-time processing requirements. *IEEE Transactions on Software Engineering* SE-3 (1): 60–69.

Alford, M. (1985). SREM at the age of eight: the distributed computing design system. *Computer* 18 (4): 36–46.

Alonso, A., Duenas, J. C., Leon, G., and de la Puente, J. A. (1995). An environment for distributed prototyping of real time systems. *Control Engineering Practice* 3 (6): 871–876.

Andrews, W. C. (1983). Prototyping information systems. *Journal of Systems Management* (September): 16–18.

Andriole, S. J. (1983). *Interactive Computer-Based Systems Design and Development*. Princeton, NJ: Petrocelli Books.

Andriole, S. J. (1988). Storyboard prototyping for requirements verification. *Large Scale Systems* 12: 231–247.

Andriole, S. J. (1992). *Rapid Application Prototyping: The Storyboard Approach to User Requirements Analysis*. Wellesley, MA: QES.

Apple Computer Corp. (1992). *Human Interface Guidelines*. Reading, MA: Addison-Wesley.

Appleton, D. S. (1983). Data-driven prototyping. *Datamation*. (November): 259–68.

Archer, M., Fincke, D., and Levitt, K. (1990). A template for rapid prototyping of operating systems. *Proceedings of the First International Workshop on Rapid Prototyping.* Research Triangle Park, NC. 119–127.

Archer, N. P., and Yuan, Y. (1995). Comparing telephone computer interface designs: Are software simulations as good as hardware prototypes? *International Journal of Human Computer Studies* 42, (2): 169–184.

Archibald, J. L., Leavenworth, B. M., and Power, L. R. (1983). Abstract design and program translator: New Tools for Software Design. *IBM Systems Journal* 22 (3): 170–187.

Arano, T., Chang, C. K., Mongkolwat, P., Lui, Y., and Shu, X. (1993). An object-oriented prototyping approach to system development. The Seventeenth Annual International Computer Software and Applications Conference.

Arthur, L. J. (1992). *Rapid Evolutionary Development: Requirements, Prototyping and Software Creation.* New York: John Wiley and Sons.

Auernheimer, B., and Kemmerer, R. A. (1986). RT-ASLAN: A specification language for real-time systems. *IEEE Transactions on Software Engineering* SE-12 (9): 879–889.

Babcock, J., Gerhart, S., Greene, K., and Ralston, T. (1989). SpecTra: A Formal Methods Environment. MCC Technical Report Number ACT-ILO-STP-324-89.

Baecker, R. M., and Buxton, A. S., eds. (1987). Readings in Human-Computer Interaction: A Multidisciplinary Approach. Los Altos, CA: Morgan Kaufmann.

Bailin, S. C. (1989). An object-oriented requirements specification method. *Communications of the ACM* 32 (5): 608–623.

Baldassari, M., Bruno, G., and Castella, A. (1991). PROTOB: An object-oriented CASE tool for modelling and prototyping distributed systems. *Software Practice and Experience* 21 (8): 823–844.

Bally, L., Brittan, J., and Wagner, K. H. (1977). A prototype approach to information systems design and development. *Information and Management* 1, 21–26.

Balzer, R., Goldman, N. M., and Wile, D. S. (1982). Operational specification as the basis of rapid prototyping. *ACM SIGSOFT Software Engineering Notes* 7 (5): 3–16.

Balzer, R. M., Cohen, D., Feather, M. S., Goldman, N. M., Swartout, W., and Wile, D. S. (1983). Operational specification as the basis for specification validation. In *Theory and Practice of Software Technology*, North Holland Publishing Company, 21–49.

Baroudi, J. J., Olson, M. H., and Ives, B. (1986). An empirical study of the impact of user involvement on system usage and information satisfaction. *Communications of the ACM* 29 (March).

Beichter, F. W., Herzog, O., and Petzsch, H. (1984). SLAN-4—A software specification and design language. *IEEE Transactions on Software Engineering* SE-10 (2): 155–162.

Belady, L. A. (1992). The 7 years of MCC's innovative software technology program. *American Programmer* 15 (1): 10–15.

Belkhouche, B. (1985). Compilation of specification languages as a basis for rapid and efficient prototyping. *Proceedings of the 3rd International Workshop on Software Specification and Design*, London.

Belkhouche, B., and Urban, J. E. (1986). Direct implementation of abstract data types from abstract specifications. *IEEE Transactions on Software Engineering* 12 (5): 649–661.

Bell, T. E., Bixler, D. C., and Dyer, M. E. (1977). An extendable approach to computer-aided software requirements engineering. *IEEE Transactions on Software Engineering* SE-3 (1): 49–60.

Bellantone, C. E., and Lanzetta, T. M. (1992). *"Works as advertised": Observations and benefits of prototyping.* (Technical Report TR-36. 0005). Southbury, CT: IBM Corporation.

Bera, R. K. (1990). Setting software requirements: Scenario for future fighters. *Information and Software Technology* 32 (9): 253–257.

Beregi, W. G. (1984). Architecture prototyping in the software engineering environment. *IBM Systems Journal* 23 (1): 4–18.

Bernstein, A. (1985). Shortcut to systems design. *Business Computer Systems* (June): 70–76.

Berzins, V., and Luqi (1990). An introduction to the specification language spec. *IEEE Software* 7 (2): 74–84.

Bewely, W. L., Roberts, T. L., Scgroit, D., and Verplank, W. L. (1983). Human factors testing in the design of Xerox's 8010 "Star" Office Workstation. In *Human Factors in Computing Systems*, 72–77.

Biemans, F., and Blonk, P. (1986). On the formal specification and verification of CIM architectures using LOTOS. *Computers in Industry* 7: 491–504.

Biewald, J., Goehner, R., Lauber, R., and Schelling, H. (1979). EPOS—A specification and design technique for computer controlled real-time automation systems. *Proceedings of the 4th International Conference on Software Engineering*, Munich.

Bischofberger, W., and Keller, R. (1989). Enhancing the software life cycle by prototyping. *Structured Programming* 10 (1): 47–59.

Bjerknes, G., Ehn, P., and Kyng, M. (1987). *Computers and Democracy: A Scandinavian Challenge.* Brookfield, VT: Gower.

Blackman, M., and Jeffreys, M. (1993). Quality systems by prototyping. *First International Conference on Software Quality Management,* 385–400.

Blee, A. (1994). Reducing lead time to rapid prototyping through the reuse of existing design data. *Proceedings of the Third European Conference on Rapid Prototyping and Manufacturing.*

Block, R. (1983). *Politics of Projects.* New York: Yourdon Press.

Blum, B. I. (1982). The life cycle—a debate over alternate models. *ACM SIGSOFT Software Engineering Notes* 7 (4): 18–20.

Blum, B. I. (1983). Still more about rapid prototyping. *ACM Sigsoft Software Engineering Notes* 8 (3) (July): 9–11.

Blum, B. I. (1986). Iterative development of information systems: A case study. *Software Practice and Experience* 16 (6): 503–515.

Blum, B. I., and Houghton, R. C. (1982). Rapid prototyping of information management systems. *ACM SIGSOFT Software Engineering Notes* 7 (5): 35–38.

Boar, B. H. (1983). Prototyping: Giving users a working model for applications development. *Computerworld,* September 12, 39–47.

Boar, B. (1984). *Application Prototyping: A Requirements Definition Strategy for the 80s.* New York: John Wiley.

Boar, B. H. (1995). Application prototyping. *Management Systems Development* 15(1): 7–10.

Bodker, S., Knudsen, J. L., Kyng, M., Ehn, P., and Halskov Madsen, K. (1988). Computer support for cooperative design. In *CSCW '88: Proceedings of the Conference on Computer Supported Cooperative Work,* Portland, OR. NY: ACM.

Boehm, B. W. (1976). Software engineering. *IEEE Transactions on Computers.* C-25 (December).

Boehm, B. W. (1981). *Software Engineering Economics.* Englewood Cliffs, NJ: Prentice-Hall.

Boehm, B. W., Gray, T. E., and Seewaldt, T. (1984). Prototyping versus specifying: A multiproject experiment. *IEEE Transactions on Software Engineering* SE-10 (3) (May): 290–302.

Boehm, B. W., and Standish, T. A. (1983). Software technology in the 1990s: Using an evolutionary paradigm. *IEEE Computer* 16 (1): 30–37.

Boies, S. J., Gould, J. D., Levy, S., Richards, J. T., and Schoonard, J. W. (1985). *The 1984 Olympic Message System—A Case Study in System Design.* IBM Research Report RC1138.

Botting, R. J. (1985). On prototyping vs. mockups vs breadboards. *ACM SIGSOFT Software Engineering Notes* 10 (1): 18.

Brooks, F. P., Jr. (1973). *The Mythical Man Month*. Reading, MA: Addison-Wesley.

Brooks, F. P., Jr. (1987). No silver bullet: Essence and accidents of software engineering. *IEEE Computer* (April): 10–19.

Brown, C. M. (1988). Human-Computer Interaction Guidelines. Norwood, NJ: Ablex.

Bruno, G., and Marchetto, G. (1986). Process-translatable petri nets for the rapid prototyping of process control systems. *IEEE Transactions on Software Engineering* 12 (2): 346–357.

Bryant, B. R., and Pan, A. (1989). Rapid prototyping of programming language semantics using Prolog. *Proceedings of the 13th International Computer Software and Applications Conference,* Orlando, FL. IEEE Computer Society Press.

Bucci, G., Mattolini, R., and Vicario, E. (1995). Automatic transition from rapid prototyping to target code for distributed systems. *Proceedings of the Second International Symposium on Autonomous Decentralized Systems.*

Budde, R., Kuhlenkamp, K., Mathiassen, L., and Zullighoven, H. (1984). *Approaches to Prototyping*. Berlin: Springer-Verlag.

Budde, R., Kautz, K., Kuhlenkamp, K., and Zullighoven, H. (1992). *Prototyping: An Approach to Evolutionary System Development*. Berlin: Springer–Verlag.

Budkowski, S., and Dembinski, P. (1987). An introduction to Estelle: A specification language for distributed systems. *Computer Networks and ISDN Systems* 14: 3–23.

Burkle, U., Gryczan, G., and Zullighoven, H. (1995). Object-oriented system development in a banking project: Methodology, experience, and conclusions. *Human Computer Interaction* 10(2–3): 293–336.

Buxton, W., and Schneiderman, B. (1980). Iteration in the design of the human-computer interface. In *Proceedings of the 13th Annual Meeting of the Human Factors Association of Canada.*

Canning, R. G. (1981). Developing systems by prototyping. *EDP Analyzer* 19 (9): 1–14.

Card, S. K., Moran, T. P., and Newell, A. (1983). *The Psychology of Human-Computer Interaction*. Hillsdale, NJ: Erlbaum.

Cardenis-Garcia, S., and Zelkowitz, M. V. (1991). A management tool for evaluation of software designs. *IEEE Transactions on Software Engineering* 17: 961–971.

Carey, J. M. (1990). Prototyping: Alternative systems development methodology. *Information and Software Technology* 32 (2): 119–126.

Carroll, J. M., ed. (1991). *Designing Interaction: Psychology at the Human-Computer Interface.* Cambridge: Cambridge University Press.

Casey, B. E., and Dasarathy, B. (1982). Modelling and validating the man-machine interface. *Software Practice and Experience* 12: 557–569.

Catchpole, P. (1986). Requirements for a successful methodology in information systems design. *Data Processing* 28 (4): 207–210.

Ceri, S., Crespi-Reghizzi, S., Di Maio, A., and Lavazza, L. A. (1988). Software prototyping by relational techniques: experiences with program construction systems. *IEEE Transactions on Software Engineering* 14 (11): 1597–1609.

Cerveny, R. P. (1987). Why software prototyping works. *Datamation*, August 15, 97–103.

Cerveny, R. P., Garrity, E. J., and Sanders, G. L. (1986). The application of prototyping to systems development: A rationale and model. *Journal of Management Information Systems* 3 (2): 53–62.

Chapanis, A. (1970). Human factors in systems engineering. In K. B. DeGreene (Ed.), *Systems Psychology.* New York: McGraw-Hill.

Cheatham, T. E. (1984). Reusability through program transformations. *IEEE Transactions on Software Engineering* 10 (5): 589–594.

Chen, J., Wang, J., and Kuo, J. (1989). An integrated framework for software prototyping. *Proceedings of the 13th International Computer Software and Applications Conference,* Orlando, FL. IEEE Computer Society Press.

Chen, P. (1990). Entity-relationship approach to data modeling. In *System and Software Requirements Engineering.* Edited by M. Dorfman and R. Thayer. IEEE Computer Society Press Tutorial, Order Number 1921.

Chen, P. M., and Chou, C. R. (1988). The requirements model in a knowledge-based rapid prototyping system. *Proceedings of the 12th International Computer Software and Applications Conference,* Chicago. IEEE Computer Society Press.

Cheng, L. L., Soffa, M. L., and Yang, Y. H. (1982). Simulation of an I/O driven requirements language. *Proceedings of the 6th International Computer Software and Applications Conference,* Chicago. IEEE Computer Society Press.

Christensen, N., and Kreplin, K. (1984). Prototyping of user-interfaces. In *Approaches to Prototyping.* Edited by R. Budde, K. Kuhlenkamp, L. Mathiassen, and H. Zullighoven. Berlin: Springer-Verlag.

Church, V., Card, D., Agresti, W., and Jordan, Q. (1986). *An Approach for Assessing System Prototypes,* Collected Software Engineering Papers, vol. IV, Software Engineering Laboratory Series, SEL-86-004. Greenbelt, MD: NASA Goddard Space Flight Center.

Cieslak, R., Fawaz, A., Sachs, S., Varaiya, P., Walrand, J., and Li, A. (1989). The programmable network prototyping system. *Computer* 22 (5): 67–76.

Clapp, J. A. (1987). Rapid Prototyping for risk management. *Proceedings of the 11th International Computer Software and Applications Conference,* Tokyo. IEEE Computer Society Press.

Clark, F., Drake, P., Kapp, M., and Wong, P. (1984). User acceptance of information technology through prototyping. *Proc. Interact 1984 Conf.,* London.

Clark, I. A. Software simulation as a tool for usable product design. *IBM Systems Journal* 20 (3): 272–293.

Coad, P., and Yourdon, E. (1990). Object-oriented analysis. In *System and Software Requirements Engineering.* Edited by M. Dorfman and R. Thayer. IEEE Computer Society Press Tutorial. Order No. 1921.

Cole, R. Novick, D. G., Fanty, M., Vermeulen, P., Sutton, S., Burnett, D., and Schalkwyk, J. (1994). A prototype voice response questionnaire for the U. S. census. *1994 International Conference on Spoken Language Processing,* no. 2: 683–686.

Collins, D. (1995). *Designing Object-Oriented User Interfaces.* Redwood City, CA: Benjamin/Cummings Publishing Company.

Commodore-Amiga, Inc. (1991). *Amiga User Interface Style Guide.* Reading, MA: Addison-Wesley.

Connell, J., and Brice, L. (1984a). Rapid prototyping. *Datamation,* August 15.

Connell, J., and Brice, L. (1984b). Prolonging the life of software. *Proceedings of the 1984 NCC.* AFIPS Press.

Connell, J., and Brice, L. (1985). Practical quality assurance. *Datamation* 31 (5): 106–114.

Connell, J. L., and Shafer, L. B. (1989). *Structured Rapid Prototyping.* Englewood Cliffs, NJ: Prentice-Hall.

Consolatti, S. (1993). *An Evaluation of Visual Basic.* IBM Technical Report 29. 1569.

Cook, S. (1986). Modeling generic user interface with functional programs. In *People and Computers: Designing for Usability.* Edited by M. D. Harrison and A. I. Monk. Cambridge: Cambridge University Press.

Coomber, C. J., and Childs, R. E. (1990). A graphical tool for the prototyping of real-time systems. *ACM SIGSOFT Software Engineering Notes* 15(2): 70–82.

Cordy, J. R., Promislow, E., and Halpern-Hamu, C. D. (1991). TXL: A rapid prototyping system for programming language dialects. *Computer Languages* 16 (1): 97–107.

Cuomo, D. L., and Mosier, J. N. (1989). *Choosing a User Interface Prototyping Tool for the Macintosh or IBM PC*. Bedford, MA: Mitre Corporation.

Darlington, J. (1983). Validation techniques for software specifications. In *Microcomputers: Developments in Industry, Business, and Education*. Edited by C. J. van Spronson. Amsterdam: North-Holland.

Davis, A. M. (1979). Formal techniques and automatic processing to ensure correctness in requirements specifications. *Proc. Conf. Specification of Reliable Software*.

Davis, A. M. (1982). Rapid prototyping using executable requirements specifications. *ACM SIGSOFT Software Engineering Notes* 7 (5): 39-42.

Davis, A. M. (1990). *Software Requirements: Analysis and Specification*. Englewood Cliffs, NJ: Prentice-Hall.

Davis, A. M., and Freeman, P. A. (1991). Guest editor's introduction—requirement engineering. *IEEE Transactions on Software Engineering* 17 (3): 210–211.

David, C. G., and Vick, C. R. (1977). The software development system. *IEEE Transactions on Software Engineering* SE-3 (1): 69–84.

Dearnley, P. A., and Mayhew, P. J. (1981). Experiments in generating system prototypes. *Proceedings of the First European Workshop on Information Systems Teaching*, Aix-en-Provence.

Dearnley, P. A., and Mayhew, P. J. (1983). In favour of system prototypes and their integration into the systems development cycle. *Computer Journal* 26 (1): 36–42.

Dearnley, P. A., and Mayhew, P. J. (1984). On the use of software development tools in the construction of data processing system prototypes. In *Approaches to Prototyping*. Edited by R. Budde, K. Kuhlenkamp, L. Mathiassen, and H. Zullighoven. Berlin: Springer-Verlag.

Dee, D. (1984). Developing PC applications. *Datamation* (April): 112–116.

Degl'Innocenti, M., Ferrari, G. L., Pacini, G., and Turini, F. (1990). RSF: A formalism for executable requirement specifications. *IEEE Transactions on Software Engineering* 16 (11): 1235–1245.

DeMarco, T. (1978). *Structured Analysis and System Specification.* New York: Yourdon Press.

DeMarco, T. (1982). *Controlling Software Projects.* New York: Yourdon Press.

Di Angelo, M.F., and Petrun, C.J. (1995). Collecting product-based usability requirements. *IBM Systems Journal*: 4–19.

Diaz-Gonzalez, J. P. (1987). *The Requirements Engineering of Real-Time Systems: A Temporal Logic Approach.* Ph. D. Dissertation, University of Southwestern Louisiana.

Diaz-Gonzalez, J. P., and Urban, J. E. (1987). ENVISAGER: A visual object–oriented specification environment for real-time systems. *Proceedings of the 4th International Workshop on Software Specification and Design,* Monterey, CA. IEEE Computer Society Press.

Diaz-Gonzalez, J. P., and Urban, J. E. (1991). Language aspects of Envisager: An object-oriented environment for the specification of real-time systems. *Computer Languages* 16 (1): 19–37.

Doberkat, E. E., and Gutenbeil, U. (1987). SETL to Ada—Tree transformations applied. *Information and Software Technology* 29 (10): 548–557.

Dodd, W. P. (1980). Prototype programs. *IEEE Computer* 13 (2): 80.

Dorfman, M., and Flynn, R. F. (1984). Arts—An automated requirements traceability system. *Journal of Systems and Software* 4 (1): 63–74.

Dorfman, M., and Thayer, R. (eds.). (1990). ANSI/IEEE Std. 830–1984: IEEE guide to software requirements specifications. In System and Software Requirements Engineering. IEEE Computer Society Press Tutorial. Order No. 1921.

Duffield, C. A., Eikenhorst, K. S., and Richards, P. H. (1992). *Designing Graphical User Interfaces.* IBM Technical Report TR 07. 1785.

Duke, E. L., Brumbaugh, R. W., and Disbrow, J. D. (1989). A rapid prototyping facility for flight research in advanced systems concepts. *Computer* 22 (5): 61–66.

Dumas, J. (1988). *Designing User Interfaces for Software.* Englewood Cliffs, NJ: Prentice-Hall.

Dumas, J. S. and Redish, J. C. (1993). *A Practical Guide to Usability Testing.* Norwood, NJ: Ablex.

Easterby, R. (1987). Trillium: An interface design prototyping tool. *Information and Software Technology* 29 (4): 207–213.

Edmonds, E. A. (1981). Adaptive man-computer interfaces. In *Computing Skills and the User Interface*. Edited by M. J. Coombs and J. L. Alty. London: Academic Press.

Edmonds, L. S., and Urban, J. E. (1984). A method for evaluating front-end life cycle tools. *Proceedings of the First International Conference on Computers and Applications*, Beijing, June 20–22.

EDP Analyzer (1984). Using fourth-generation languages and prototyping. *EDP Analyzer*. Special Report. Vista, CA: Canning Publications.

EDP Analyzer (1985). Speeding up application development. *EDP Analyzer*. Special Report. Vista, CA: Canning Publications.

Ehn, P. (1990). *Work Oriented Design of Computer Artifacts*. Hillsdale, NJ: Erlbaum.

Ehrich, R. W., and Williges, R. C. (1986). *Human-Computer Dialog Design*. Amsterdam: Elsevier.

Eisner, H. (1988). *Computer-Aided Systems Engineering*. Englewood Cliffs, NJ: Prentice-Hall.

Ellenbogen, E., Phillips, F., and Zucker, D. (1991). User Interface Prototyping and Development Tools. IBM Technical Report 85. 0117. July 1.

Fagan, M. (1976). Design and code inspections to reduce errors in program development. *IBM Systems Journal* 15 (3): 182–207.

Fairley, R. E. (1985). *Software Engineering Concepts*. New York: McGraw-Hill.

Feather, M. S. (1982). Mappings for rapid prototyping. *ACM SIGSOFT Software Engineering Notes* 7 (5): 17–24.

Flavin, M. (1981). *Fundamental Concepts of Information Modeling*. New York: Yourdon Press.

Fleischman, E. A., Quaintance, M. K., and Broedling, L. A. (1984). *Taxonomies of Human Performance*. New York: Academic Press.

Floyd, C. (1984). A systematic look at prototyping. In *Approaches to Prototyping*. Edited by R. Budde, K. Kuhlenkamp, L. Mathiassen, and H. Zullighoven. Berlin: Springer-Verlag.

Flynn, S. (1995). Prototyping learning tools for special needs using multimedia. *Proceedings of the 1st Conference on Computer Art and Design Education*, Brighton, UK.

Foley, J., Kim, W., Kovacevic, S., and Murray, K. (1991). UIDE—An intelligent user interface design environment. In J. Sullivan and S. Tyler (eds.), *Architectures for Intelligent User Interfaces: Elements and Prototypes*. Reading, MA: Addison-Wesley.

Fraser, M. D., Kumar, K., and Vaishnavi, V. K. (1991). Informal and formal requirements specification languages: Bridging the gap. *IEEE Transactions on Software Engineering* 17 (5): 454–466.

Galitz, W. O. (1984). *Humanizing Office Automation.* Wellesley, MA: QED Information Sciences.

Gane, C. (1987). *Rapid System Development: Using Structured Techniques and Relational Technology.* New York: Rapid System Development.

Gehani, N. H. (1982). A study in prototyping. *ACM SIGSOFT Software Engineering Notes* 7 (5): 71–75.

Gilb, T. (1981). Evolutionary development. *ACM SIGSOFT Software Engineering Notes* 6 (2): 17.

Gilb, T. (1985). Evolutionary delivery versus the waterfall model. *ACM SIGSOFT Software Engineering Notes* 10 (3): 49–62.

Gilhooley, I. A. (1984). Prototyping. In *Systems Development Management.* Auerbach Publishers.

Gladden, G. R. (1982). Stop the life-cycle, I want to get off. *ACM SIGSOFT Software Engineering Notes* 7 (2): 35–39.

Glass, R. (1985). Some thoughts on prototyping. *System Development* 5 (8): 7–8.

Godfrey, M. W., Holt, R. C., and Mancoridis, S. (1994). Prototyping: A visual formalism for system modelling. *Research Issues in Intersection Between Software Engineering and Human Computer Interaction Conference.*

Goedicke, M. (1986). The use of formal requirements specifications in EDE in a software development environment. *Proceedings of the 10th International Computer Software and Applications Conference,* Chicago. IEEE Computer Society Press.

Goguen, J. A., and Tardo, J. J. (1979). An introduction to OBJ: A language for writing and testing formal algebraic program specifications. *Proceedings of the Conference on Specifications of Reliable Software.*

Goldsack, S. J., and Finkelstein, A. C. W. (1991). Requirements engineering for real-time systems. *Software Engineering Journal* 6 (3): 101–115.

Gomaa, H. (1983). The impact of rapid prototyping on specifying user requirements. *ACM Software Engineering Notes* 8 (2) (April): 17–28.

Gomaa, H. (1984). A software design method for real-time systems. *Communications of the ACM 27* (9): 938–949.

Gomaa, H., and Scott, D. B. H. (1981). Prototyping as a tool in the specification of user requirements. *Proceedings of the 5th International Conference on Software Engineering.*

Gorden, U. S., and Bieman, J. M. (1995). Rapid prototyping: Lessons learned. *IEEE Software* 12 (1): 85–95.

Gould, J. D., and Lewis, C. H. (1985). Designing for usability—key principles and what designers think. *Communications of the ACM* 28(3): 300–311.

Greenbaum, J., and Kyng, M. (1991). *Design at Work: Cooperative Design of Computer Systems.* Hillsdale, NJ: Erlbaum.

Gregory, S. T. (1984). On prototypes versus mockups. *ACM SIGSOFT Software Engineering Notes* 9 (5): 13.

Greitzer, F. L., Wunderlich, D., and Weinberg, M. (1993). Hypermedia-based rapid interface prototyping. *Journal of the Society for Information Display* 1(1): 111–119.

Gronbaek, K., Kyng, M., and Mogensen, P. (1993). CSCW challenges: Cooperative design in engineering projects. *Communications of the ACM* 36 (6) (June): 67–77.

Guest, S. P. (1982). The use of software tools for dialogue design. *International Journal of Man-Machine Studies* 16: 263–285.

Guimaraes, T. (1987). Prototyping: Orchestrating for success. *Datamation,* December 1, 101–106.

Gupta, R., Cheng, W. H., Hardonag, I., and Breuer, M. A. (1989). An object-oriented VLSI CAD framework. *Computer* 22 (5): 28–37.

Guthrie, W. (1995). An overview of portable GUI software. *SIGCHI Bulletin* 27 (1): 55–70.

Guttag, J. V., Horning, J. J., and Wing, J. M. (1985). The Larch family of languages. *IEEE Software* 2 (5): 24–26.

Hackiel, S. (1995). A deliverables oriented approach to the integration of HCI into the design and development of software products. *IEEE Colloquium on Integrating HCI in the Lifecycle.*

Hallman, M. (1988). Incorporating transactions in a requirements engineering method. *Proceedings of the 12th Annual International Computer Software and Applications Conference,* Chicago. IEEE Computer Society.

Hamilton, M. H., and Hackler, W. R. (1990). 001: A rapid development approach for rapid prototyping based on a system that supports its own life cycle. *Proceedings of the First International Workshop on Rapid System Prototyping,* Research Triangle Park, NC.

Hanau, P. R., and Lenorovitz, D. R. (1980). Prototyping and simulation tools for user/computer dialogue design. *Computer Graphics* 14 (2): 271–278.

Harbert, A., Lively, W., and Sheppard, S. (1990). A graphical specification system for user-interface design. *IEEE Software* 7 (4): 12–20.

Hardgrave, B. C. (1995). When to prototype: Decision variables used in industry. *Information Software Technology* 37(2): 113–118.

Harel, D., Lachover, H., Naamad, A., Pnueli, A., Poti, M., Sherman, R., Shtull-Tauring, A., and Trakhtenbrot, M. (1990). STATEMATE: A working environment for the development of complex reactive systems. *IEEE Transactions on Software Engineering* 16 (4): 403–414.

Hartson, H. R., and Hix, D. (1989). Human-computer interface development: Concepts and systems for its management. *ACM Computing Surveys* 21 (1): 5–92.

Hartson, H. R., and Smith, E. C. (1991). Rapid prototyping in human-computer interface development. *Interacting with Computers* 3 (1): 51–91.

Hawgood, J. (ed.). (1982). *Evolutionary Information Systems*. Amsterdam: North-Holland.

Heaton, N. (1992). What's wrong with the user interface. How rapid protoyping can help. In *IEE Colloquium on Software Prototyping and Evolutionary Digest (Digest No. 202): Part 7*. London: IEE.

Heck, M.P., and Rudd, J. (1993). First impressions are everything: A CUA-compliant installation program. In D. Conklin (Ed.) *OS/2 2.X Notebook: The Best of OS/2 Developer Magazine*. New York: Van Nostrand Reinhold: 425–443.

Heckel, P. (1991). *The Elements of Friendly Software Design: The New Edition*. San Francisco, CA: Sybex.

Heitmeyer, C., Landwehr, C., and Cornwell, M. (1982). The use of quick prototypes in the secure military message systems project. *ACM SIGSOFT Software Engineering Notes* 7 (5): 85–87.

Heitmeyer, C., and McLean, J. D. (1983). Abstract requirements specification: A new approach and its application. *IEEE Transactions on Software Engineering* SE-9 (5): 580–589.

Hekmatpour, S., and Ince, D. (1988). *Software Prototyping, Formal Methods, and VDR*. Reading, MA: Addison-Wesley.

Helander, M. (1990). *Handbook of Human-Computer Interaction*. Amsterdam: Elsevier.

Helmbold, D. P. (1988). *The Meaning of TSL: An Abstract Implementation of TSL–1*. Stanford University Computer Systems Laboratory Technical Report CSL-TR-88-353.

Hemenway, K., and McCusker, L. X. (1982). Prototyping and evaluating a user interface. *Proceedings of the 6th International Computer Software and Applications Conference,* Chicago.

Henderson, P. (1986). Functional programming, formal specification, and rapid prototyping. *IEEE Transactions on Software Engineering* 12 (2): 241–250.

Herndon, R. M., and Berzins, V. A. (1988). The realizable benefits of a language prototyping language. *IEEE Transactions on Software Engineering* 14 (6): 803–809.

Hice, G. F., Turner, W. S., and Cashwell, L. F. (1978). *System Development Methodology.* New York: North-Holland.

Hix, D. (1989). A procedure for evaluating human-computer interface development tools. *Proceedings of the ACM SIGGRAPH Symposium on User Interface Software and Technology.*

Hix, D. (1990). Evaluation of human-computer interface development tools: Problems and promises. In P. Zunde and D. Hocking (eds.), *Empirical Foundations of Information and Software Science V.* New York: Plenum Press.

Hix, D., and Hartson, H. R. (1993). *Developing User Interfaces: Ensuring Usability Through Product and Process.* New York: John Wiley.

Hix, D., and Schulman, R. S. (1991). Human-computer interface development tools: A methodology for their evaluation. *Communications of the ACM* 34 (3): 74–87.

Hoffman, D. (1989). Practical interface specification. *Software Practice and Experience* 19 (2): 127–148.

Hoffman, D., and Snodgrass, R. (1988). Trace specifications: Methodology and models. *IEEE Transactions on Software Engineering* 14 (6)803–809.

Holbrook, H. (1990). A scenario-based methodology for conducting requirements elicitation. *ACM SIGSOFT Software Engineering Notes* 15(1): 95–104.

Hooper, J. W. (1989). Language features for prototyping and simulation support of the software life cycle. *Computer Languages* 14 (2): 83–92.

Hooper, J. W., and Hsia, P. (1982). Scenario-based protoyping of requirements identification. ACM SIGSOFT Software Engineering Notes 7(5): 89–93.

Hopgood, F. R., and Duce, D. A. (1980). A production approach to interactive graphic program design. In *Methodology of Interaction.* Edited by R. A. Guedj et al. Amsterdam: North-Holland.

Horowitz, E. (1975). *Practical Strategies for Developing Large Scale Software Systems.* Reading, MA: Addison-Wesley.

Hsia, P., Yaung, A. T., and Jiam, S. H. (1986). Requirements clustering for incremental construction of software systems. *Proceedings of the 10th International Computer Software and Applications Conference,* Chicago. IEEE Computer Society Press.

IBM Corp. (1991). *IBM Systems Application Architecture: Common User Access Guide to Interface Design.* SC34-4289-00. Cary, NC: IBM.

IBM Corp. (1992). *Object-Oriented Interface Design: IBM Common User Access Guidelines.* Carmel, IN: Que.

Iivari, J. (1984). Prototyping in the context of information systems design. In *Approaches to Prototyping.* Edited by R. Budde, K. Kuhlenkamp, L. Mathiassen, and H. Zullighoven. Berlin: Springer-Verlag.

i-Logix, Inc. (1990). *The STATEMATE Approach to Complex Systems.* i–Logix Report. Burlington, MA.

Ince, D. C., and Hekmatpour, S. (1987). Software prototyping—Progress and prospects. *Information and Software Technology* 29 (1): 8–14.

Isensee, S. (1991). *Controls for Graphical User Interfaces: The M&M Rule.* Master's thesis, University of North Carolina at Charlotte.

Isensee, S. (1992a). Software prototyping. *Midnight Engineering* (January/February): 53–43.

Isensee, S. (1992b). *Visual Programming Prototype.* IBM Technical Report 83. 290.

Isensee, S. (1992c). *Smalltalk Prototype of an MDI Application.* IBM Technical Report 83.277.

Isensee, S. (1992d). *Smalltalk Power Company Prototype.* IBM Technical Report 83.274.

Isensee, S., and Heck, M. (1993). *Charlotte Icon Development Process.* IBM Technical Report 83.302.

Isensee, S., Jones, J., Krizan, B., Levine, R., Lundell, J., Poston, R., and Wagner, A. (1993). Designing the user interface. In *Proceedings of the Common Operating System Environment Developers' Conference,* San Jose, CA.

Isensee, S., and Poston, R. (1994). CDE human interface design. In *UNITE '94 Proceedings,* Austin, TX.

Isensee, S., and Rudd, J. (1991). Prototyping software user interfaces: Usability as a competitive edge. *IBM Personal Systems Developer*: 29–34.

Isensee, S., and Rudd, J. (1992a). Smalltalk/V PM, Version 1. 4. In *User Interface Prototyping and Development Tools*. IBM Technical Report 85. 0168.

Isensee, S., and Rudd, J. (1992b). The Software studio: A new model for software development. *Creativity* (September): 2–5.

Isensee, S., and Rudd, J. (1992c). *A Do-It-Yourself Guide for Multimedia Video*. IBM Technical Report 83.272.

Isensee, S., and Rudd, J. (1993). Prototyping software user interfaces: Usability as a competitive edge. In *OS/2 2. X Notebook*. New York: Van Nostrand Reinhold: 405–413.

Isensee, S., Rudd. J., and Douyotas, D. (1992). *Multimedia Prototype Development*. IBM Technical Report 83. 293.

Jackson, M. I. (1985). Developing Ada programs using the Vienna development method. *Software Practice and Experience* 15 (3): 305–318.

Jackson, R. B., Embley, D. W., and Woodfield, S. N. (1995). Developing formal object-oriented requirements specifications: A model, tool, and technique. *Information Systems* 20 (4): 273–289.

Jaffe, M. S., Leveson, N. G., Heimdahl, M. P. E., and Melhart, B. E. (1991). Software requirements analysis for real-time process-control systems. *IEEE Transactions on Software Engineering* 17 (3): 241–258.

James, E. B. (1980): The user interface. *Computer Journal* 23 (1): 25–28.

Janson, M. A., and Douglas Smith, L. D. (1985). Prototyping for systems development: A critical appraisal. *MIS Quarterly* (December): 305–316.

Jarvinen, H. M., Kurki–Suonio, R., Sakkinen, M., and Systa, K. (1990). Object-oriented specification of reactive systems. *Proceedings of the 12th International Conference on Software Engineering*, Nice, France. IEEE Computer Society Press.

Johnson, J., Ehn, P., Grudin, J., Nardi, B., and Thoresen, K. (1990). Participatory design of computer systems. In *Proceedings of CHI '90*, Seattle, WA.

Johnson, J. R. (1983). A prototypical success story. *Datamation*. (November): 251–256.

Jones, C. A. (1992). *An Evaluation of ENFIN/3*. IBM Technical Report 29. 1534.

Jones, C. A., and King, D. D. (1993). *An Evaluation of KASE:VIP.* IBM Technical Report 29. 1513.

Jones, C. A., King, D. D., and Eckhoff, R. P. (1993). *An Evaluation of XVT.* IBM Technical Report 29. 1683.

Jones, C. A., King, D. D., and Hanks, B. S. (1993). *An Evaluation of PowerBuilder.* IBM Technical Report 29. 1568.

Jones, K., and Shepard, T. (1994). Focusing software requirements through rapid prototyping. *1994 Canadian Conference on Electrical and Computer Engineering,* 2.

Jordan, P. W., Keller, K. S., Tucker, R. W., and Vogel, D. (1989). Software storming: Combining rapid prototyping and knowledge engineering. *Computer* 22 (5): 39–48.

Jorgensen, P. (1986). Complete specifications and the sorcerer's apprentice problem. *Proceedings of the 10th International Computer Software and Applications Conference,* Chicago. IEEE Computer Society Press.

Karakostas, V. (1989). Requirements for CASE tools in early software reuse. *ACM SIGSOFT Software Engineering* 14 (2): 39–41.

Karat, J., ed. (1991). *Taking Software Design Seriously: Practical Techniques for Human-Computer Interaction Design.* Boston, MA: Academic Press.

Kato, J., and Morisawa, Y. (1987). Direct execution of a JSD specification. *Proceedings of the 11th Computer Software and Applications Conference,* Tokyo. IEEE Computer Society Press.

Kauber, P. G. (1985). Prototyping: Not a method but a philosophy. *Journal of Systems Management* (September): 28–33.

Kensing, F., and Munk-Madsen, A. (1993). PD: Structure in the toolbox. *Communications of the ACM* 36(6): 78–85.

Kinoe, Y., and Horikawa, Y. (1991). *Eliciting Requirements For A New Product's User Interface Design: The Customer Prototype Express.* Technical Report TR58–0963. Yamato, Japan: IBM.

Knoll, H. D., and Suk, W. (1989). A graphic language for business application systems to improve communication concerning requirements specification and the user. *ACM SIGSOFT Software Engineering Notes* 14 (6): 68–72.

Krista, R., and Rozman, I. (1989). A computer aided prototyping methodology. *ACM SIGSOFT Software Engineering Notes* 14 (6): 68–72.

Kruchten, P., and Schonberg, E. (1984). The Ada/Ed system: A large-scale experiment in software prototyping using SETL. In *Approaches to Prototyping.* Edited by R. Budde, K. Kuhlenkamp, L. Mathiassen, and H. Zullighoven. Berlin: Springer-Verlag.

Kuo, J. H., and Tu, H. C. (1987). Prototyping a software information base for software engineering environments. *Proceedings of the 11th International Computer Software and Applications Conference,* Tokyo. IEEE Computer Society Press.

Kyng, M. (1991). Designing for cooperation: Cooperating in design. *Communications of the ACM,* 34(12): 64.

LaLonde, W.R., and Pugh, J.R. (1990). *Inside Smalltalk, Volume I.* Englewood Cliffs, NJ: Prentice-Hall.

Lanergan, R. G., and Grasso, C. A. (1984). Software engineering with reusable designs and code. *IEEE Transactions on Software Engineering* 10 (5): 498–501.

Langle, G. B., Leitheiser, R. L., and Naumann, J. D. (1984). A survey of applications systems prototyping in industry. *Information and Management* 7: 273–284.

Lantz, K. S. (1986a). *The Prototyping Methodology.* Englewood Cliffs, NJ: Prentice-Hall.

Lantz, K. (1986b). The prototyping methodology: designing it right the first time. *Computerworld,* April 7, 69–72.

Larsen, L. B., and Baekgaard, A. (1994). Rapid prototyping of a dialogue system using a generic dialogue development platform. *1994 International Conference on Spoken Language Processing,* 2.

Laurel, B. (1990). *The Art of Human-Computer Design.* Reading, MA: Addison-Wesley.

Laurel, B. (1991). *Computers as Theater.* Reading, MA: Addison-Wesley.

Lea, R. J., and Chung, C. G. (1990). Rapid prototyping from structured analysis: executable specification approach. *Information and Software Technology* 32 (9): 589–597.

Lee, H. J., and Tsai, W. T. (1993). Object prototyping: Concept and specification language. *The Seventeenth Annual International Computer Software and Applications Conference.*

Lee, S. (1985). On executable models for rule-based prototyping. *Proceedings of the 8th International Conference on Software Engineering,* London.

Lee, S., and Sluizer, S. (1985). On using executable specifications for high-level prototyping. *Proceedings of the 3rd International Workshop on Software Specification and Design,* London.

Leibrandt, U., and Schnupp, P. (1984). An evaluation of Prolog as a prototyping system. In *Approaches to Prototyping.* Edited by R. Budde, K. Kuhlenkamp, L. Mathiassen, and H. Zullighoven. Berlin: Springer-Verlag.

Lenorovitz, D. R., and Ramsey, H. R. (1977). A dialogue simulation tool for use in the design of interactive computer systems. *Proceedings of the 21st Annual Meeting of the Human Factors Society,* Santa Monica, CA.

Leslie, R. E. (1986). *Systems Analysis and Design: Method and Invention.* Englewood Cliffs, NJ: Prentice-Hall.

Leszczylowski, J., and Bieman, J. M. (1989). Prosper: A language for specification by prototyping. *Computer Languages* 14 (3): 165–180.

Lewis, T. G., Handloser III, F., Bose, S., and Yang, S. (1989). Prototypes from standard user interface management systems. *Computer* 22 (5): 51–60.

Lichter, H., Schneider-Hufschmidt, M., and Zullighoven, H. (1994). Prototyping in industrial software projects: Bridging the gap between theory and practice. *IEEE Transactions on Software Engineering* 20(11): 825–832.

Life, M. A., Narborough-Hall, C. S., and Hamilton, W. I. (eds.). (1990). *Simulation and the User Interface.* London: Taylor & Francis.

Linthicum, D. S. (1995). The end of programming. *BYTE* (August): 69–72.

Lintulampi, R., and Pulli, P. (1990). Graphics based prototyping of real-time systems. *Proceedings of the First International Workshop on Rapid System Prototyping,* Research Triangle Park, NC.

Lor, K. W. E. (1991). Operational definitions for system requirements as the basis of design automation. *Software Practice and Experience* 21 (10). 1103–1124.

Loucopoulos, P., and Champion, R. E. M. (1989). Knowledge-based support for requirements engineering. *Information and Software Technology* 31 (3). 124–135.

Luckham, D. C., Kenney, J. J., Augustin, L. M., Vera, J., Bryan, D., and Mann, W. (1995). Specification and analysis of system architecture using Rapide. *IEEE Transactions on Software Engineering* 21 (4): 336–354.

Luckham, D. C., Neff, R., and Rosenblum, S. (1987). An environment for Ada software development based on formal specification: Status and development plan. *ACM SIGADA Ada Letters* 2 (3): 94–106.

Luckham, D. C., and von Henke, F. W. (1985). An overview of Anna: A specification language for Ada. *IEEE Software* 2 (2): 9–22.

Ludewig, J. (1983). ESPRESO—A system for process control software specification. *IEEE Transactions on Software Engineering* SE-9 (4): 427–436.

Ludewig, J., Glinz, M., Huser, H., Matheis, G., Matheis, H., and Schmidt, M. F. (1985). SPADES—A specification and design system and its graphical interface. *Proceedings of the 8th International Conference on Software Engineering.*

Luker, P. A., and Burns, A. (1986). Program generators and generation software. *Computer Journal* 29 (4): 315–321.

Luqi (1988). Knowledge-based support for rapid software prototyping. *IEEE Expert* 3 (4): 9–18.

Luqi (1989). Software evolution through rapid prototyping. *Computer* 22 (5): 13–25.

Luqi (1992). Computer-aided prototyping for a command-and-control system using CAPS. *IEEE Software*, 9 (1): 56–67.

Luqi, Barnes, P. D., and Zyda, M. (1990). Graphical tool for computer-aided prototyping. *Information and Software Technology* 32 (3): 199–206.

Luqi, and Berzins, V. (1988). Rapidly prototyping real-time systems. *IEEE Software* 2 (5): 25–36.

Luqi, Berzins, V., and Yeh, R. (1988). A prototyping language for real-time software. *IEEE Transactions on Software Engineering* 14 (10). 1409–1423.

Luqi, and Ketabchi, M. (1988). A computer-aided prototyping system. *IEEE Software* 5 (2): 66–72.

Luqi, and Lee, Y. K. (1989). Interactive control of prototyping process. *Proceedings of the 13th International Computer Software and Applications Conference,* Orlando, FL. IEEE Computer Society Press.

MacEwen, G. H. (1982). Specification prototyping. *ACM SIGSOFT Software Engineering Notes* 7 (5): 112–119.

Mandel, T. (1994). The GUI-OOUI War: Windows vs. OS/2. *The Designer's Guide to Human-Computer Interfaces*. New York: John Wiley.

Mantei, M. (1986). Techniques for incorporating human factors in the software lifecycle. *Proceedings of the Structured Techniques Association Third Annual Conference,* 177–203.

Marcus, A. (1992). *Graphic Design for Electronic Documents and User Interfaces*. Reading, MA: Addison-Wesley.

Martin, J. (1982). *Application Development without Programmers*. Englewood Cliffs, NJ: Prentice-Hall.

Martin, J., and McClure, C. (1983). *Software Maintenance: The Problem and Its Solution*. Englewood Cliffs, NJ: Prentice-Hall.

Martin, J., and McClure, C. (1985). *Diagraming Techniques for Analysts and Programmers*. Englewood Cliffs, NJ: Prentice-Hall.

Mason, R. E. A., and Carey, T. T. (1983). Prototyping interactive information systems. *Communications of the ACM 26* (5) (May): 347–354.

Mathiassen, L., Seewaldt, T., and Stage, J. (1995). Prototyping and specifying: Principles and practices of a mixed approach. *Scandinavian Journal of Information Systems* 7(1): 55–72.

Matsumoto, A. S. (1984). Some experience in promoting reusable software presentation in higher abstract levels. *IEEE Transactions on Software Engineering* 10 (5): 502–512.

Mayhew, D. J. (1992). *Principles and Guidelines in Software User InterFace Design.* Englewood Cliffs, NJ: Prentice-Hall.

Mayhew, D. J., and Dearnly, P. A. (1987). An alternative prototyping classification. *Computer Journal* 30 (6): 481–484.

Mayhew, D. J., and Dearnley, P. A. (1990). Organization and management of systems prototyping. *Information and Software Technology* 32 (4): 245–252.

Mayhew, D. . J., Worsley, C. J., and Dearnley, P. A. (1989). Control of software prototyping process: Change classification approach. *Information and Software Technology* 31 (2): 59–67.

Mayr, H. C., Bever, M., and Lockemann, P. C. (1984). Prototyping interactive application systems. In *Approaches to Prototyping.* Edited by R. Budde, K. Kuhlenkamp, L. Mathiassen, and H. Zullighoven. Berlin: Springer-Verlag.

McCormick, E. J., and Sanders, M. S. (1982). *Human Factors in Engineering and Design.* New York: McGraw-Hill.

McCracken, D. D., and Jackson, M. A. (1982). Life cycle concept considered harmful. *ACM SIGSOFT Software Engineering Notes* 7 (2): 29–32.

McLean, E. R. (1976). The use of APL for production applications: The concept of throwaway code. *APL 76 Conference Proceedings,* ACM.

McLuhan, M. (1964). *Understanding Media.* New York: Signet Books.

McMenamin, S., and Palmer, J. (1984). *Essential Systems Analysis.* New York: Yourdon Press.

McNurlin, B. C. (1981). Developing systems by prototyping. *EDP Analyzer* 19 (9) (September): 1–12.

Meister, D. (1976). *Behavioral Foundations of System Development.* New York: John Wiley.

Melkus, L. A., & Torres, R. (1988). Guidelines for the use of a prototype in user interface design. In *Proceedings of the Human Factors Society 32nd Annual Meeting*. Santa Monica, CA: Human Factors Society.

Meyer, G. J. (1978). *The Art of Software Testing*. New York: Wiley.

Michaelson, G. (1988). Interpreter prototypes from language definition style specifications. *Information and Software Technology* 30 (1): 23–31.

Microsoft Corp. (1992). *The Windows Interface: An Application Design Guide*. Seattle: Microsoft Press.

Miler, D. S., Smith, J. G., and Muller, M. J. (1992). TelePICTIVE: Computer-supported collaborative GUI design for designers with diverse expertise. In *UIST'92 Proceedings*.

Misra, S. K., and Jalics, P. J. (1988). Third-generation versus fourth-generation software development. *IEEE Software* 5 (4): 8–14.

Mittermeir, R. T. (1982). HIBOL, A language for fast prototyping in data processing environments. *ACM SIGSOFT Software Engineering Notes* 7 (5): 133–140.

Moran, T. P. (1981). The command language grammar: A representation for the user interface of interactive computer systems. *International Journal of Man-Machine Studies* 15, 3–50.

Morgan, C., Williams, G., and Lemmons, P. (1983). An interview with Wayne Rosig, Bruce Danials and Larry Tesler. *BYTE* 8(2): 90–114.

Mosse, D., Gudmundsson, O., and Agrawala, A. K. (1990). Prototyping real time operating systems: A case study. *Proceedings of the First International Workshop on Rapid Systems Prototyping*. Research Triangle Park, NC.

Muller, M. J. (1991a). Panel: Participatory design in Britain and North America: Responses to the "Scandinavian challenge. " In *Reaching Through Technology: CHI '91 Conference Proceedings*.

Muller, M. J. (1991b). PICTIVE—An exploration in participatory design. In *Reaching Through Technology: CHI '91 Conference Proceedings*.

Muller, M. J. (1992). Retrospective on a year of participatory design using the PICTIVE technique. In *Striking a Balance: Proceedings of CHI '92*.

Muller, M. J., Smith, J. G., Goldberg, H., and Shoher, J. Z. (1991). Privacy, anonymity, and interpersonal competition issues identified during participatory design of project management groupware. *SIGCHI Bulletin* 23(1): 82–87.

Mullin, M. (1990). *Rapid Prototyping for Object-Oriented Systems*. Reading, MA: Addison-Wesley.

Mumford, E., and Henshall, D. (1979). *A Participatory Approach to Computer Systems Design*. New York: John Wiley.

Murch, G. (1984). Physiological principles for the effective use of color. *IEEE CG&A* (November).

Musser, D. R. (1980). Abstract data type specification in the AFFIRM system. *IEEE Transactions on Software Engineering* SE-6 (1): 24–32.

Myers, B. A. (1987). Creating dynamic interaction techniques by demonstration. *Proceedings of ACM CHI+GI'87 Conference on Human Factors in Computing Systems and Graphics Interface*.

Myers, B. A. (1992). State of the art in user interface software tools. In H. Rex Hartson and Deborah Hix (eds.), *Advances in Human-Computer Interaction*, Vol. 4. Norwood, NJ: Ablex.

Myers, B. A., and Rosson, M. B. (1992). Survey on user interface programming. *Proceedings of CHI'92, The National Conference on Computer-Human Interaction*.

Myers, B. A., Vander Zanden, B., and Dannenberg, R. B. (1989). Creating graphical interactive application objects by demonstration. *Proceedings of ACM SIGGRAPH 1989 Symposium on User Interface Software and Technology (UIST'89)*.

Naumann, J. D., and Jenkins, A. M. (1982). Prototyping: The new paradigm for systems development. *MIS Quarterly* (September): 29–44.

Newcombe, R., and Rudd, J. (1992). *The Development of an Object-Oriented Relationship Banking Prototype Using Smalltalk*. IBM Technical Report TR 83.279.

NeXT Computer Inc. (1992). *NeXTSTEP User Interface Guidelines Release 3*. Reading, MA: Addison-Wesley.

Nielsen, J. (1987). Using scenarios to develop user friendly videotex systems. *Proceedings of NordData87, Joint Scandinavian Computer Conference*.

Nielsen. J. (ed.) (1989). *Coordinating User Interfaces for Consistency*. Boston, MA: Academic Press.

Nielsen, J. (1990). Paper versus computer implementations as mockup scenarios for heuristic evaluation. In H. Draper et al. (eds.), *Human-Computer Interaction—INTERACT '90*. Amsterdam: Elsevier.

Nielsen, J. (1993). *Usability Engineering*. Boston, MA: Academic Press.

Nielsen, J. (1995). Using paper prototypes in home page design. *IEEE Software* 12(4): 88–89.

Nielsen, J., Bush, R. M., Dayton, J. T., Mond, N. E., Muller, M. J., and Root, R. W. (1992). Teaching experienced developers to design graphical user interfaces. In *Striking a Balance: Proceedings of CHI '92.*

Niitsu, Y., Yoshida, T., and Izumi, N. (1995). Design method of user interface specifications for new telephone services. *Transactions of the Information Processing Society of Japan* 36 (5): 1138–1150.

Nopachai, S., Baker, K. L., and Randell, R. E. (1995). User interface design of an electronic curbside parking and charging system. *Proceedings of the 3rd Annual Mid Atlantic Human Factors Conference,* Blacksburg, VA.

Norman, D. A. (1983). Design rules based on analysis of human error. *Communications of the ACM* 26 (4): 254–258.

Norman, D. (1988). *Design of Everyday Things.* New York: Basic Books.

Norris, M. (1990). A formal specification method. In *System and Software Requirements Engineering.* Edited by M. Dorfman and R. Thayer. IEEE Computer Society Press Tutorial. Order No. 1921.

Nosek, J. T. (1984). Organisation design changes to facilitate evolutionary development of prototype information systems. In *Approaches to Prototyping.* Edited by R. Budde, K. Kuhlenkamp, L. Mathiassen, and H. Zullighoven. Berlin: Springer-Verlag.

Oerder, M., and Aust, H. (1994). A realtime prototype of an automatic inquiry system. *1994 International Conference on Spoken Language Processing,* no. 2.

Open Software Foundation. (1990). *OSF/Motif Style Guide.* Englewood Cliffs, NJ: Prentice-Hall.

Orr, K. T. (1977). *Structured Systems Development.* New York: Yourdon Press.

Overmyer, S. P. (1990). *Survey of Rapid Prototyping Tools for Requirements Definition and User-Computer Interface Design.* Fairfax, VA: School of Information Technology and Engineering, George Mason University.

Page-Jones, M. (1980). *The Practical Guide to Structured Systems Design.* New York: Yourdon Press.

Parnas, D. L. (1969). The use of transition diagrams in the design of a user interface for an interactive computer system. *Proceedings of the 24th National ACM Conference.*

Parnas, D. L., and Clements, P. C. (1986). A rational design process: How and why to fake it. *IEEE Transactions on Software Engineering* 12 (2): 251–257.

Patton, B. (1983). Prototyping—A nomenclature problem. *ACM SIGSOFT Software Engineering Notes* 8 (2): 14–16.

Payton, T., Keller, S., Perkins, J., Rowan, S., and Mardinly, S. (1982). SSAGS: A Syntax and Semantics Analysis and Generation System. *Proceedings of the 6th International Computer Software and Applications Conference,* Chicago.

Pencilkowski, P. (1995). Tool-based development of man-machine interfaces. *1995 IEEE Aerospace Applications Conference,* no. 1, 343–349.

Petropoulos, L. (1995). Prototyping beats simulation for complex real time designs. *EDN* 40(12): 136–140.

Pfaff G. E. (ed.). (1985). *User Interface Management Systems.* Berlin: Springer-Verlag.

Pfauth, M., Hammer, A., and Fissel J. (1985). Software prototyping as a human factors tool. In *Proceedings of the Human Factors Society 29th Annual Meeting.* Santa Monica, CA: Human Factors Society.

Podger, D. N. (1979). High-level languages—A basis for participative design. In *Design and Implementation of Computer-Based Information Systems.* Edited by E. Grochla. Oslo: Sijthoff and Noordhoff.

Polster, F. J. (1986). Reuse of software through generation of partial systems. *IEEE Transactions on Software Engineering* 12 (3): 402–416.

Porras, L. H., and Giodano, D. (1995). Developing hypermedia with a rapid prototyping approach: A case study. *British Journal of Educational Technology* 26(1): 59–61.

Pressman, R. S. (1987). *Software Engineering: A Practitioner's Approach.* New York: McGraw-Hill.

Prizant, A. (1986). Prototyping counterproductive? *Data Processing* 28 (7): 379.

Prywes, N. S., and Pnueli, A. (1983). Compilation of nonprocedural specifications into computer programs. *IEEE Transactions on Software Engineering* 9 (3): 267–279.

Purtilo, J. M., and Jalote, P. (1991). An environment for prototyping distributed applications. *Computer Languages* 16 (3/4): 197–207.

Ramamoorthy, C. V., Garg, V., and Prakash, A. (1986). Programming in the large. *IEEE Transactions on Software Engineering* 12 (7): 769–783.

Ramsey, H. R. (1979). *Human Factors in Computer Systems: A Review of the Literature.* Boulder, CO: Science Applications.

Ratcliff, B. (1988). Early and not-so-early prototyping—Rationale and tool support. *Proceedings of the 12th Annual International Computer Software and Applications Conference,* Chicago.

Ravden, S., and Johnson, G. (1989). *Evaluating Usability of Human-Computer Interface.* New York: Wiley.

Reisman, S., and Carr, W. (1991). Perspectives on multimedia systems in education. *IBM Systems Journal.*

Rettig, M. (1994). Prototyping for tiny fingers. *Communications of the ACM* 37(4): 21–27.

Reubenstein, H. B., and Waters, R. C. (1991). The requirements apprentice: Automated assistance for requirements acquisition. *IEEE Transaction on Software Engineering* 17 (3): 226–240.

Rich, C., and Waters, R. C. (1982). The disciplined use of simplifying assumptions. *ACM SIGSOFT Software Engineering Notes* 7 (5): 150–154.

Richards, J. T., Boies, S. J., and Gould, J. D. (1986). Rapid prototyping and system development: Examination of an interface toolkit for voice and telephony applications. *Proceedings of CHI Conference on Human Factors in Computing Systems.* New York: ACM.

Riddle, W. E. (1984). Advancing the state of the art in software system prototyping. In *Approaches to Prototyping.* Edited by R. Budde, K. Kuhlenkamp, L. Mathiassen, and H. Zullighoven. Berlin: Springer-Verlag.

Rolland, C., and Benci, G. (1983). An event-driven methodology for technical software design. *Proceedings of the Real-Time Systems Symposium.*

Roman, G. C. (1985). A taxonomy of current issues in requirements engineering. *Computer* 18 (4): 14–21.

Ross, D. (1977). Structured analysis (SA): A language for communicating ideas. *IEEE Transactions on Software Engineering* SE-4(3) (May).

Ross, D. T., and Schoman, K. E., Jr. (1977). Structured analysis for requirements definition. *IEEE Transactions on Software Engineering* SE-3 (1): 6–15.

Rosson, M. B., and Carroll, J. M. (1990). Climbing the Smalltalk mountain. *ACM SIGCHI Bulletin* 21(3): 76–79.

Rosson, M. B., Maass, S., and Kellogg, W. A. (1987). Designing for designers: An analysis of design practices in the real world: Human factors in computing systems. *CHI+GI'87.*

Rowe, L. A., and Shoens, K. (1983). Programming language constructs for screen definition. *IEEE Transactions on Software Engineering* 9(1): 31–39.

Rowley, D. E., and Rhoades, D. G. (1992). The cognitive jogthrough: A fast-paced user interface evaluation procedure. *Proceedings of the ACM CHI '92 Conference,* Monterey, CA, May 3–7.

Royce, W. W. (1970). *Managing the development of large software systems: Concepts and techniques.* Redondo Beach, CA: TRW.

Rudd, J., and Isensee, S. (1991a). Twenty-two tips for a healthier, happier prototype. *Proceedings of the 35th Annual Meeting of the Human Factors Society.*

Rudd J., and Isensee, S. (1991b). *An OS/2 CUA-Compliant Bank Loan Program.* IBM Technical Report 83. 248.

Rudd, J., and Isensee, S. (1992). *Walk-Up-and-Use Personal Banking Kiosk Prototype.* IBM Technical Report 83. 265.

Rudd, J., and Isensee, S. (1994a). Origins of the vacuous prototyping problem. *Interactions* (April): 52–53.

Rudd, J. R. & Isensee, S. H. (1994b). 22 tips for a happier, healthier prototype. ACM *Interactions* 1(1): 35–40.

Rudd, J. R., and Isensee, S. H. (1994). Smalltalk for user-interface rapid prototyping. *Ergo in Design*, Santa Monica: Human Factors and Ergonomics Society.

Rudd, J., Isensee, S., and Beechler R. (1990). *A Software Usability Design Process.* IBM Technical Report 83. 223.

Rudd, J., Isensee, S., and Ominsky, M. (1993). *The Art of Rapid Prototyping: A Process for Designing Usable User Interfaces.* IBM Technical Report 83. 305.

Rudd, J. R., and Ominsky, M. (1993). *User-interface Design for Finance Industry Applications.* IBM Technical Report 83.318.

Rudd, J. R., Stern, K. R., and Isensee, S. H. (In press). The low- versus high-fidelity prototyping debate. *ALM Interactions.*

Rzepka, W., and Ohno, Y. (1985). Guest editor's introduction—Requirements environments: Software tools for modeling user needs. *Computer* 18 (4): 9–12.

Rzevski, G. (1984). Prototype versus pilot systems: Strategies for evolutionary information system development. In *Approaches to Prototyping.* Edited by R. Budde, K. Kuhlenkamp, L. Mathiassen, and H. Zullighoven. Berlin: Springer-Verlag.

Sarna, D. E. Y., and Febish, G. (1993). *Windows Rapid Application Development.* Ziff-Davis Press.

Scheffer, P. A., Stone III, A. H., and Rzepka, W. E. (1985). A case study of SREM. *Computer* 18 (4): 47–54.

Schmidt, H. W. (1991). Prototyping and analysis of non-sequential systems using predicate-event nets. *Journal of Systems and Software* 15 (1): 43–62.

Scheiderman, B. (1979). Human factors experiments in designing interactive systems. *IEEE Computer* 12 (1): 9–19.

Schneiderman, B. (1980). *Software Psychology: Human Factors in Computer and Information Systems.* Englewood Cliffs, NJ: Prentice-Hall.

Schneiderman, B. (1992). *Designing the User Interface.* Reading, MA: Addison-Wesley.

Schuler, D., and Namioka, A. (eds.) (1993). *Participatory Design: Principles and Practices.* Hillsdale, NJ: Erlbaum.

Shannon, R. E. (1975). *System Simulation—The Art and Science.* Englewood Cliffs, NJ: Prentice-Hall.

Shea, J. G., and Ragada, R. K. (1993). Virtual prototyping: Object-oriented modeling and intelligent knowledge capture for system design. *Fourth Annual Conference on AI, Simulation, and Planning in High Autonomy Systems.*

Shiz, K. (1991). *Visual Design with OSF/Motif.* Reading, MA: Addison-Wesley.

Sievert, G. E., and Mizell, T. A. (1985). Specification-based software engineering with TAGS. *Computer* 18 (4): 56–65.

Singh, G., Kok, C. H., and Ngan, T. Y. (1990). Druid: A system for demonstrational rapid user interface development. *Proceedings of ACM SIGGRAPH 1990 Symposium on User Interface Software and Technology (UIST'90).*

Skillcorn, D. B., and Glasgow, J. I. (1989). Real-time specification using Lucid. *IEEE Transactions on Software Engineering* 15 (2): 221–229.

Slusky, L. (1987). Integrating software modelling and prototyping tools. *Information and Software Technology* 27 (7): 79–87.

Smith, D. A. (1982). *Rapid Software Prototyping.* Ph.D. dissertation, University of California, Irvine.

Smith, D. C., Irby, C., Kimball, R., Verplank, W., and Harslem, E. (1982). Designing the Star user interface. *BYTE* 7 (4): 242–282.

Smith, S. L. (1986). Standards versus guidelines for designing user interface software. *Behaviour and Information Technology* 5 (1): 47–61.

Smith, S. L., and Gerhart, S. L. (1988). STATEMATE and cruise control: A case study. *Proceedings of the 12th International Computer Software and Applications Conference,* Chicago. IEEE Computer Society Press.

Smith, S. L., and Mosier, J. N. (1984). *Design Guidelines for the User Interface to Computer-Based Information Systems.* Bedford, MA: MITRE Corporation.

Smith, S. L., and Mosier, J. N. (1986). *Guidelines for Designing User Interface Software.* Technical Report MTR-10090, ESD-TR-86-278. Bedford, MA: MITRE Corporation.

Sol, H. G. (1984). Prototyping: A methodological assessment. In *Approaches to Prototyping.* Edited by R. Budde, K. Kuhlenkamp, L. Mathiassen, and H. Zullighoven. Berlin: Springer-Verlag.

Sommerville, I. (1982). *Software Engineering.* Reading, MA: Addison-Wesley.

Somogyi, E. K. (1981). Prototyping—a method not to be missed. *EDP Analyzer* (October): 13–14.

Srinivasan, A., and Kaiser, K. M. (1987). Relationships between selected organizational factors and systems development. *Communications of the ACM* 30(6) (June).

Staknis, M. E. (1990). Software quality assurance through prototyping and automated testing. *Information and Software Technology* 32 (1): 26–33.

Stamps, D. (1987). CASE: Cranking out productivity. *Datamation,* July 1.

Stasko, J. T. (1990). A practical animation language for software development. *Proceedings of the International Conference on Computer Languages,* New Orleans. IEEE Computer Society Press.

Stephens, M. A., and Bates, P. E. (1990). Requirements engineering by prototyping: Experiences in development of estimating system. *Information and Software Technology* 32 (4): 253–257.

Suchman, L. (1988). Designing with the user. *ACM Transactions for Office Information Systems* 6: 173–183.

Sufrin, B. (1986). Formal methods and the design of effective user interfaces. In *People and Computers: Designing for Usability.* Edited by M. D. Harrison and A. I. Monk. Cambridge: Cambridge University Press.

Sun Microsystems, Inc. (1989). *OPEN LOOK Graphical User Interface: Application Style Guidelines.* Reading, MA: Addison-Wesley.

Sunshine, C. A., Thompson, D. H., Erickson, R. W., Gerhart, S. L., and Schwabe, D. (1982). Specification and verification of communication protocols in AFFIRM using state transition models. *IEEE Transactions on Software Engineering* SE-8 (5): 460–489.

Suydam, W. (1987). CASE makes strides toward automated software development. *Computer Design* (January).

Swartout, W., and Balzer, R. (1982). On the inevitable intertwining of specification and implementation. *Communications of the ACM* 25(7): 438–440.

Szekely, P. (1994). User interface prototyping: Tools and techniques. *Research Issues in Intersection Between Software Engineering and Human Computer Interaction Conference.*

Szekely, P., Luo, P., and Neches, R. (1992). Facilitating the exploration of interface design alternatives: The HUMANOID model of interface design. *Proceeding of SIGCHI'92.*

Szekely, P., Luo, P., and Neches, R. (1993). Beyond interface builders: Model-based interface tools. In *Proceedings of INTERCHI'93.*

Tate, G., and Verner, J. (1990). Case study of risk management, incremental development, and evolutionary prototyping. *Information and Software Technology* 32 (3): 207–214.

Tavendale, R. D. (1985). A technique for prototyping directly from a specification. *Proceedings of the 8th International Conference on Software Engineering,* London.

Tavolato, P., and Vincena, K. (1984). A prototyping methodology and its tools. In *Approaches to Prototyping.* Edited by R. Budde, K. Kuhlenkamp, L. Mathiassen, and H. Zullighoven. Berlin: Springer-Verlag.

Taylor, T., and Standish, T. (1986). Initial thoughts on rapid prototyping techniques. In *New Paradigms for Software Development.* Edited by William W. Agresti. IEEE Computer Society Press.

Teichroew, D., and Hershey III, E. A. (1977). PSL/PSA: A computer-aided technique for structured documentation and analysis of information processing systems. *IEEE Transactions on Software Engineering* SE-3 (1): 41–48.

Telek, M. J., and Schell, D. A. (1992). The user interface design team (UIDT) process. In *Proceedings of the 1992 GSD Technical Symposium.* Bethesda, MD: IBM Corporation.

Terwilliger, R. B., and Campbell, R. H. (1989). PLEASE: Executable specifications for incremental software development. *Journal of Systems and Software* 10 (2): 97–112.

Tetzlaff, L. & Schwartz, D. (1991). The use of guidelines in interface design. *Human Factors in Computer Systems (CHI '91).*

Thayer, R. H., and Dorfman, M. (eds.). (1990). *System and Software Requirements Engineering.* IEEE Computer Society Press Tutorial. Order No. 1921.

Tognazzini, B. (1992). *TOG on Interface.* Reading, MA: Addison-Wesley.

Tomeski, E. A., and Lazarus, H. (1975). *People-oriented Computer Systems.* New York: Van Nostrand Reinhold.

Topping, P., McInroy, J., Lively, W., and Sheppard, S. (1987). Express—rapid prototyping and product development via integrated, knowledge-based executable specifications. *Proceedings of the 1987 Fall Joint Computer Conference, Dallas.* IEEE Computer Society Press.

Tozer, J. E. (1987). Prototyping as a system development methodology: Opportunities and pitfalls. *Information and Software Technology* 29 (5): 265–269.

Trenner, L. (1995). Prototyping for usability: The benefits of peer group review. *IEEE Colloquium on Integrating HCI in the Lifecycle.*

Tsai, J. J. P., Aoyama, M., and Chang, Y. L. (1988). Rapid prototyping using FRORL language. *Proceedings of the 12th International Computer Software and Applications Conference,* Chicago. IEEE Computer Society Press.

Tsai, J. J. P., and Weigert, T. (1989). Exploratory prototyping through the use of frames and production rules. *Proceedings of the 13th International Computer Software and Applications Conference.* Orlando, FL. IEEE Computer Society Press.

Tsai, J. J. P., and Weigert, T. (1991). HCLIE: A logic-based requirement language for new software engineering paradigms. *Software Engineering Journal* 6 (4): 137–151.

Tsai, S. T., Yang, C. C., and Lien, C. C. (1990). Automated retrieval of consistent documentation for rapid prototyping systems and software maintenance. *Information and Software Technology* 32 (8): 521–530.

Tseng, J. S., Szymanski, B., Shi, Y., and Prywes, N. S. (1986). Real-time software life cycle with the model system. *IEEE Transactions on Software Engineering* 12 (2): 358–373.

Tullis, T. S. (1990). High-fidelity prototyping throughout the design process. In *Proceedings of the Human Factors Society 34th Annual Meeting.* Santa Monica, CA: Human Factors Society.

Urban, J. E. (1977). *A Specification Language and Its Predecessor.* Ph. D. dissertation, University of Southwestern Louisiana.

Urban, J. E. (1990). The Descartes specification language. In *System and Software Requirements Engineering.* Edited by M. Dorfman and R. Thayer. IEEE Computer Society Press Tutorial. Order No. 1921.

Urban, J. E. (1992). *Software Prototyping and Requirements Engineering.* Utica, NY: Data Analysis Center for Software.

Urban, S. D., Urban, J. E., and Dominick, W. D. (1985). Utilizing an executable specification language for an information system. *IEEE Transactions on Software Engineering* 11 (7): 598–605.

van Delft, A. J. E. (1989). Express: Proposal for uniform notations. *Information and Software Technology* 31 (3): 143–159.

van Harmelen, M. (1989). Exploratory user interface design using scenarios and prototypes. In A. Sutcliffe and L. Macaulay (ed.), *People and Computers V: Proceedings of the Fifth Conference of the British Computer Society.* Cambridge: Cambridge University Press.

van Hoeve, F. A., and Engmann, R. (1984). The TUBA project: A set of tools for application development and prototyping. In *Approaches to Prototyping.* Edited by R. Budde, K. Kuhlenkamp, L. Mathiassen, and H. Zullighoven. Berlin: Springer-Verlag.

Venken, R., and Bruynooghe, M. (1984). Prolog as a language for prototyping of information systems. In *Approaches to Prototyping.* Edited by R. Budde, K. Kuhlenkamp, L. Mathiassen, and H. Zullighoven. Berlin: Springer-Verlag.

Virzi, R. A. (1989). What can you learn from a low-fidelity prototype? *Proceedings of the Human Factors Society 33rd Annual Meeting.* Denver, CO, October 16–20.

Virzi, R. A. (1990). Low-fidelity prototyping. In *Proceedings of the Human Factors Society 33rd Annual Meeting.* Santa Monica, CA: Human Factors Society.

Walters, N. (1991a). Requirements specification for Ada software under DoD-STD-2167A. *Journal of Systems and Software* 15 (2): 173–183.

Walters, N. (1991b). An Ada object-based analysis and design approach. *ACM SIGADA Ada Letters* 11(5): 62–78.

Wang, Y. (1988). A distributed specification model and its prototyping. *IEEE Transactions on Software Engineering* 14 (8): 1090–1097.

Ward, P., and Mellor, S. (1985). *Structured Development of Real-Time Systems.* New York: Yourdon Press.

Wasserman, A. I., Pircher, P. A., Shewmake, D. T., and Kersten, M. L. (1986). Developing interactive information systems with the user software engineering methodology. *IEEE Transactions on Software Engineering* 12 (2): 326–345.

Wasserman, A. I., and Shewmake, D. T. (1982). Automating the development and evolution of user dialogue in an interactive information system. In *Evolutionary Information Systems*. Edited by J. Hawgood. Amsterdam: North-Holland.

Wasserman, A. I., and Shewmake, D. T. (1985). The role of prototypes in the user software engineering methodology. In H. R. Hartson (ed.), *Advances in Human-Computer Interaction*. Norwood, NJ: Ablex.

Wasserman, A. I., and Stinson, S. K. (1979). A specification method for interactive information systems. *Proceedings of the Conference on Specification of Reliable Software*.

Webb, B. R. (1994). Teaching usability to Visual Basic programmers: A case study. *Proceedings of Software Engineering in Higher Education*.

Weiser, M. (1982). Scale models and rapid prototyping. *ACM SIGSOFT Software Engineering Notes* 7 (5): 181–185.

Whiteside, J., and Wixon, D. (1985). Developmental theory as a framework for studying human-computer interaction. In H. R. Hartson (ed.), *Advances in Human-Computer Interaction*, Vol. 1. Norwood, NJ: Ablex.

Wiecha, C., Bennett, W., Boies, S., Gould, J., and Greene, S. (1990). ITS: A tool for rapidly developing interactive applications. *ACM Transactions on Information Systems* 8(3): 204–236.

Williges, R. C., Williges, B. H., and Elkerton, J. (1987). Software interface design. In G. Salvendy (ed.), *Handbook of Human Factors*. New York: Wiley.

Windsor, P., and Storrs, G. (1992). Prototyping user interfaces. In *IEE Colloquium on Software Prototyping and Evolutionary Development, Part 4*. London: IEE.

Wing, J. M. (1988). A study of 12 specifications of the library problem. *IEEE Software* 5 (4): 66–76.

Yang, Y. (1990). Experimental rapid prototype of undo support. *Information and Software Technology* 32 (9): 625–635.

Yeh, R. T. (1982). Requirements analysis—A management perspective. *Proceedings of the 6th International Software and Applications Conference*, Chicago. IEEE Computer Society.

Yeh, R. T., Zave, P., Conn, A. P., and Cole, G. E., Jr. (1984). Software requirements: New directions and perspectives. In *Handbook of Software Engineering*. Edited by C. R. Vick and C. V. Ramamoorthy. New York: Van Nostrand Reinhold Company.

Young, R. M. (1981). The machine inside the machine: User's models of pocket calculators. *International Journal of Man-Machine Studies* 15: 51–58.

Young, T. R. (1984). Superior prototypes. *Datamation,* May 15, 152–158.

Yourdon, E. (1978). *Structured Walkthroughs.* New York: Yourdon Press.

Yourdon, E. (1982). *Managing the System Life Cycle: A Software Development Methodology Overview.* New York: Yourdon Press.

Yourdon, E., and Constantine, L. (1979). *Structured Design: Fundamentals of a Discipline of Computer Program and System Design.* Englewood Cliffs, NJ: Prentice-Hall.

Zachary, W. (1986). A cognitively based functional taxonomy of decision support techniques. *Human-Computer Interaction* 2: 25–63.

Zave, P. (1991). An insider's evaluation of Paisley. *IEEE Transactions on Software Engineering* 17 (3): 212–225.

Zelkowitz, M. V. (1980). A case study in rapid prototyping. *Software Practice and Experience* 10: 1037–1042.

Zelkowitz, M. V. (1984). A taxonomy of prototype designs. *ACM SIGSOFT Software Engineering Notes* 9 (5): 11–12.

Zelkowitz, M. V., Shaw, A. C., and Gannon, J. D. (1979). *Principles of Software Engineering and Design.* Englewood Cliffs, NJ: Prentice-Hall.

Zhou, W. (1990). PM: A system for prototyping and monitoring remote procedure call programs. *ACM SIGSOFT Software Engineering Notes* 15 (1): 59–63.

Zucconi, L. (1989). Techniques and experiences capturing requirements for several real-time applications. *ACM SIGSOFT Software Engineering Notes* 14 (6): 51–55.

INDEX

Accuracy, 27
Action! prototyping tool, 62
Actor prototyping tool, 62
Add-ons, 56
AIXWindows Interface Composer (AIC) prototyping
    tool, 62
AlphaWindow prototyping tool, 62
Andrew prototyping tool, 62
Apple Macintosh, 16
AppleMaker prototyping tool, 62
Aspect prototyping tool, 62
ATK prototyping tool, 62
ATM prototype, 79, 80, 113, 114
Authorware prototyping tool, 62
Autocode prototyping tool, 62

Banking kiosk example, 156–173
    account balance, 163
    Audio Visual Connection (AVC) selection,
        156–157
    check ordering function, 160–162, 163
    code (AVC), 165–173
    operational description, 157–164
    personal information number (PIN), 157, 158
    product video, 163
    rate information, 158–159
Banking multimedia kiosk example, 111–120
    account information, 113, 114
    automated teller machine (ATM) instruction,
        113, 114
    branch locator, 112
    customer service, 114
    digital video interactive (DVI) technology, 113
    encapsulation, 115
    MediaScript code for branch locator, 119–120
    object-oriented prototyping, 114–115
    product information, 113
    scenario, 79–82, 111–112
    Smalltalk code for branch locator, 116–119
    Smalltalk implementation, 114–116
Builder Xcessory prototyping tool, 63

CASE tools, 43, 76. *See also* Tools, prototyping
Check ordering
    banking kiosk example, 160–162, 163
    Easel banking scenario, 106–107
Chiron prototyping tool, 63

Choreographer prototyping tool, 63
CLIM prototyping tool, 63
Code
    banking kiosk code (AVC), 165–173
    branch locator (MediaScript), 119–120
    branch locator (Smalltalk), 116–119
    credit card workstation (Easel), 183–202
    final prototype development, 40
    low-level, 21
    modular code, 17, 30–31
    Power Company Customer Service System
        (Smalltalk), 128–156
    reusable libraries, 30–31, 42
Common User Access (CUA), IBM, 2, 60, 72
Competition, 49, 60
Concept validation, 36–38
Control of prototyping project, 57, 59
Costs
    of development, 47, 53, 60
    maintenance costs, 16–17
    savings, 17–18
    using low-fidelity prototypes, 51
Credit card workstation example, 173–311
    audio mail, 175
    bubble help feature, 177
    correspondence, 178–179
    credit card adjustment, 182
    credit card information, 179–182
    customer account information, 175–177
    desktop and icons, 174–182
    Easel code, 183–311
    object-oriented user interface, 173–174
    operational description, 174–182
    relationship mix information, 178
C-scape prototyping tool, 63
Customer requirements and task specification (CRTS),
    32, 34–35
Customers
    buy-in, 50
    early prototypes, 56
    feedback, 37, 39, 42, 56
    input, 34–35, 52
    operational needs, 32–36
    presentations, 40
    requirements, 18–19, 58
    treated as king, 58
    wants and needs, identifying, 32–36

Dan Bricklin's Demo II prototyping tool, 63
Data flow diagrams, 35
Data Views prototyping tool, 63
DEC Forms prototyping tool, 63
Decision support center, 34
Delphi prototyping tool, 63
Demonstrations
    aesthetics, 59
    benefits of, 52, 55
    of early progress, 21, 56
Design
    alternatives, 13, 51
    graphics design, 59
    hardware design evaluation, 23
    improvements, 22
    iterative, 16, 22, 31, 51, 55
    initial, and functional specification 38, 56
    joint application design (JAD), 32, 35
    overdesigning/underdesigning, 33
    rationale, 42
    tools and, 75
    user interface design teams (UIDT), 47–48
Development
    input, 35, 38, 51, 57
    iterative, 16, 22, 31, 51, 55
    tools. *See* Tools, prototyping
DevGuide prototyping tool, 64
Display Construction Set prototyping tool, 64
Domain
    becoming multidisciplinary, 59
    expertise, 31
    specific prototypes, 7, 8, 30–31

Easel, 64, 104–109
    advantages, 109
    audio support, 105
    client/server support, 105
    coding language, 108–109
    creating windows and dialog boxes, 108
    credit card workstation code, 183–202
    description, 105–106
    disadvantages, 109
    dynamic data exchange (DDE) support, 106
    ease of use, 108–109
    Editors, 106
    ESL Wizard, 106
    National Language Support, 106
    recommendation, 110
    supported hardware/software platform, 105
    usage scenario, 107–108
    WYSIWYG, 108
Easel-EE prototyping tool, 40
Easel prototyping tool, 64

Encapsulation, 78
End user characteristics, 33
Ending prototyping, 27
Enfin/2 and Enfin/3 prototyping tools, 64
Error conditions, 33
Error messages, 55
Examples
    banking kiosk, 156–173
        account balance, 163
        Audio Visual Connection (AVC) selection, 156–157
        check ordering function, 160–162, 163
        code (AVC), 165–173
        operational description, 157–164
        personal information number (PIN), 157, 158
        product video, 163
        rate information, 158–159
    credit card workstation, 173–311
        audio mail, 175
        bubble help feature, 177
        correspondence, 178–179
        credit card adjustment, 182
        credit card information, 179–182
        customer account information, 175–177
        desktop and icons, 174–182
        Easel code, 183–202
        object-oriented user interface, 173–174
        operational description, 174–182
        relationship mix information, 178
    multimedia kiosk, 111–120
        account information, 113, 114
        automated teller machine (ATM) instruction, 113, 114
        branch locator, 112
        customer service, 114
        digital video interactive (DVI) technology, 113
        encapsulation, 115
        MediaScript code for branch locator, 119–120
        object-oriented prototyping, 114–115
        product information, 113
        scenario, 79–82, 111–112
        Smalltalk code for branch locator, 116–119
        Smalltalk implementation, 114–116
    power company customer service system, 121–156
        alerts, 125, 126, 127
        code listings, 128–156
        customer information, 122–124, 127
        E-mail, 124–125, 127
        logo, 121, 126
        primary window, 121–122, 127
        radar, 125, 127
        scenario, 121
        service response, 125, 127
        Smalltalk code, 128–156

ExoCODE prototyping tool, 64
EZX prototyping tool, 64

Feasibility, 20, 38
Final prototype development, 39–40
    actual code, 40
    customer presentations, 40
    help panels, 40, 55
    idealistic prototypes, 40, 57
    living specification, 39, 49, 52, 56
    publications and training input, 40, 51
    test data results, 40
Functional specifications, 41, 56
    initial design and, 38, 56
    prototype as, 56

Galaxy prototyping tool, 64
Garnet prototyping tool, 64
GIB prototyping tool, 64
Global prototypes, 13
GMW and Guide prototyping tool, 65
Graphical user interface (GUI), 18–19
Graphics design, 59
GUI Programming Facility (Gpf) prototyping tool, 65
Guidelines
    concept validation and, 37
    corporate, 59, 60
    Human Interface Guidelines, Apple Computer, 2, 72
    user interface, 2, 29
Guide 2 prototyping tool, 65
GX Series Developer's Pak prototyping tool, 65

Hardware design evaluation, 23
Hardware support, 74
Help panels, 40, 55
High-fidelity prototypes
    advantages, 49–50, 54, 55
    creating living specifications, 52
    demonstrations, 52
    disadvantages, 50–51, 54
    effectiveness of (table), 54
    overview, 47
    requirements gathering and, 53
    skills, schedule and budget considerations, 53
    testing user interface issues, 52–53
    using, 52–53
    versus low-fidelity, 45, 54
Horizontal prototypes, 12, 47
HP Interface Architech prototyping tool, 65
Human factors, spreading information, 59
Human Interface Guidelines, Apple Computer, 2, 72
Humanoid, 10
Hypercard prototyping tool, 7, 65, 73

IBM Proprinter hardware prototype, 23
Icon Author prototyping tool, 65
Icons, 29, 37
Idealistic prototypes, 40, 57
Information Presentation Facility (IPF), 40
Interactive prototypes, 47
Interface
    builder prototypes, 7–9
    functionality specifications, 41
    techniques and functions, 19–20
InterMAPHics prototyping tool, 66
International development, 58
Interviews, 34

JAM prototyping tool, 65
Joint application design (JAD), 32, 35

KASE:PM prototyping tool, 40, 66
KASE:VIP, 87–93
    32-bit capabilities, 90
    animation errors, 92
    Application Designer, 88
    code generation, 90
    code reuse, 91
    compliance checking, 91
    Container Designer, 88
    Data Object Designer, 89
    description, 88
    DLL Designer, 88
    documentation/online help/tutorial advantages, 91
    documentation/online help/tutorial disadvantages, 91
    drag and drop, 90
    easy to use, 91
    extensibility, 90
    functional capability advantages, 90
    functional capability disadvantages, 91–92
    icon creation, 89
    incomplete team support, 99
    installation, 92
    KASEWORKS, 88
    logic separation, 91
    maintenance features, 90
    memory optimization, 90
    Menu Designer, 89
    no WPS classes, 91
    Notebook Designer, 89
    Panel Designer, 89
    Process Designer, 89
    programming skill required, 92
    recommendation, 92–93
    regeneration, 90
    reliability, 90

KASE:VIP, *continued*
  shortcuts, 91
  size, 90
  source control, 92
  speed, 92
  supported hardware/software platform, 87–88
  team development, 91
  test and animation facilities, 92
  threads, 90
  usability advantages, 90
  usability disadvantages, 91–92
  usage scenario, 88–90
  User-Defined Code Designer, 89
  Window Designer, 89
  Workbench, 88
  WYSIWYG, 91
KEE prototyping tool, 66
Kiosk examples. *See* Examples
Knowledge Pro prototyping tool, 66

Language prototypes, 10–11
Languages, fourth-generation prototyping tools, 7, 11, 40
Layout prototyping tool, 66
Learning curve, 24
Libraries reusable code, 30–31, 42
Lisa, 16
Living specification, 56
  programming from, 39, 49, 52
Local prototypes, 13
Low-fidelity prototypes
  advantages, 47–48, 54
  coding and, 52
  depicting concepts, 51
  disadvantages, 48–49, 54
  effectiveness of (table), 54
  eliciting customer input, 51
  evaluating design alternatives, 51
  identifying markets and user requirements, 51
  investigating early concepts, 51
  overview, 46
  product requirements and, 52
  providing common language among developers and support groups, 51
  testing user interface issues, 52
  using, 51–52
  versus high-fidelity, 45, 54
LUIS prototyping tool, 66

Macintosh Toolbox prototyping tool, 66
Macromedia Director and storyboard prototypes, 7
Macromind Director prototyping tool, 66
Maintenance costs, 16–17
Management support, 55

Marketing input, 34, 38, 51, 57
Marketing tool, 20, 50
Menuet prototyping tool, 66
Microsoft Windows Style Guide, 72
Model-based prototypes, 9–10
Modular code, 17, 30–31
Motif prototyping tool, 66

New Wave prototyping tool, 67
NeXT Interface Builder, 9, 67
Non-interactive prototypes, 46

Object-oriented programming, 43
  credit card workstation, 173–311
ObjectVision prototyping tool, 67
OLIT prototyping tool, 67
Olympic Messaging System, 16
Open Dialogue prototyping tool, 67
Open Interface prototyping tool, 67
Operational environment, 33–34
Oracle Tools prototyping tool, 67
OS/2 help panels, 40, 55
OSF/Motif Style Guide, 72
Overdesigning, 33

Paper-and-pencil prototypes, 5–6, 46–49
Paradigm shift, 19
Performance criteria, 42
Personnel
  attitudes towards prototyping, 26
  undefined roles during prototyping, 25
  volunteering, 58
PLUS prototyping tool, 67
Power company customer service system, 121–156
  alerts, 125, 126, 127
  customer information, 122–124, 127
  E-mail, 124–125, 127
  logo, 121, 126
  primary window, 121–122, 127
  radar, 125, 127
  scenario, 121
  service response, 125, 127
  Smalltalk code, 128–156
PowerBuilder prototyping tool, 68, 101–105
  access to OS features, 102
  Application Painter, 101
  client-server, 103
  control support, 103
  Data Window Painter, 102
  Database Painter, 102
  Debug Tool, 102
  description, 101

documentation/online help/tutorial advantages, 103–104
documentation/online help/tutorial disadvantages, 105
drag and drop, 103, 104
easy to learn/program, 103
error checking, 103
extensible, 103
fast paths, 103
Function Painter, 102
functional capability advantages, 102–103
functional capability disadvantages, 104
high productivity, 103
hooks, 103
iterative development, 103
lags OS changes, 104
library facilities, 103
Library Painter, 102
Menu Painter, 102
online help, 102
Picture Tool, 102
poor development team support, 104
PowerScript, 101
Preferences Tool, 102
programming required, 104
recommendation, 105
reliability, 104
Run Tool, 102
run time required, 104
supported hardware/software platform, 101
usability advantages, 102–104
usability disadvantages, 104–105
usage scenario, 101–102
User Object Painter, 102
Window Painter, 101
WYSIWYG, 103
Product, final and prototype, 25–26
Productivity expectations, 34
Programmers
    and low-fidelity prototypes, 48–49
    productivity, 18
Prograph prototyping tool, 68
Project control, 57, 59
Proof-of-concept prototypes, 46
Proteus prototyping tool, 68
Protofinish prototyping tool, 68
Protoscreens prototyping tool, 68
Prototyper for the Macintosh, 9
Prototyper, Now prototyping tool, 68
Prototypes
    compared, 11–12
    description of, 3–5
    as functional specification, 56

high fidelity
    advantages, 49–50, 54, 55
    creating living specifications, 52
    demonstrations, 52
    disadvantages, 50–51, 54
    effectiveness of (table), 54
    overview, 47
    requirements gathering and, 53
    skills, schedule and budget considerations, 53
    testing user interface issues, 52–53
    using, 52–53
    versus low fidelity, 45, 54
idealistic, 40, 57
initial, 38, 39
low fidelity
    advantages, 47–48, 54
    coding and, 52
    depicting concepts, 51
    disadvantages, 48–49, 54
    effectiveness of (table), 54
    eliciting customer input, 51
    evaluating design alternatives, 51
    identifying markets and user requirements, 51
    investigating early concepts, 51
    overview, 46
    product requirements and, 52
    providing common language among developers and support groups, 51
    testing user interface issues, 52
    using, 51–52
    versus high fidelity, 45, 54
scope of, 12–13
tips for successful, 53–60
types of, 5–12
Prototyping
    advantages 16–23
    considerations, 54
    ending, 27
    future of, 42–43
    history of, 13–14
    need for usable interfaces, 1–2
    pitfalls, 24–27
    structured rapid, 13
    tips for success, 53–60
    tools. *See* Tools, prototyping
Prototyping process
    basis for successful, 30–31
    concept validation, 36–38
    domain expertise, 31
    early completion, 31
Prototyping process, *continued*
    final prototype development, 39–40
    identification of customer wants and needs, 32–36

initial design and functional specification 38, 56
initial prototype, 38, 39
iterative development, 16, 22, 31, 51, 55
modular code, 17, 30–31
overview, 29–30
reusable code libraries, 30–31, 42
specifications and information, 41–42
test data results, 38, 39, 40

Quality improvement, 19

Rapid application development (RAD), 11
Rapid prototyping. *See* Prototyping
Representativeness, 25
Requirements phase, 18–19, 53
  identifying markets and user requirements, 51
Reusable code libraries, 30–31, 42
RIPL prototyping tool, 68

Sales tools, 20, 50
Scenarios, low-fidelity prototypes, 46
Schedule
  ending prototyping, 27
  traditional development, 60
Screen layouts and behavior, 41, 51
SET prototyping tool, 68
Simulations, 23
Smalltalk prototyping tool, 77–87
  access to system primitives, 83
  automatic garbage collection, 83
  change management, 86
  code reuse, 82
  description, 78
  development schedule, 81
  documentation/online help/tutorial advantages, 84
  documentation/online help/tutorial
    disadvantages, 87
  functional capability advantages, 82–84
  functional capability disadvantages, 85–86
  functionality, 86
  high-fidelity prototyping, 47
  image management, 86
  incremental compile environment, 83
  independence, 83
  integrated programming environment, 82
  interface layout tool, 86
  language tool, 11, 40
  late binding, 83–84
  learning curve, 85
  National Language Support, 84
  no design guide compliant window classes, 86
  no reference to model-view-controller, 86
  no run-time licensing fees, 84

other support, 84
recommendation, 87
simple syntax, 83
supported hardware/software platform, 77–78
usability advantages, 84
usability disadvantages, 86–87
usage scenario, 79–81
Software development
  software engineering, 13
  software life cycle, 15–17, 22
Software prototyping. *See* Prototyping
Specifications
  clear, 20
  user interface, 39–40
Speed. *See* Performance
Star Information System, 1, 16
Storyboard prototypes, 6–7, 46–49
Structured rapid prototyping, 13–14
SUIT prototyping tool, 68
Supercard prototyping tool, 69
Survey questionnaires, 34
System/task analysis, 30–36, 37, 41, 51–52

TAE Plus prototyping tool, 69
Task specifications, 41
Team building, 57, 58
TeamFocus groupware, 34–35
Technology and prototyping, 34, 60
Teleuse prototyping tool, 69
TIGERS prototyping tool, 69
Tigre Interface Designer prototyping tool, 69
Tk/Tcl prototyping tool, 69
ToolBook prototyping tool, 69
  and storyboard prototypes, 7
Tools, prototyping. *See* Easel, KASE:VP,
    PowerBuilder, Smalltalk, Visual Basic, XVT
  efficiency, 24
  overview, 58
  product summary (table), 62–71
Tools, selecting
  application requirements, 72
  budget considerations, 76
  calls to external procedures and programs, 74
  control over interface features, 76
  data collection capabilities, 76–77
  determining project-specific criteria, 71–72
  easy to learn, 75
  easy to use, 74
  easy to develop and modify screens, 73
  features, 73–77
  fits design process, 75
  goals, 71
  identifying tools, 71

imports text, graphics, other media 75
operating system, 72
prioritizing project-specific criteria, 72
process for, 71–77
project size considerations, 76
prototype distribution, 77
support for chosen interface, 73
support for input-output devices, 74
team development, 76
user interface style or standard, 72
vendor support, 75
version control, 77
Trade shows, 52
Trade-off studies, 37–38

UIDE model-based prototyping, 10
UIMX for X Windows and Motif, 9, 69
Ultimedia Audio Visual Connection (AVC), 157
Underdesigning, 33
Usability testing
design alternatives, 13, 51
early testing, 21
high-fidelity prototypes, 49, 52–53
Usable interfaces, 1–2
User interfaces, 1–2
graphical user interface (GUI), 18–19
guidelines, 2, 29
concept validation and, 37
corporate, 59, 60
object-oriented (Easel), 173–174
prototyping tools and, 72
specifications, 39–40
testing. See Usability testing
user interface design teams (UIDT), 47–48
User requirements, identifying markets and 51
User satisfaction, 21–22
User tasks and scenarios, 30–36, 37, 41, 51–52
User's manual, 40

VAPS prototyping tool, 69
Vertical prototypes, 12, 47, 53
Videotapes as living specifications, 39
Visual Age prototyping tool, 67
Visual Basic prototyping tool, 96–100
controls, 98
creating help, 100
database connectivity, 98
debugger, 97
description, 96–97
designer, 97
documentation/online help/tutorial advantages, 99
documentation/online help/tutorial
disadvantages, 100

easy to learn, 99
extensibility, 98
flexibility, 98
forms, 97
functional capability advantages, 98–99
functional capability disadvantages, 100
high-fidelity prototyping, 47
integrated programming environment, 99
interactive, 99
language tool, 7
links to other languages, 98
no CASE tools, 100
programming language, 100
prototype size considerations, 100
recommendation, 100
supported hardware/software platform, 96
usability advantages, 99
usability disadvantages, 100
usage scenario, 97–98
VUIT prototyping tool, 70

Waterfall life cycle model, 13, 15
Windowcraft prototyping tool, 70
Windows Development Kit prototyping tool, 70
WindowsMAKER for Microsoft Windows, 9, 70
Work complexity and customer wants and needs, 33
WYSIWYG (what you see is what you get) interface-
builder, 9

Xbuild prototyping tool, 70
Xerox Palo Alto Research Center (PARC), 1, 77
XView prototyping tool, 70
XVT (Extensive Virtual toolkit), 70, 93–96
description, 93
documentation/online help/tutorial advantages, 95
documentation/online help/tutorial
disadvantages, 96
events, 94
fonts, 94
functional capability advantages, 94
functional capability disadvantages, 95
graphics, 94
help, 94
recommendation, 96
supported hardware/software platform, 93
usability advantages, 94
usability disadvantages, 95
usage scenario, 93–94
windows, menus, and controls, 94

Zinc prototyping tool, 71